Harry Ulrich

Fun with Marzipan

Harry Ulrich

Fun with Marzipan

MATTHAES VERLAG GMBH

Die Modellierhölzer *Modelling tools*

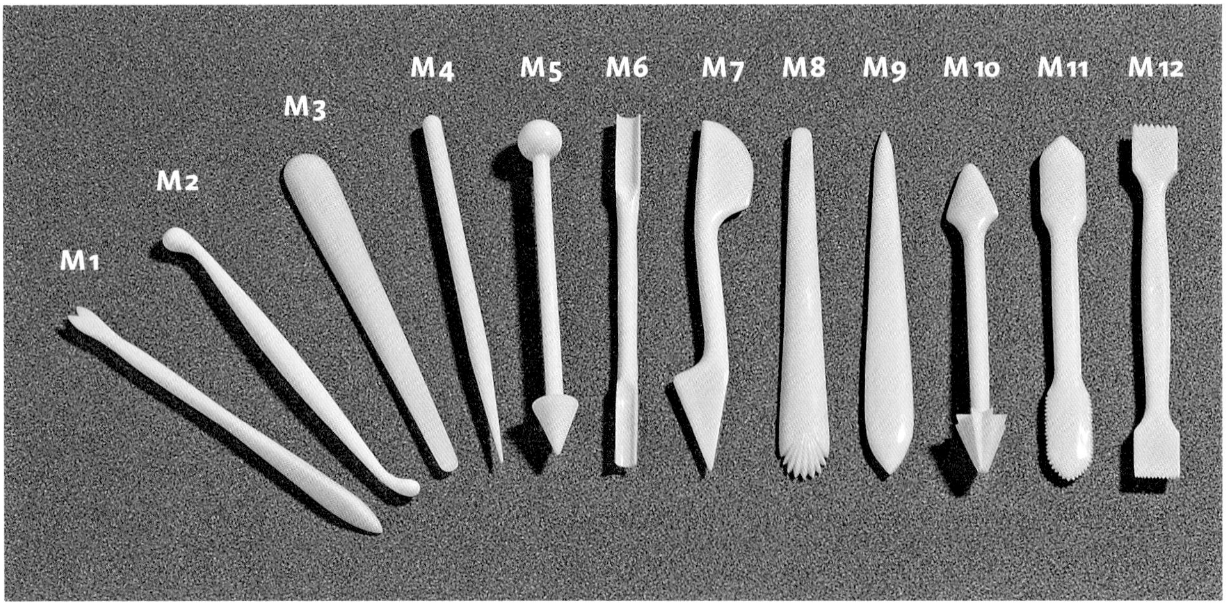

M = Modellierholz *M = Modelling tool*

ISBN 3-87516-332-X

Fotografie: Fotostudio Leupold, Stuttgart
Grafische Gestaltung und Producing:
Petra Bachmann, Weinheim
Projektbetreuung: Silvia Leitz

ISBN 3-87516-332-X

Photography: Fotostudio Leupold, Stuttgart
Graphic design and production:
Petra Bachmann, Weinheim
Project management: Silvia Leitz

Vorwort
Foreword

Liebe Leserin, lieber Leser,

schön, dass Sie sich für das Gestalten mit Marzipan interessieren und mehr darüber wissen wollen. Mich selbst hat die Faszination dieser vielfältig formbaren Masse schon früh ergriffen. Durch einen schlichten Hasen – modelliert von meinem damaligen Berufsschullehrer – bin ich auf den süßen Rohstoff gekommen. Mein Vater und Ausbilder Heinz Ulrich war es, der die Situation erkannte und mich forderte. Positive Reaktionen unserer Kundschaft belohnten die Mühe und gaben Ansporn für viele weitere Versuche.

Heute kann ich behaupten, dass es fast nichts gibt, was sich nicht aus Marzipan modellieren ließe. Selbst einen Elefanten kann man auf dem Rüssel balancierend modellieren, wenn man eine „Wand“ aus Schokolade als Stütze nutzt.

Fest steht: Es gibt keinen Anlass, zu dem man nicht irgendetwas – mit vergleichweise geringen Mitteln – modellieren könnte! Bei der Herstellung der Exponate habe ich deshalb absichtlich auf besondere Geräte verzichtet, nicht zuletzt auch um zu zeigen, dass es vor allem unsere Hände und unsere Vorstellungskraft sind, die die oft humorvollen Figuren und Szenen entstehen lassen.

Wenn wir es schaffen, den Betrachter, Gast und Kunden für einen kurzen Augenblick zu fesseln oder zu amüsieren, wenn wir ihn vielleicht sogar so weit bringen, dass er unsere Arbeit aufbewahren und nicht verzehren möchte, dann haben wir erreicht, was wir wollten. Solche Kunden sind zufriedene Kunden – und genau darum geht es im täglichen Geschäft!

Ihnen wünsche ich eine anregende Lektüre, Freude und Mut beim (Nach-)Modellieren und viel Phantasie bei der Umsetzung Ihrer eigenen Ideen.

Herzlich,
Ihr

Harry Ulrich

Dear Reader

A warm welcome to the techniques and artistry of working and modelling with marzipan. I myself became involved with the fascination of this versatile mixture from an early age. It was just a simple rabbit modelled by my teacher at technical college that fired my enthusiasm for the sweet material. Then it was my father and trainer, Heinz Ulrich, who recognised my talent and provided a challenging and supportive situation for my further development. Positive reactions from our customers were the reward for my efforts and encouraged me to venture further afield.

Today I am convinced that there is almost nothing that cannot be represented in a marzipan model. Even an elephant balancing on its trunk can be modelled and made to hold up by using a “wall” of chocolate as support.

One thing is certain: there is no event or celebration for which one cannot model something – at relatively little expense! For this reason, I have intentionally avoided using special equipment in making the exhibits, not least in order to demonstrate that it is primarily our hands and imagination which create the often humorous figures and scenes.

If we succeed in capturing the attention of and amusing our visitors, guests or customers for a short moment, if we perhaps even stimulate them into keeping our work rather than eating it, then we have achieved what we were aiming for. These kinds of customers are satisfied customers – precisely what matters in our daily business!

I hope you enjoy this book and that you have fun when you start modelling some of the scenes in this book or start composing your own exhibits.

Best wishes,
yours

Harry Ulrich

Inhalt
Content

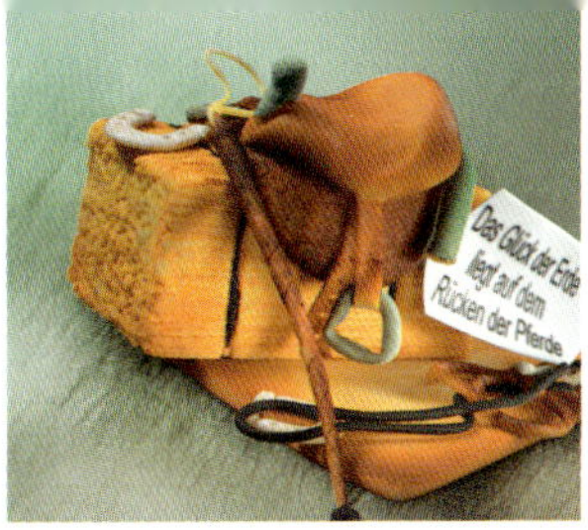

1000
You're a winner

Früh übt sich ......

Happy diet !!

Let's celebrate

Wir feiern

Das ideale Ostergeschenk für große Kinder!

The ideal Easter present for the small and not so small!

Frohe Ostern

Happy Easter

› Aus einer Kugel den Grundkörper formen. Mit M 2 die vormodellierten Beine abgrenzen. |1|
Zwischen Daumen und Zeigefinger beide Beine ausmodellieren. |2|
Auf der Vorderseite eine zweite Beuge mit M 2 eindrücken. Im Gegenzug die „Kniekehle“ auf der Rückseite einkerben. Durch ständiges Tippen die Oberfläche glatt halten. Beine in Form bringen und die Figur abstützen. Mit M 1 die Pfoten einkerben. |3|
Für die Arme den Grundkörper seitlich einschneiden und entsprechend formen. Kopf modellieren und nahtlos ansetzen. Die Figur gut abstützen und über Nacht trocknen lassen. Mit gelber Farbe grundieren und mit Brauntönen hauptsächlich von oben besprühen. Hauttöne mit dem Pinsel aufbringen.

› Use a marzipan ball to model the basic body shape. Roughly form the legs and then use an M 2 to accentuate the line between the body and legs. |1|
Complete the two legs by shaping them between your thumb and forefinger. |2|
Use the M 2 again to shape the front bend of the leg and then model the knee at the back.
Keep the surface smooth by constantly tapping with your fingers. Arrange the legs in the required position and support the figure. Use an M 1 to make a notch for the paws. |3|
To form the arms, make an incision on the side of the body and shape to suit. Model the head separately and attach without a seam. Support the figure well and leave to dry overnight. Apply a base coat in yellow and then spray on brown shades, mainly from the top. Apply the skin colours with a brush.

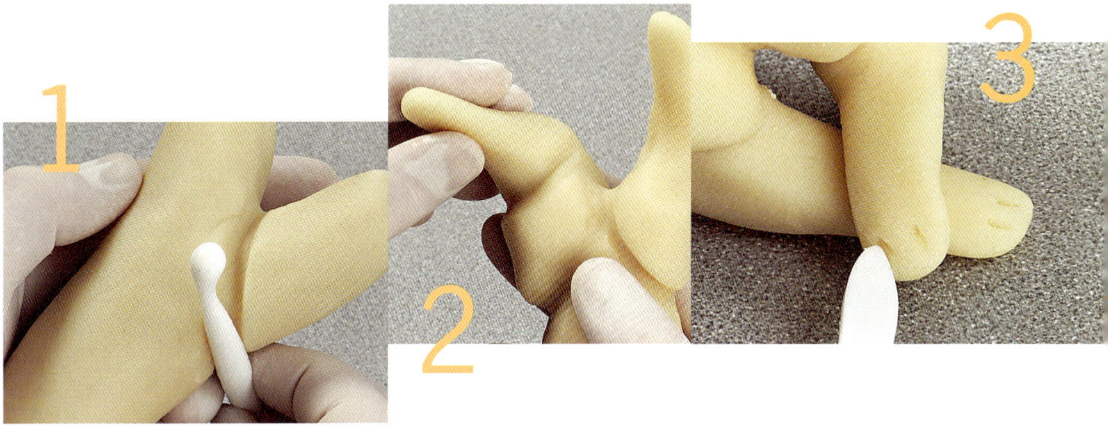

PROFI **TIPP** *Zum nahtlosen Anbringen von Einzelteilen werden diese am Ansatz stumpf modelliert und gut angefeuchtet. Beherztes Andrücken und sofortiges Verstreichen der Wülste mit M 2 oder M 3 lassen die Nähte verschwinden.*

Join up additional parts by modelling a flat surface and wetting it well. Put the part in place and press home firmly, immediately smooth out the bulges with an M 2 or M 3 so that the joins are no longer visible.

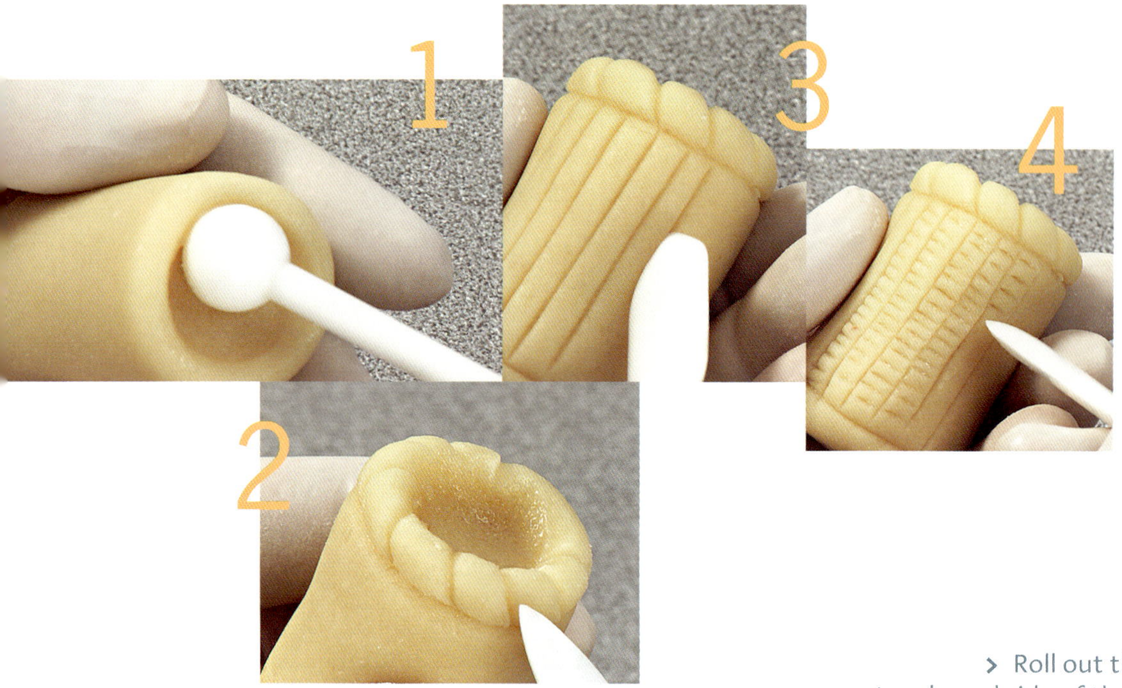

› Grundplatte ausrollen und mit der gesternten Seite des M 10 das Gras durch Rollen einkerben. Für das Nest marmoriert gefärbtes Marzipan durch ein Sieb drücken und formen.
Körper des Huhns modellieren, weiß absprühen und einsetzen. Schnabel und Kamm mit durchgefärbtem Marzipan ausführen.
Den Hasen wie gewohnt formen und schminken.
Korb aus einem Zylinder beginnen.
Mit M 5 durch ständiges Kreisen eine runde Vertiefung formen. | 1 |
Mit M 1 den oberen und unteren Korbrand abgrenzen. Oben Querrillen eindrücken. | 2 |
Mit M 3 den inneren Korbrand horizontal einkerben. Die Längsrillen außen entstehen mit M 11, möglichst im gleichen Abstand und parallel. | 3 |
Die Flechtstruktur ergibt sich durch feine Kerbungen. | 4 |
Mit Gelb grundieren, sehr leicht mit Braun nachspritzen und schließlich mit Wasser übersprühen. Die braune Farbe sammelt sich in den Vertiefungen und erhöht den Kontrast. Mit dem Pinsel nachschminken.

› Roll out the base slab and use the star-shaped side of the M 10 to produce the grass texture by rolling. Make the nest by pressing marble-coloured marzipan through a strainer and forming it into the nest shape.
Model the body of the chicken, spray with white and place on the nest. Create the beak and the crest with tinted marzipan.
Form the rabbit in the usual way and apply colouring.
Start the basket from a basic cylinder shape.
Use an M 5 in a continuous circular motion to hollow out a round shape. | 1 |
Use an M 1 to mark the top and bottom edge of the basket. Mark the cross pattern at the top. | 2 |
Use an M 3 to score the inner edge of the basket.
The vertical grooves are made with an M 11, taking care to keep them parallel and at an equal distance. | 3 |
Finish the weaving pattern by adding further slight indentations horizontally. | 4 |
Apply a yellow base coat and then spray over lightly with brown, finishing off with a spray of water.
The brown colouring will then run into the indentations and heighten the contrast. Add extra touches by brush.

Wo bleibt die Ware?
Where are the goodies?

> Hostien ausstechen und mit Eiweißspritzglasur verzieren. Kelch aus verschiedenen, platt oder lang geformten Kugeln zusammensetzen. Für die Gefäßschale eine Kugel mit M 5 hohl formen. Trocknen lassen und erst dann befestigen. Mit gelber Farbe grundieren, danach auf einer Seite rot ansprühen.
Für die Äste der Palmkätzchen lange, spitz zulaufende Stangen formen. Aus kleinen Tropfen die einzelnen Knospen ansetzen. | 1 |
Mit den Fingern gut andrücken und die Übergänge durch Tippen kaschieren. | 2 |
Äste braun schminken, auf Grundplatte platzieren und die Palmkätzchen mit Glasur anspritzen.
Für den Blätterkranz einen Marzipanring herstellen. Ausgestochene Blättchen in gleich bleibender Richtung anbringen. | 3 |
Gelb grundieren und mit Grün nachspritzen. Leicht mit Wasser übersprühen.

> Cut out the hosts and decorate with piped royal icing. Build up the chalice. To make the actual bowl, hollow out a ball using an M 5. Leave to dry and do not attach to the stem until dry. Apply a yellow base coat and then spray in red from one side.
To make the branches of the palm catkins, roll some sticks until long and pointed. Add the small buds made from small elongated drops. | 1 |
Use your fingers to join the buds to the branches and smooth out the joins by tapping lightly. | 2 |
Apply brown colour to the branches, place them on the base slab and add on the palm catkins in icing.
To make the wreath of leaves, first make a ring of marzipan and then attach the cut-out leaves, following the same direction all round. | 3 |
Apply a yellow base coat and follow up with green spray. Lightly spray with water.

PROFI **TIPP** *Zum Anbringen von Marzipanteilen genügt es gewöhnlich, diese etwas anzufeuchten. Festere Verbindungen erhält man durch das Benetzen mit flüssigem Eiweiß.*

To join marzipan parts it is usually sufficient to slightly wet the touching surfaces. Stronger joins are formed by wetting with liquid egg white.

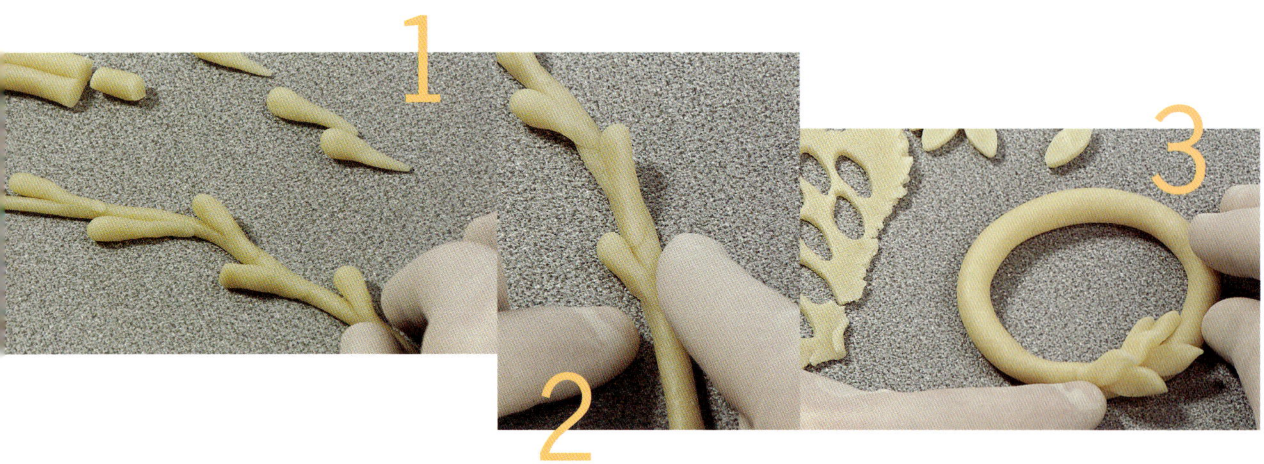

Kelch und Hostie – die Symbole dieses Festes

Chalice and host – the holy symbols

Zur Kommunion

Holy Communion

1

2

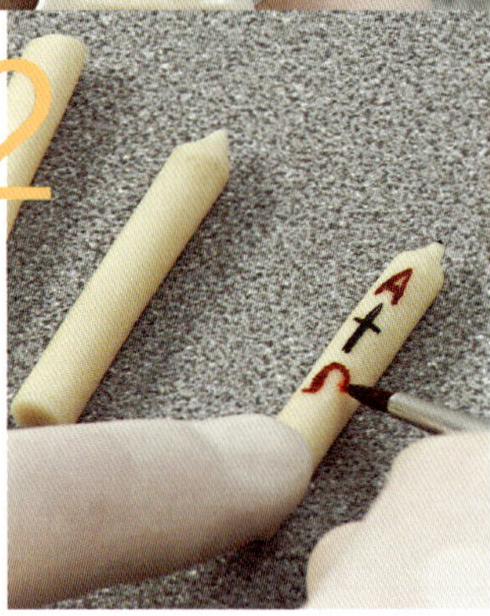

3

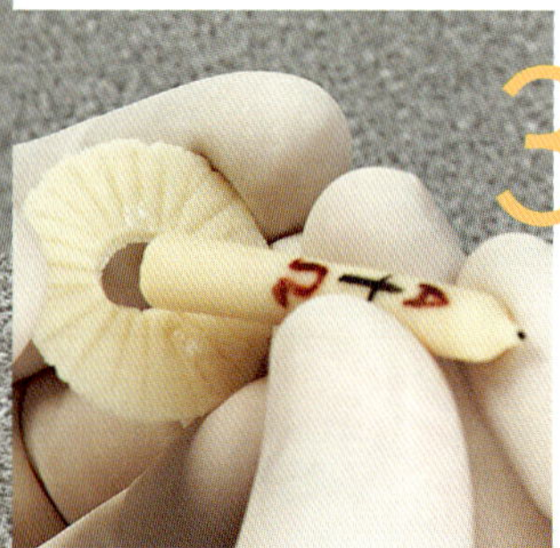

PROFI**TIPP** *Auf weiß grundierten Flächen lassen sich Pinselstriche besser aufbringen, da die Grundierung ein Breitlaufen der Linien verhindert.*

It is easier to apply brush strokes on surfaces that have been given a white base coat as this stops the brush lines from "bleeding".

› Grundplatte ausschneiden und mit Buchstaben-Ausstechern den Schriftzug eindrücken. Gelb grundieren, den Rand mit etwas brauner Farbe besprühen und mit Wasser in die Vertiefungen spülen.
Kinderfigur modellieren. Das Kleid weiß grundieren. Arme und Gesicht mit dem Pinsel rosa, die Haare schwarz färben. Das Gesicht ausarbeiten.
Zur Herstellung der Kerzenmanschette aus einer Kugel eine runde Scheibe formen. Diese mit M 10 rundum einkerben. | 1 |
Die Mitte herausstechen. Für die Kerze eine kleine Marzipanstange spitz modellieren und mit dem Pinsel die Verzierungen auftragen. | 2 |
Die Kerze durch die vorbereitete Manschette stecken. | 3 |
Kerze auf ein Holzstück legen, Faltenwurf in die Manschette kerben.
Die getrocknete Kerze mit der Figur verbinden.

› Cut out the base slab and add the writing with letter cutting shapes. Apply yellow base coat and then a little brown colour to the edge, flushing the indentations with water. Model the child's figure. Apply a white base coat to the dress. Model the face and then apply pink colour to the arms and face and black to the hair.
To make the "skirt" for the candle, shape a round disc from a ball. Apply indentations all round using an M 10. | 1 |
Cut out the central hole. Roll a small marzipan stick to make the candle and apply the embellishments by brush. | 2 |
Push the candle through the prepared "skirt". | 3 |
Place the candle onto a piece of wood and carve the folds into the "skirt".
Join up the dried candle with the figure.

Kommunion

Communion

Als Tortenaufsatz bestens geeignet

Ideally suited for placing on decorative cakes

Big Barbecue

Big Barbecue

> Zur Herstellung der Einladungskarte benötigt man einen Lebensmittelfarbdrucker und die passenden Trägerfolien. (Im Fachhandel erhältlich.) Sollte kein Lebensmittelfarbdrucker zur Verfügung stehen, kann die Karte auch mit der Spritztüte hergestellt werden. Fertig gestaltete Einladungskarte knicken und in einem entsprechend gefalteten Karton trocknen lassen. So bleibt der Knick erhalten.
Zwei Marzipanstangen oben und unten mit M 1 abmodellieren, bis Würstchen mit „Zipfeln" entstehen.
Mit M 10 den „Wurstzipfel" eindrücken und ausmodellieren. Die Augen mit M 2 eindrücken, dabei leicht nach oben drehen. Die dadurch entstehenden Wülste über den Augenhöhlen wirken sehr natürlich. Mit M 3 die Münder und Zornfalten einkerben. Gut trocknen lassen.
„Würstchen" senkrecht stellen, Arme und Beine anbringen. Gut abstützen und trocknen lassen.
„Würstchen" weiß grundieren, mit Braun nachschminken und zum Schluss noch einen Hauch Rot aufbringen. Münder und Falten mit dem Pinsel dunkel nachziehen. Augen einspritzen.

> In order to produce the invitation card one needs a colour printer for food colouring as well as the appropriate edible paper (available in specialist shops). If such a printer is not available, it is also possible to produce the card with the help of an icing bag. Once you have completed the invitation card, fold it over and leave to dry against a piece of card folded into the appropriate shape. This helps to retain the crease.
Work the ends of two marzipan rolls at top and bottom with an M 1 until they look like sausages with tied ends. Use an M 10 for the shaping of the tied end. Use an M 2 to push in the eye sockets, turning slightly upwards to form the bulges above the eyes that naturally form the eyebrows. Use an M 3 to indent the mouths and frown lines. Leave to dry well. Arrange the "sausages" vertically and apply arms and legs. Support well and leave to dry. Apply white base coat to the sausages, follow up with brown and finally add a touch of red. Use the brush to paint on mouths and the frown lines in darker colour. Pipe on the eyes.

PROFI **TIPP** *Zum ordentlichen Abstützen der Figuren bis zur vollständigen Trocknung eignen sich naturbelassene Bauklötzchen aus dem Spielzeugladen ganz hervorragend. Mit den verschiedenen Klötzchen können ganz unterschiedliche Stützkonstruktionen gestapelt werden.*

To support the figures until they are completely dry you can use natural wood blocks (i.e. without any finishing) available from toy shops. Blocks of different sizes can be used to make up all kinds of supporting structures.

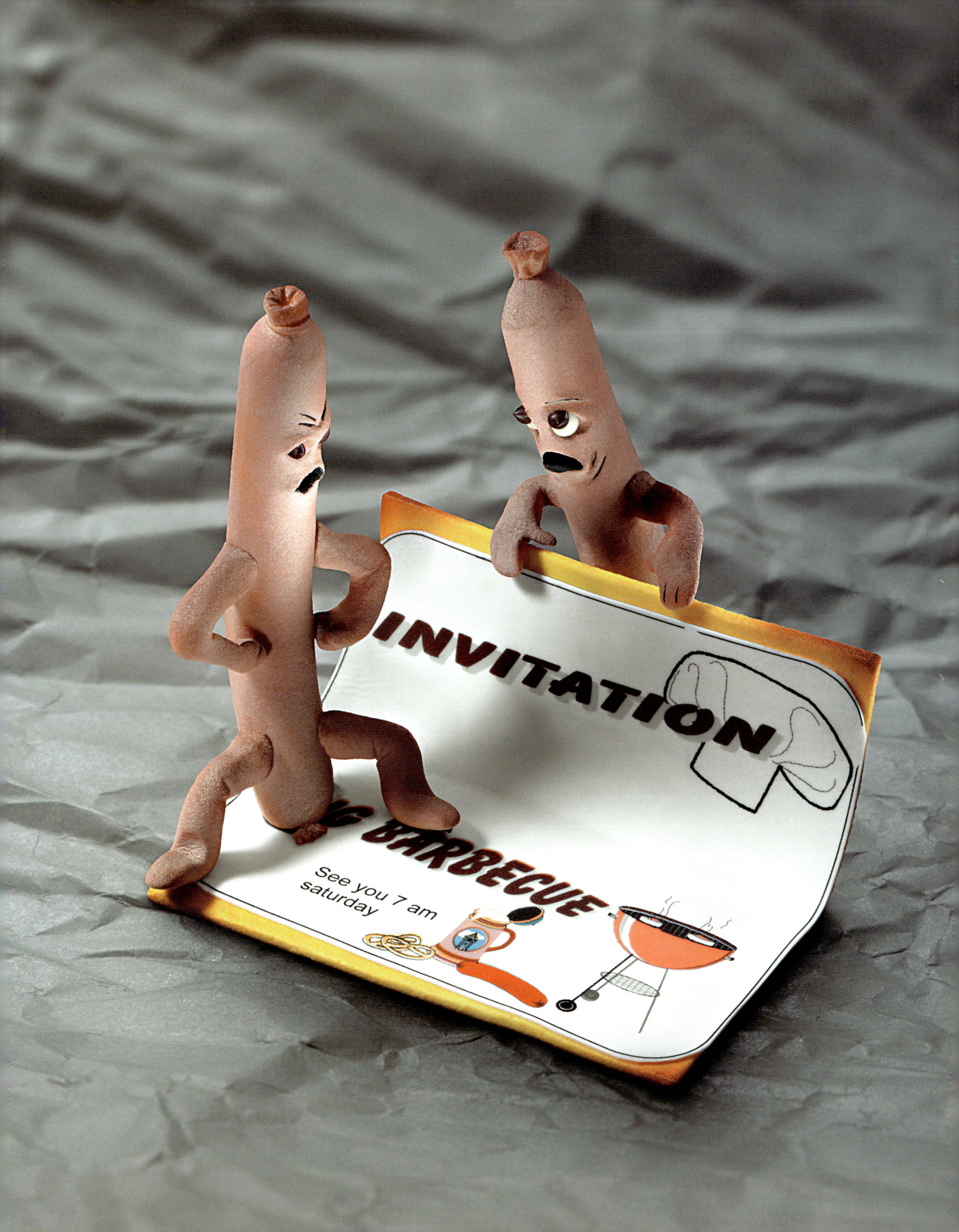
INVITATION
BARBECUE
See you 7 am
saturday

Freunde der Nacht

Spooky!

Für die nächste Halloween-Party

For the next Halloween party

› Grundplatte aus halber Marzipankugel durch grobes Ausstreichen aus der Mitte herstellen. Gelb-braun grundieren und mit Wasser übersprühen.
Blätter vorbereiten, schminken, leicht wölben und trocknen lassen.
Für den Kürbis eine Kugel leicht platt drücken.
Mit M 1 den Kürbis ringsum gleichmäßig einkerben. | 1 |
Augen und Nase mit M 1 beherzt eindrücken.
Den Mund ebenfalls mit M 1 unregelmäßig bogenförmig eindrücken. | 2 |
Den Strunk einkleben. | 3 |
Mit Gelb grundieren, leicht mit Rot übersprühen und mit Wasser Schattierungen aufbringen. Den Strunk mit dem Pinsel grün färben, Schnittstelle weiß nachziehen. Kürbis nass in nass schminken. So ergeben sich interessante Schattierungen. Mund, Nase und Augen schwarz aufzeichnen. Trocknen lassen und mit weißen Strichen hervorheben.
Fledermaus modellieren und zum Trocknen an den Kürbis lehnen. So passt am Ende alles wieder zusammen. Fledermaus gelb grundieren, mit Braun und schließlich mit Schwarz besprühen. Hände und Ohren rosa schminken, Augen einspritzen.
Szene zusammensetzen, Schild fertigen und anbringen.

› Make the base slab from a ball of marzipan that has been cut in half, using rough strokes from the centre. Apply a yellow/brown base coat and spray with water.
Prepare the leaves and bend them, then apply the colour and leave to dry.
To make the pumpkin, slightly flatten a ball of marzipan. Use an M 1 to evenly indent the pumpkin all around. | 1 |
Use an M 1 to indent quite distinct shapes for eyes and nose. Again use the M 1 to shape the mouth in an uneven curve. | 2 |
Attach the stalk. | 3 |
Apply a yellow base coat, lightly spray with red and then apply the highlighting with water. Use the brush to colour the stalk green, accentuate the cut in white. Colour the pumpkin "wet in wet", which results in interesting colour shadings. Paint the mouth, nose and eyes in black. Leave to dry and outline the edges in white.
Model the bat and leave to dry leaning up against the pumpkin. In this way everything will fit together at the end. Apply a yellow base coat to the bat and spray with brown and finally black. Paint hands and ears in pink and pipe on the eyes.
Assemble the set, then prepare and fix the sign.

> Einen Klecks temperierte Kuvertüre auf eine strukturierte Platte gießen und erstarren lassen. Grundplatte ausschneiden oder ausstechen. Für den Käse ein Marzipanstück als Quader zurechtschneiden. Mit den M 2, 4 und M 5 die Löcher unregelmäßig eindrücken. Mit gelber Farbe kräftig schminken.
Für das Geschenkband ein Stück Marzipan mit Rot, ein anderes mit Grün durchfärben. Dünne Stangen ausrollen und diese zwischen zwei Folien platt walzen. Deckfolie vorsichtig abziehen. | 1 |
Mit Lineal und Schneiderad zwei unterschiedlich breite Bänder schneiden. | 2 |
Das breite Band von überschüssigem Marzipan befreien. Das schmale sehr gefühlvoll abziehen. Das schmale Band mittig auf das breite auflegen und leicht andrücken. | 3 |
Die Maus aus einem Stück Marzipan formen, Ohren, Schwanz und Nase ansetzen. Figur mit Weiß grundieren und zaghaft mit Schwarz nachspritzen. Rosa Stellen werden mit dem Airbrush aufgetragen. So entsteht in der Fellpartie ein zarter Farbverlauf, vor allem an der Schnauze. Erst jetzt die Zähne einsetzen und Mütze anbringen.

> Pour a small drop of tempered couverture onto a textured slab and leave to go hard. Cut out the base slab with a knife or cutting shape.
To make the cheese, cut a piece of marzipan into the shape of a cube. Use an M 2, M 4 and M 5 to push in the holes in an irregular fashion. Apply yellow paint in strong shades.
To make the gift ribbon, dye a piece of marzipan with red and another one with green. Roll out thin strips, place in between two foils and roll out until flat. Carefully pull off the cover foil. | 1 |
Use the ruler and a cutting wheel to cut two ribbons of different widths. | 2 |
Take the wider ribbon and clear off any excess marzipan. Then take the narrower ribbon and carefully pull off the foil. Place the narrow ribbon centrally onto the wider one and press on lightly. | 3 |
Make the mouse from a piece of marzipan, applying the ears, tail and nose as separate pieces. Apply a white base coat to the figure and gently spray over in black. Apply the pink areas with the airbrush. This will create a delicate merging of the colours in the fur, particularly at the mouth. Now add the teeth and hat.

PROFI **TIPP** *Das Band sofort nach Herstellung in die endgültige Form bringen, denn schon nach wenigen Minuten ist es so trocken, dass es nicht mehr formbar ist. Es bricht.*

Bend the ribbon into its final shape immediately after making it since it will dry out in just a few minutes, when it can no longer be formed without breaking.

1

2

3

Niko-Maus
Santa Mouse

Für die glanzvolle Zeit

For the festive season

Weihnachts-Engelchen – zum Fressen süß!

Sweet Christmas angels!

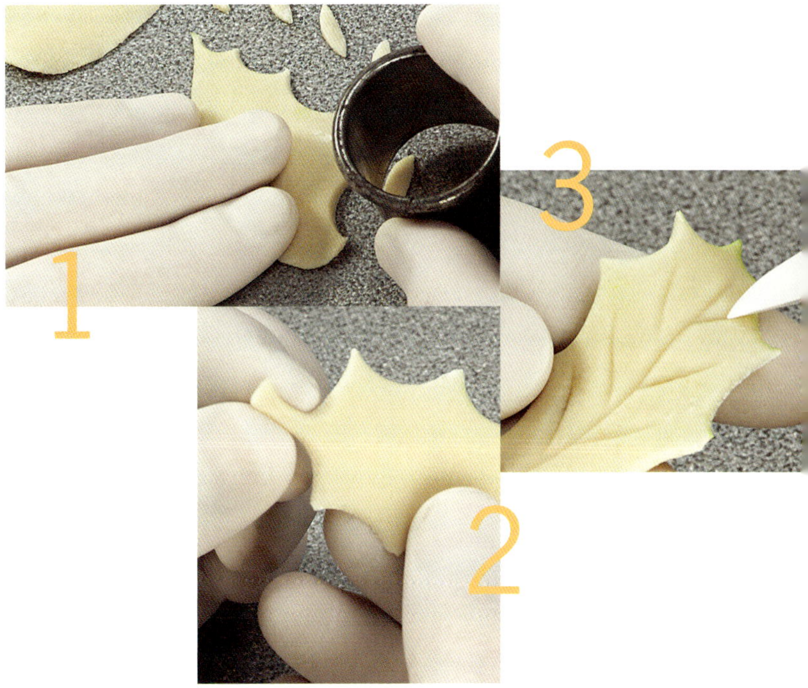

> Christbaumkugel aus ganz gedrungener Birne formen. Spitze knapp abschneiden. Mit Zackenausstecher Deckelchen herstellen, auflegen und bordieren. Marzipanringchen fertigen, trocknen lassen und ankleben. Kugel gelb grundieren und mit Rot nachschminken. Obere Wölbung gelb lassen. Deckelchen und Ring mit Lebensmittel-Silber färben.
Das Engelchen modellieren, an die Kugel andrücken, etwas fixieren und trocknen lassen. Nach der Trocknung rosa grundieren. Alle anderen Farben mit dem Pinsel auftragen.
Für die Stechpalmenblätter längliche Tropfen platt drücken. Mit verschieden großen Ausstechern oder Tüllen die typische Blattform gestalten. | 1 |
Am unteren Ende mit Daumen und Zeigefinger einen kurzen Stiel formen. | 2 |
Mit M 1 Adern einkerben. | 3 |
Blätter gelb grundieren, mit Grün färben und mit Wasser übersprühen.
Schild mit dem Lebensmittelfarbdrucker auf Zuckerfolie fertigen.

> Make the bauble from a fairly squat bulb and cut off the tip. Use a jagged edge cutter to make the attachment, put it on the bauble and drape the edges over. Make the small marzipan ring, leave to dry and stick on. Apply yellow base coat to the ball and follow up with red. Leave the top part in yellow. Colour the attachment with ring with silver food colouring.
Model the little angel, attach it to the bauble and leave to dry. Once dry, apply a pink base coat. Apply all other colours by brush. To make the palm leaves, use drops in a long shape and press flat. Use different type of cutting tools or points to make the typical shape of the leaves. | 1 |
At the lower end, form a short stalk between thumb and forefinger. | 2 |
Use an M 1 to indent the veins. | 3 |
Apply yellow base coat to the leaves, then follow up with green and spray with water.
Make the sign with the food colour printer on sugar paper.

Happy Xmas

Happy Xmas

› Für den Tannenbaum einen lang gezogenen Tropfen modellieren, mit der Schere ringsum kleine Ecken einschneiden. | 1 |
Für die Girlanden dünne Marzipanrollen fertigen. Mit M 10 Oberseite einkerben. | 2 |
Girlanden nacheinander in die Handfläche legen und seitlich einkerben. | 3 |
Girlanden unregelmäßig um den Baum legen, Enden leicht andrücken. | 4 |
Mit Gelb grundieren und mit Grün kräftig nachfärben. Die Girlanden gut mit Wasser abspritzen. Sternchen ausstechen, an der Spitze anbringen und gelb färben. Wenn der Tannenbaum fertig geschminkt ist, sofort Silberperlen eindrücken. Ansonsten dunkle Kuvertüre sehr sparsam mit der Spritztüte anspritzen und Perlen eindrücken. Eiweißspritzglasur eignet sich nur, wenn sie grün gefärbt wurde, sonst sticht die weiße Farbe zu sehr hervor.
Aus einer Platte den Bodenstern ausschneiden, gelb grundieren und von den Spitzen zur Mitte mit Rot schattieren. Mit weißer Kuvertüre die dunkleren Kanten nachziehen.
Für die Geschenkpakete Marzipanquader ausschneiden. Für die Geschenkbänder Doppelkerben mit M 10 eindrücken. Geschenke und Bänder bunt färben. Schild mit Lebensmittelfarbdrucker herstellen. Schilder und Geschenke um den Tannenbaum platzieren.

› Make the Christmas tree by modelling a long drawn-out drop, using scissors to cut in little corners all around the tree. | 1 |
To make the garlands, make some marzipan sticks into rolls. Use an M 10 to indent the top side. | 2 |
Place the garlands one after the other on your hand and indent on the side. | 3 |
Place the garlands irregularly around the tree and press the ends slightly down. | 4 |
Apply a yellow base coat followed by a strong green colour. Spray the garlands well with water. Cut out the small star and fix to the top, colouring it yellow. Once you have finished colouring the Christmas tree, immediately press on the silver beads. Otherwise you can apply a little dark couverture very sparingly with the icing bag and then press the beads into these. Royal icing can only be used if it is coloured green, otherwise the white colour will be too prominent.
Cut out the floor star from a slab, apply yellow base coat and then red shading from the tips to the centre. Outline the darker edges in white couverture.
To make the present parcels, cut out marzipan cubes. The ribbons are formed by scoring a double groove with an M 10. Apply different colours to parcels and ribbons. Make the sign using the food colour printer. Place the sign and presents around the Christmas tree.

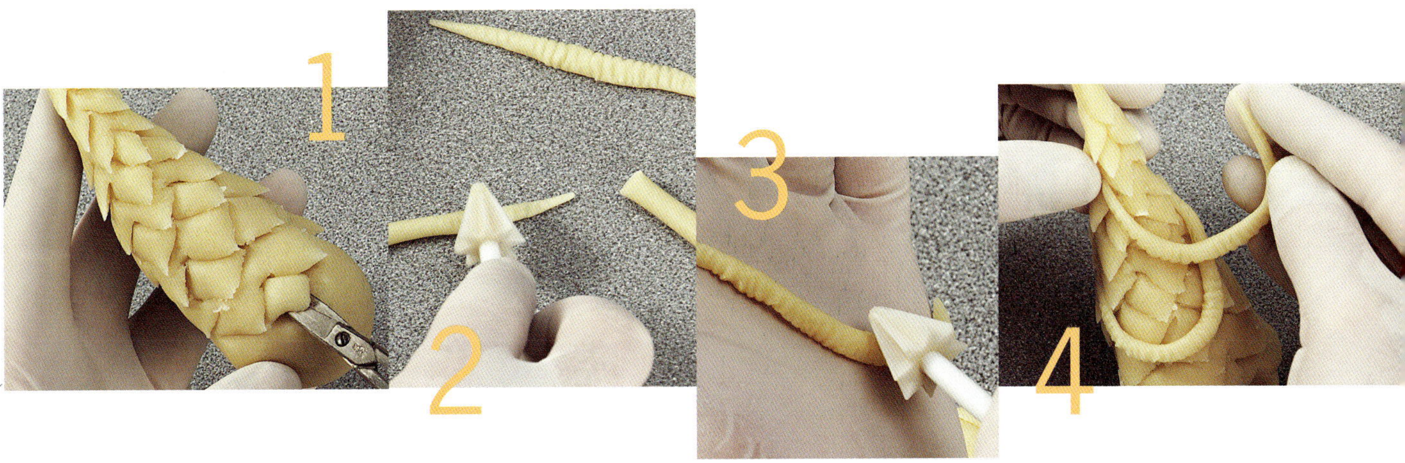

Liebe

In love engaged in wedlock

Verliebt verlobt verheiratet

It's time for a kiss!

It's time for a kiss!

Die Spatzen pfeifens von den Dächern!
As happy as a lark!

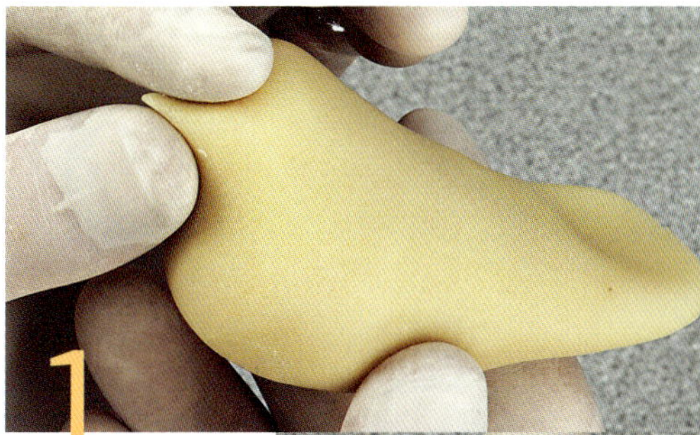
1

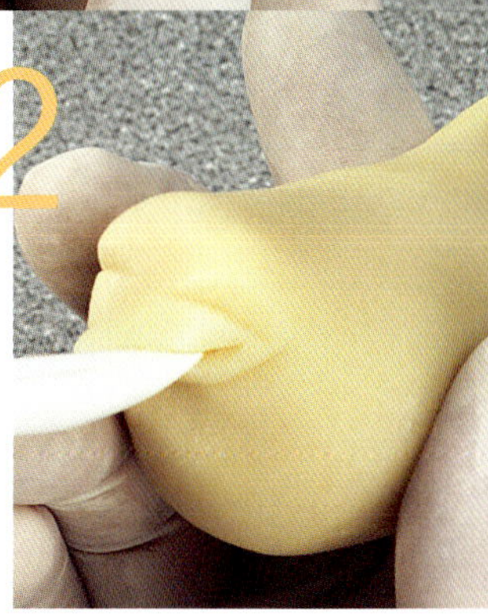
2

3

> Blätter mit Silikonform ausformen oder modellieren. Gelb grundieren, mit Grün ungleichmäßig färben und mit Wasser nachsprühen. Blätter leicht wölben und trocknen lassen. Ast naturgetreu aus einer Marzipanstange formen und braun färben. Blätter am Ast platzieren.

Für den Vogel die Grundform des stumpfen Tropfens fertigen. Das dünne Ende flach und breit drücken. Den Kopf mit beiden Zeigefingern leicht herausmodellieren. Mit Daumen und Zeigefinger den Schnabel formen. | 1 |

Ständiges Tippen verhindert ein Reißen des Marzipans. Augen mit M 2 eindrücken. Mit dem spitzen Winkel des M 1 den Schnabel sauber einkerben. | 2 |

Mit dem stumpfen Winkel des M 1 die Flügel und die Schwungfedern eindrücken. Die Flaumfedern mit M 6 andeuten. | 3 |

Zur Farbgebung am besten eine Abbildung des Originalvogels hinzuziehen. Für das Gefieder ohne Grundierung Brauntöne aufsprühen.

Charakteristische Federmuster mit dem Pinsel nacharbeiten.

Vögel auf dem Ast anordnen. Schild mit dem Lebensmittelfarbdrucker herstellen und anbringen.

Achtung: Gefieder der Vögel nicht nass in nass färben, sondern jeden Farbauftrag trocknen lassen.

> Make the leaves by modelling them yourself or using a silicone shape. Apply a yellow base coat, then an irregular colouring with green and finally spray with water. Slightly bend the leaves and leave to dry. Form the branch from a rolled marzipan strip as naturally as possible and colour brown. Place the leaves on the branch.

To make the bird, start with the basic shape of a bulb, the thin end of which you push flat so that it widens out. Use both forefingers to model the head. Form the beak between thumb and forefinger. | 1 |

Keep tapping the marzipan with your fingers to prevent cracks forming. Use an M 2 to indent the eye sockets. Use the sharp edge of the M 1 to make a neat line along the beak. | 2 |

Use the blunt end of the M 1 to shape the wings and the main feathers. Use an M 6 to give a light indication of the soft feathers. | 3 |

For the colouring it is best to copy a picture of an actual bird. Colour the feathers without base coat in shades of brown, sprayed on. Characteristic patterns of the plumage can be worked in with the brush. Arrange the birds on the branch. Make the sign with the printer for food colouring and fix to the ensemble.

Important: When colouring the feathers of the birds it is best to let each coat dry out before applying the next one, rather than working wet-in-wet.

> Marzipanring aus einer Stange formen. Zwei Marzipanrollen in Stücke schneiden und daraus Tropfen modellieren. Zwischen zwei Folien legen und zu Blütenblättern ausstreichen. Es werden etwa 30 Blütenblätter benötigt. | 1 |
Jedes Blatt mit M 1 in der Mitte profilieren und ringsum versetzt über den Ring legen. | 2 |
Aus einer platt gedrückten Kugel das Gesicht formen. Mit M 9 Rauten einkerben. | 3 |
Mit leichter Drehung des M 2 die Augen und den Mund mit M 3 eindrücken. Eine kleine Raute bildet die Nase. Gesicht mit Gelb und Braun grundieren. Wasser nachsprühen, um die Vertiefungen hervorzuheben. Mund mit Pinsel schminken und Augen einspritzen. Den Blütenring mit Gelb grundieren und die Spitzen sehr leicht mit Rot nachsprühen. Gesicht in noch feuchtem Zustand in den Ring einsetzen.
Das große Blatt aus einer dünnen Marzipanplatte ausschneiden, einkerben und mit Gelb sowie Grün färben. Ebenfalls Wasser nachsprühen. In leichter Wölbung trocknen lassen.
Die Sonnenblumenblüte und ein Schildchen auf dem Blatt anbringen.

> Make a marzipan ring from a rolled strip. Cut two marzipan rolls into pieces and model into drops. Place between two foils and flatten out to make petals. You need 30 petals. | 1 |
Each leaf is shaped along the middle using an M 1 and then the leaves are attached all along the ring with a half overlap for each leaf. | 2 |
Model the face from a squashed marzipan ball. Score the diamond shapes with an M 9. | 3 |
Use the M 2 with a slight twisting motion to indent holes for eyes.
Mark the outline of the mouth with an M 3. Use a small diamond to form the nose. Apply yellow and brown base coat to the face, followed by a spray of water to highlight the indentations. Use the brush to colour the mouth and then pipe on the eyes. Apply yellow base coat to the ring of petals and add a slight touch of red to the tips. Place the face into the ring while it is still moist.
Cut out the large leaf from a thin marzipan slab, score the lines and colour with yellow and green, following up with a spray of water. Slightly bend and leave to dry.
Fix the sunflower head and a small sign on the leaf.

PROFI**TIPP** *Sanft gewölbte Blätter am besten auf einer Folie, die man entsprechend unterbaut, trocknen lassen. Die Folienwölbung ergibt eine natürliche Form.*

It is best to allow the slightly curved leaves to dry on a piece of foil with the necessary support underneath. The curve of the foil results in a natural form.

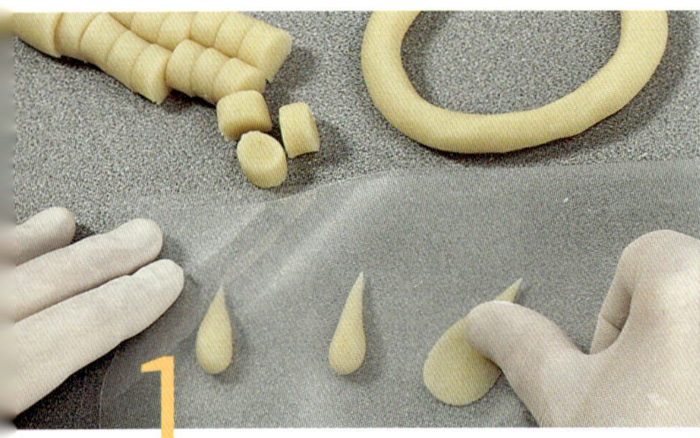
1

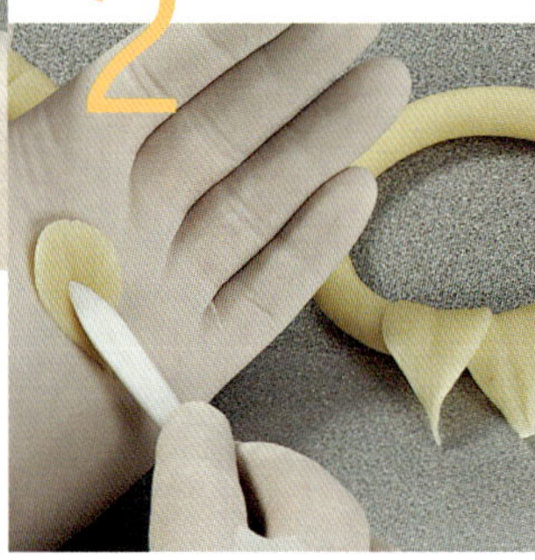
2

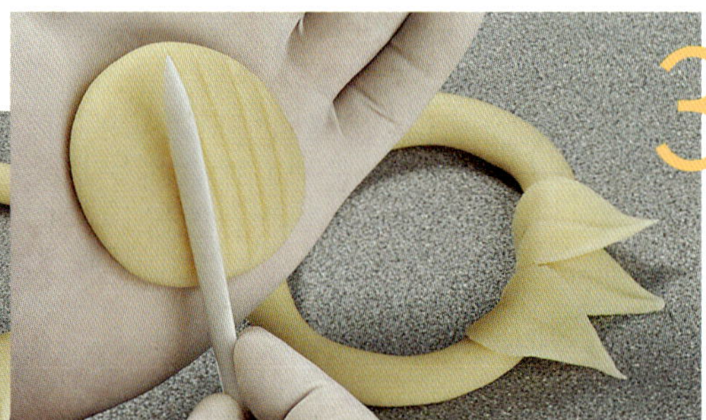
3

Bring me sunshine

Bring me sunshine

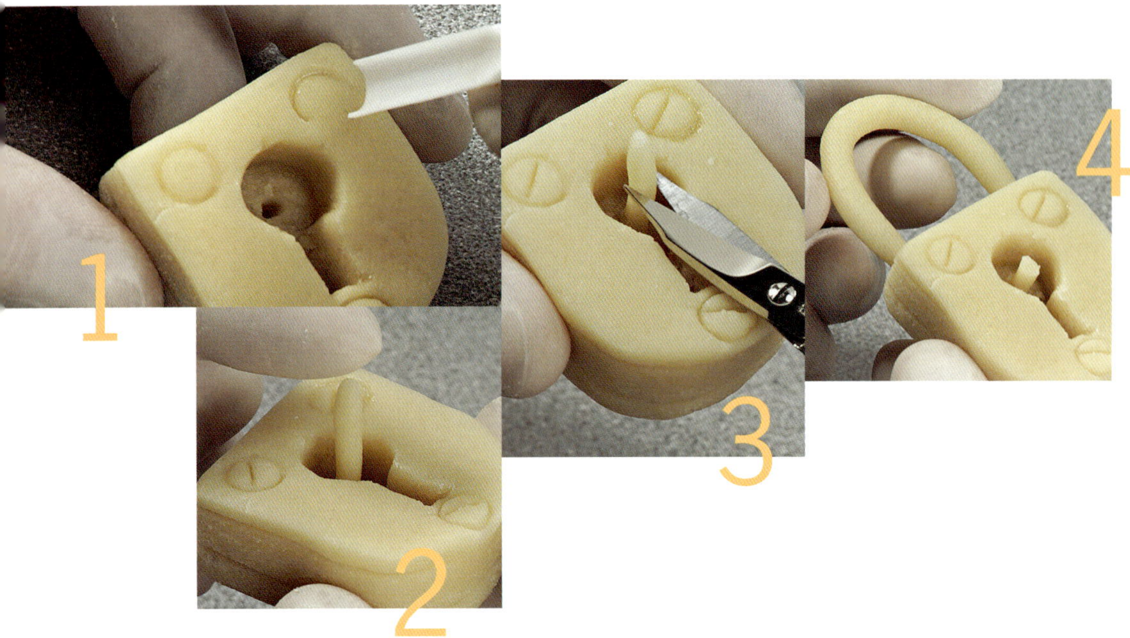

› Aus einem Tropfen ein Herz formen. Mit M 1 und M 11 die Holztore einkerben. Kurze Stangensegmente bilden die Scharniere der Türen und des Verschlusses.
Den Bart des Schlüssels aus einer Platte schneiden und an einer Marzipanstange befestigen. Den Griff aus einer Stange formen, ankleben und trocknen lassen.
Das Vorhängeschloss aus einer 1,5 cm dicken Marzipanplatte schneiden. Mit M 6 und einem Skalpell die Schlüsselöffnung herausheben.
Die Schrauben werden mit einem kleinen runden Ausstecher oder mit M 6 und M 11 eingedrückt. |1|
Eine kurze Stange bildet die Führung. |2|
Mit der Schere zurechtkürzen. |3|
Schließlich den Bügel anbringen. |4|
Das Herz gelb grundieren. Rote und braune Farbe möglichst sauber getrennt aufsprühen. Die „Holztore“ mit Wasser nachsprühen. Alle „Beschläge“ weiß grundieren und zart mit Schwarz nachsprühen. Erst jetzt alle Teile zusammenfügen.
Mit etwas Kuvertüre die Punkte der Scharniere und das Innere des Schlosses spritzen.

› Form the shape of a heart from a drop. Score the wooden shutters using an M 1 and M 11. The hinges of the shutters as well as the latch are made from short rolled pieces.
Cut the web of the key from a slab and fix to a marzipan roll. Shape the end of the key from a rolled strip, attach and leave to dry. Cut the padlock from a 1,5 cm thick marzipan slab. Use an M 6 and a scalpel to lift out the opening for the keyhole.
The screws are impressed with a small round cutting tool or with an M 6 or M 11. |1|
A short roll is used to make the guide pin. |2|
Use scissors to trim as required. |3|
Finally attach the shackles. |4|
Apply a yellow base coat to the heart. Spray on the red and brown colours, keeping them neatly separate as far as possible. Apply some water spray to the wooden shutters. Apply white base coat to all “metal” parts and then follow up with a light black spray. Now all the parts can be assembled.
Use a little couverture to pipe on the points of the hinges as well as the inner part of the lock.

You’ve got the key to my heart

... the key to my heart

› Grundplatte unregelmäßig aus einer Marzipankugel ausdrücken. Gelb grundieren und mit verwässertem Braun nachsprühen. Grünes Marzipan in Streifen schneiden und als Algen auflegen.
Die Muschel aus einer Kugel formen. Muschelrand vorne stark zusammendrücken. Hinten eher stumpf belassen. Mit M 1 Rillen eindrücken. Mit M 3 den geschwungenen Mund, mit M 2 oder M 4 die Augen eindrücken. Die Muschel weiß grundieren und mit Braun leicht schattieren. Den Mund mit dem Pinsel nachziehen.
Für den Hummer eine nach hinten dünner zulaufende Stange fertigen. Den Schwanz breit drücken, den Rückenpanzer mit M 1 einkerben. Den Kopf spitz modellieren, den Mund einschneiden und die Augen eindrücken. | 1 |
Aus kleinen Marzipanstückchen fast rechteckige Platten formen und vom Schwanz zum Kopf hin aufdrücken. | 2 |
Mit M 1 die Panzerteile nachformen. | 3 |
Mit demselben Modellierholz die Schwanzflosse profilieren. | 4 |
Aus drei Stangen Beine formen und unter dem Körper befestigen. Kleine Winkel aus Pappe halten sie in Form, bis sie getrocknet sind. Die Scheren identisch aus einer Stange formen. Hier helfen hauptsächlich M 1 und M 3. Figur rot grundieren. Mit etwas Gelb übersprühen und mit Braun schattieren. Um Lichtreflexionen des Körpers und der Scheren zu verstärken, Hummerkörper mit Weiß mittig übersprühen.
Hummer, Muschel und ein Schildchen auf der Grundplatte platzieren.

› Press out an irregular base slab from a marzipan ball. Apply a yellow base coat and follow up with a watered-down brown spray. Cut out green marzipan in strips and put in place to simulate seaweed. Make the shell from a marzipan ball. Squeeze the edge of the shell together at the front. At the back it is best to leave it blunter. Use an M 1 to score the grooves. Use an M 3 to shape the curvy mouth and an M 2 or M 4 to press in the eye sockets. Apply white base coat to the shell followed by a light brown shading. Highlight the mouth using the brush.
To make the lobster, use a rolled piece that reduces in diameter towards the end. Squash the end to form the tail, use an M 1 to score the scale pattern on the back. Model the head to a rounded point, cut in the mouth and press in the eye sockets. | 1 |
Cut almost rectangular plates from small marzipan pieces and attach to the body, starting from the tail towards the head. | 2 |
Use M 1 to accentuate the shape of the scales. | 3 |
Use the same modelling tool to score the profile of the tail fin. | 4 |
Form legs from three rolled strips and attach underneath the body. Use small pieces of bent cardboard to support them until they have dried. Make identical pincers from a roll – the M 1 and M 3 tools can be helpful for this. Apply red base coat to the figure. Overspray with a little yellow and add shadows with brown. In order to increase the light reflection of the body and pincers it is best to apply a white spray to the centre of the lobster body.
Place the lobster, the shell and a little sign on the base slab.

1
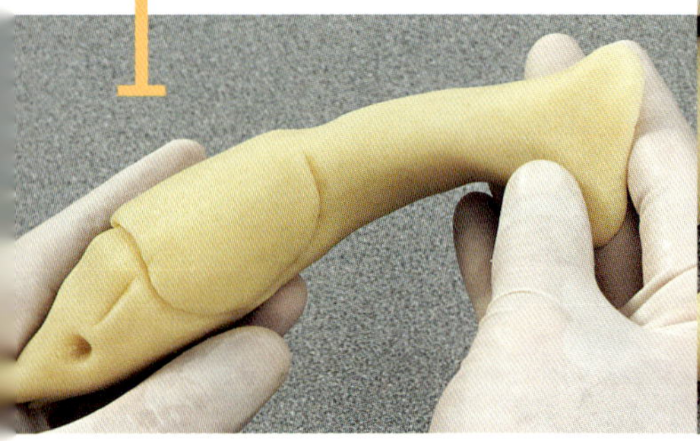
2
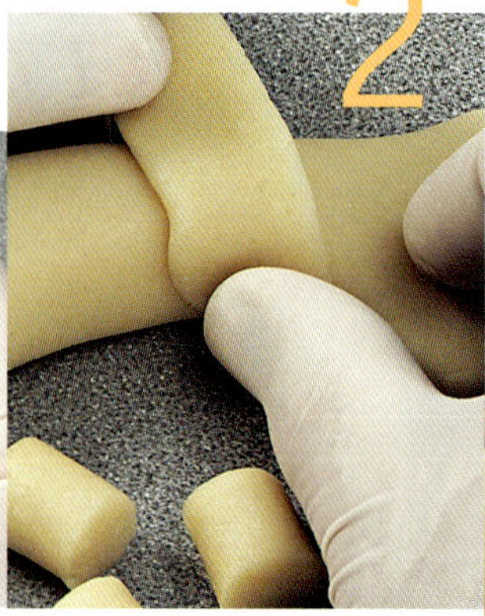
3
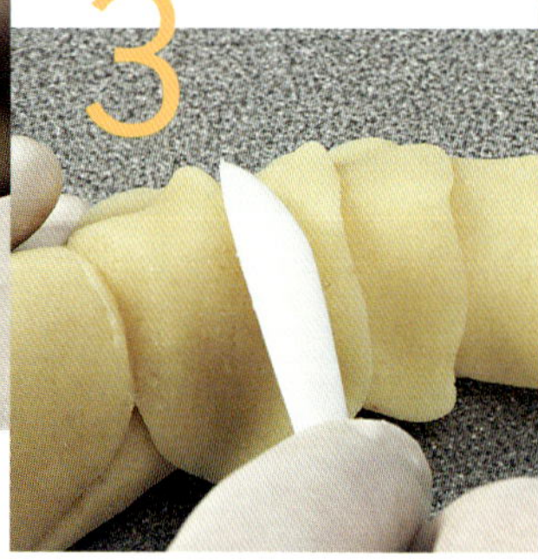
4
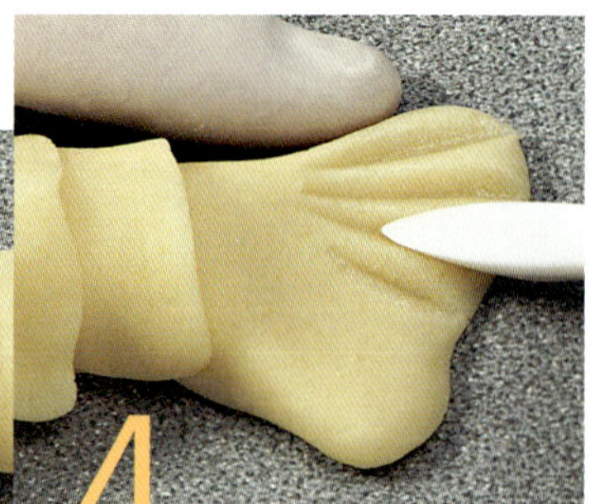

Ich liebe Deine „Inneren Werte“

I love your inner values

In Liebe
In love

› Aus zwei unterschiedlich großen Tropfen die Herzen formen. Mit passendem Ausstecher eine Öffnung in das große Herz stechen und das kleine einpassen. Weiß grundieren und mit Rot nachsprühen.
Das Tuch aus einer dünnen Marzipanplatte schneiden, sofort in Falten legen und anpassen. Hier mit dem Färben warten, bis das Marzipan durchgetrocknet ist, damit keine Verformung mehr stattfindet. Von den Herzen trennen und blau grundieren. Mit Weiß Schattierungen aufsprühen.
Das Käferchen aus einer Kugel formen, Flügel und Kopf mit M 1 einkerben. Mit dem Pinsel schminken, Punkte und Beine mit Kuvertüre aufspritzen.
Die Grundplatte hat das Aussehen eines Spitzendeckchens. Sie besteht hier aus weißer Dekormasse, kann aber auch aus weiß gefärbtem Marzipan hergestellt werden. Mit einem kleinen Tortenring die ungefähre Größe auf Dekormasse oder Marzipan aufzeichnen. Einen Zackenausstecher zum Profilieren verwenden. | 1 |
Dekorausstecher geben mehr Transparenz. | 2 |
Die anfallenden Teile sorgfältig auslösen. | 3 |
Mit M 8 Muster in die ausgestochenen Dekorformen eindrücken und auf die Grundplatte auflegen. Herzen, Tuch und Käferchen auf der Grundplatte zurechtlegen. Schriftzug und Dekor auf die Herzen aufspritzen.

› Form the hearts from two drops of different sizes. Use a suitable cutting tool to cut an opening in the larger heart and fit the small one into the opening. Apply white base coat and follow up with a red spray.
Cut the cloth from a thin marzipan slab, immediately shape the folds and arrange the overall form. Wait for the colouring until the marzipan has fully dried out so that it doesn't lose its shape when the wet colouring is applied. Separate from the hearts and apply blue base coat. Spray on white to create variations in the blue.
Make the little beetle by starting from a ball, using an M 1 to score the wings and the head. Use the brush to apply paint, pipe on the dots and the legs with couverture.
The base slab looks like a round piece of lace. It is made from white icing but can also be made from marzipan that is dyed white. Use a small cake ring to draw the rough size onto the icing or marzipan. Cut out the patterns with a jagged edge cutter. | 1 |
You can achieve greater transparency with special decoration cutters. | 2 |
Carefully remove the cut-out shapes. | 3 |
Use an M 8 to score patterns into the cut-out decorative shapes and place onto the lace base; also arrange the hearts, the cloth and the little beetle and then pipe the writing and decoration onto the hearts.

PROFI **TIPP** *Diese essbaren Spitzendeckchen lassen sich gut in Serie fertigen.*

These edible lace work pieces lend themselves to being made in series.

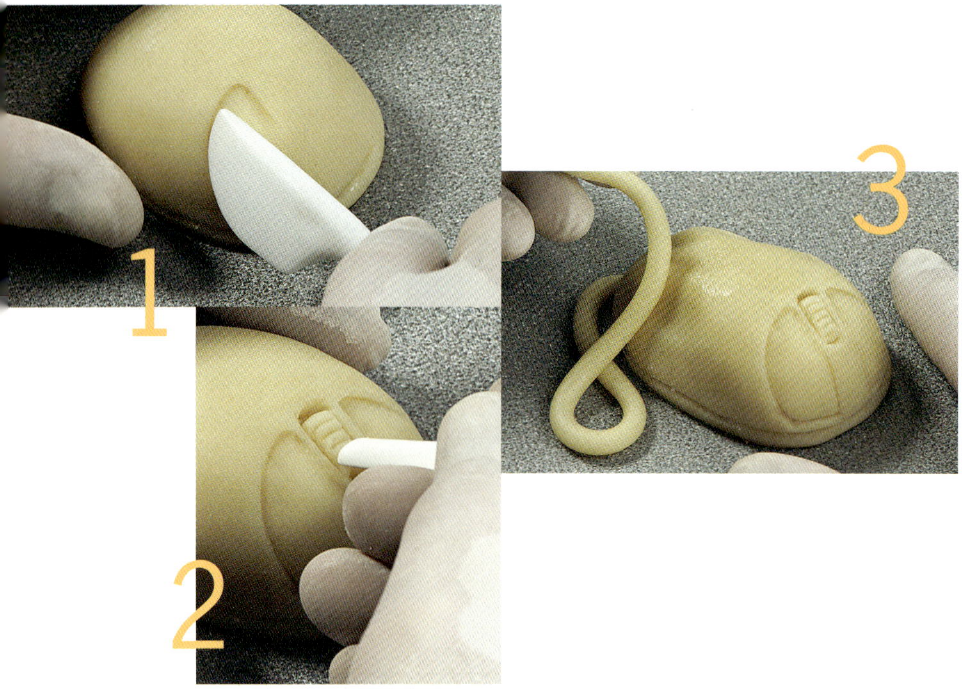

› Halb liegendes Mäuschen modellieren, Kopf abstützen und trocknen lassen. Gelb grundieren und mit Braun fertig färben. Mund und Innenseite der Ohren mit dem Pinsel hautfarben nachschminken. Schwanz, Hände und Füße rosa besprühen. Dabei auf einen weichen Übergang zum Braun des Fells achten.
Für die PC-Maus eine länglich geformte Kugel herstellen. Diese halbieren oder auf der Unterlage bündig anmodellieren. Die Oberfläche mit den Fingern in die typische Form tippen. Mit M 7 Tasten einkerben. Hier die Form des Modellierholzes nutzen. | 1 |
Mit der scharfen Kante noch mal nachkerben. Das Scroll-Rad mit M 3 oder M 8 eindrücken. | 2 |
Marzipankabel herstellen, an der Maus anbringen und schön legen. | 3 |
Die Computermaus mit schwarzer Farbe leicht grau färben und mit Wasser nachsprühen, um die eingekerbten Spalten hervorzuheben.
Schild herstellen und mit der PC-Maus sowie dem liegenden Mäuschen arrangieren.

› Model the little mouse, half lying down, support the head and leave to dry. Apply yellow base coat and finish off in brown. Go over the mouth and the inside of the ears with a brush to add the skin colour. Spray pink colouring onto tail, hands and feet. Make sure that you achieve a soft transition to the brown of the fur.
To make the PC mouse, start by forming a slightly oblong ball. Cut this in half or, alternatively, model it into shape on the base.
Tap the surface with your fingers to give it the typical form. Use an M 7 to score the buttons, making use of the shape of the modelling tool. | 1 |
Score again using the sharp edge of the tool. Use an M 3 or an M 8 to mark the scrolling wheel. | 2 |
Make the cable in marzipan, attach to the mouse and drape it so that it looks right. | 3 |
Apply black colour to the computer mouse until it is light grey and follow on with a spray of water in order to highlight the scored shapes.
Make the sign and arrange together with the PC mouse and the "real" mouse.

We are two of a kind

We are two of a kind

Für Computerfreaks und Mäusefans

For computer freaks and fans of mice

> Igelkörper aus einem Tropfen modellieren. Den Mund einkerben und mit M 3 ausformen. Die Beine aus der Grundform modellieren. Die Stacheln mit M 10 in das Marzipan rollen. Nase und Arme ansetzen. Figur gelb grundieren, dabei Bauch und Schnauze auslassen. Mit Braun nachsprühen. Stacheln schwarz grundieren und mit Wasser hervorheben. Nach der Trocknung mit fast trockenem Weiß die Stacheln quer schattieren. Bauch und Schnauze rosa besprühen. Nase mit dem Pinsel dunkel färben, Bartstoppeln aufzeichnen.
Für den Kaktus eine abgerundete Stange mit M 1 längs einkerben. Von einer etwas größeren Marzipanrolle ein Stück abschneiden, den Blumentopf formen, eine Vertiefung eindrücken und den oberen Topfrand mit M 3 ausmodellieren. Kaktus einsetzen. Kaktus und Topf gelb grundieren. Topf mit Rot, Kaktus mit Grün nachsprühen.
Die Erde mit dem Pinsel anlegen.
Die Herzen aus Tropfen formen. Dafür eine Kugel zwischen den Handballen anspitzen. | 1 |
Tropfenform vorsichtig tippend zwischen Daumen und Zeigefinger platt drücken. | 2 |
Mit M 1 hin- und herwiegend die Herzkerbe eindrücken und vertiefen. Mit den Fingern alle Kanten und Grate wegtippen, bis das Herz gleichmäßig glatt ist. | 3 |
Mit Weiß grundieren und mit Rot leicht schattieren.

> Model the body of the hedgehog from a drop. Cut the opening of the mouth and use an M 3 to finish its shape. Work the legs by modelling from the basic shape. Use an M 10 to roll the spikes into the marzipan. Attach nose and arms. Apply yellow base coat to the figure, leaving out the belly and snout. Follow on with a brown spray. Apply black base coat to the spikes and highlight with water. Once they have dried, apply cross strokes in nearly dry white to add contrast. Spray on pink for belly and snout. Apply darker colour to the nose and carefully paint on the whiskers.
To make the cactus, score a rounded roll along the side with an M 1 tool. Cut off a piece from a slightly larger marzipan roll, shape the flower pot, press the top down a little and model the top edge of the pot with an M 3. Place the cactus on the pot. Apply yellow base coat to the cactus and the pot. Spray the pot with red and the cactus with green. Use the brush to paint on the colour for the earth.
Shape the hearts from drops. To make these, use a ball and roll it between both hands until a point is formed. | 1 |
Carefully tap the drop between thumb and forefinger to flatten it. | 2 |
Use an M 1 to gradually work in the cleavage of the heart. Tap with your fingers to smooth out all edges and burs until the heart is smooth all over. | 3 |
Apply white base coat and follow on with a light shade of red.

PROFI **TIPP** *Um die Herzen wie abgebildet zu befestigen, muss das Exponat entweder liegen und/oder abgestützt sein, bis die Verbindung ausgehärtet ist. Hier wurden die Herzen mit kurzen Holzstäbchen einfach angesteckt.*

In order to fix the hearts as shown, the item has to either lie on its side or the hearts have to be supported until the join has hardened. In our example here the hearts have been fastened with short wooden sticks.

Liebe auf den ersten Blick

Love at first sight

1

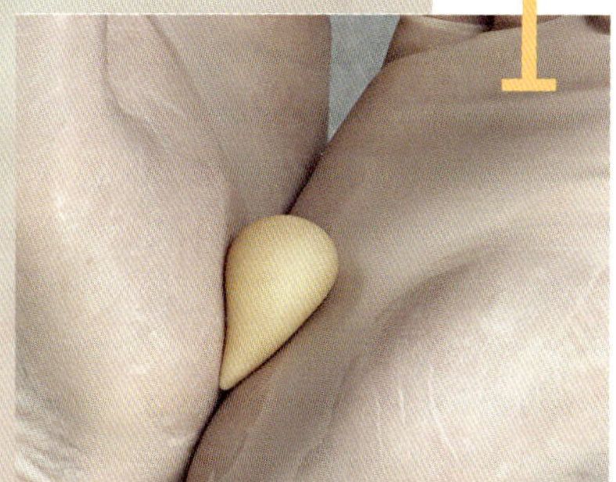

2

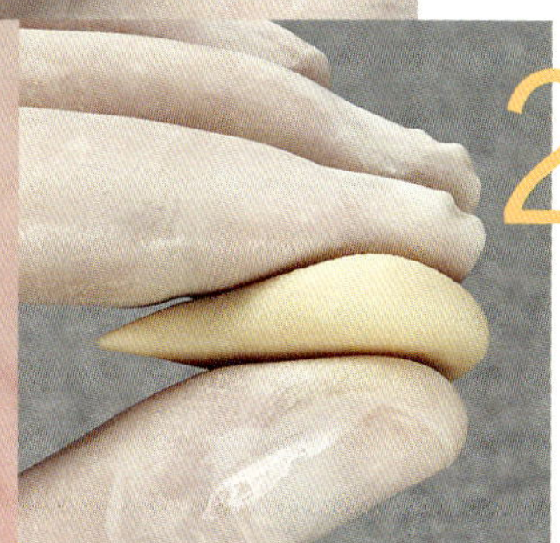

3

Nein Schatz, ich habe Kopf-Schmerz

Sorry darling …

› Für den Nagel eine Marzipanstange rollen, durch Plattdrehen auf einer Unterlage den Kopf herstellen. Riffelung mit M 9 eindrücken. Mundform mit M 1 andeuten. Augenbrauen ansetzen. Mit Weiß grundieren und mit Schwarz schattieren. Aufschlagfläche mit Wasser nachsprühen. Augen und Mund aufspritzen.
Den Hammer aus einer konisch zulaufenden Stange und einem Quader herstellen. Für die Nase ein Stück des Stiels abschneiden und auf den Hammer wieder aufkleben, so dass der Eindruck entsteht, der Stiel wäre fortgesetzt. Hammer farbig schminken und Augen aufspritzen. Mundform ebenfalls mit M 1 andeuten. Zunge und Augenbrauen ansetzen.
Für das Brett Marzipan ausrollen. Mit M 8 die Astlöcher und die Brettmaserung einkerben. | 1 |
Brett mit scharfem Messer zurechtschneiden. Gelbe Grundierung gleichmäßig auftragen. Braune Farbe schräg aufsprühen. So entsteht eine gewisse Tiefenwirkung der Rillen. | 2 |
Durch das Nachsprühen mit Wasser verstärkt sich die Tiefenwirkung. | 3 |
Hammer und Nagel auf dem Brett anbringen. Schrift aufspritzen.

› To make the nail, roll the marzipan strip and then form the head by turning the nail on its end on a hard surface until the head is shaped. Use an M 9 to score the cross pattern. Use an M 1 to indicate the shape of the mouth. Apply the eyebrows separately. Use a white base coat followed by shading in black. Follow up with a spray of water on the top surface, pipe on eyes and mouth.
Make the hammer from a tapering roll and an oblong block of marzipan. Cut a piece of the handle to form the nose and attach to the end of hammerhead so that one gets the impression that the handle sticks out of the head. Colour the hammer and pipe on the eyes. Score the line of the mouth with an M 1. Add on shapes for the tongue and the eyebrows.
To make the board, roll out some marzipan. Use an M 8 to score the knots and the grain. | 1 |
Use a sharp knife to cut the board into the required shape. Apply an even base coat of yellow. Spray on brown colour at an angle. This creates the illusion of a certain depth to the grain. | 2 |
This effect is further highlighted by spraying on water. | 3 |
Arrange the hammer and nail on the board, then pipe on the writing.

PROFI **TIPP** *Kerben und Vertiefungen werden durch das Übersprühen des gefärbten Objekts mit Wasser sehr schön hervorgehoben. In der Vertiefung sammelt sich die Farbe und lässt diese dunkler hervortreten.*

The scoring and indentations can be very nicely accentuated by spraying the coloured object with water. The paint collects in the indentations and makes them appear darker.

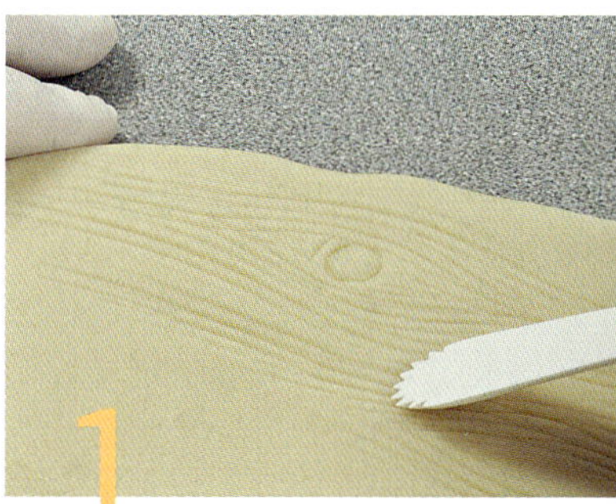
1

2

3

> Die Pilzfüße aus einer Tropfenform modellieren. Den Schirm der Pilze jeweils aus einer platt gedrückten Kugel herstellen und mit M 10 an der Unterseite fächerformig einkerben. Die Pilzränder dürfen, wie bei einem echten Pilz auch, etwas einbrechen. Gegebenenfalls durch Einschneiden etwas nachhelfen. Pilzschirme auf die jeweiligen Fußteile setzen und nur von oben mit Braun besprühen. Ein Hauch Schwarz am Pilzrand verleiht dem Pilz mehr Struktur.
Eine kleine Ameise modellieren, schminken und auf den größeren Pilzschirm aufsetzen. Bei Bedarf kann die Ameise auch durch ein anderes Insekt, zum Beispiel ein Bienchen (siehe "Have fun at the concert", Seite 228), ersetzt werden.
Blätter modellieren, in natürlicher Form trocknen lassen und herbstlich schminken.
Die Regenwürmchen nacheinander aus einer Stange formen. Mit M 1 die einzelnen Glieder gleichmäßig einkerben. Ein Stangenende durch Abrunden zum Kopf formen. Augen und Mund mit M 1 eindrücken. | 1 |
Danach die Figur sofort in Form bringen und zwischen den Stützhölzchen ausrichten. | 2 |
Eine Korrektur der Form ist später kaum möglich, da das Marzipan sehr schnell antrocknet und dann an den Kerben brechen würde. Würmchen herzförmig zusammenstellen und sofort ankleben. | 3 |
Mit Weiß grundieren und zart mit Rot nachsprühen. Grundplatte aus einer Marzipankugel ausstreichen, schminken, Pilze, Blätter und Herzwürmchen arrangieren, mit Schildchen fertig stellen.

> Model the mushroom stalks from a drop shape. Make the head of the mushrooms from a ball flattened on one side and apply the radial scoring on the underside with an M 10. It is OK if the edges of the mushroom are slightly jagged, just as with natural mushrooms. You can even help the process by making small insertions with a knife. Place the heads of the mushrooms on their stalks and spray from the top with brown colour. A touch of black at the edge of the mushroom gives the shape more depth.
Model a small ant, colour it and place it on the larger mushroom head. If you want, you can also replace the ant with another insect such as, for example, a small bee (see "Have fun at the concert", page 228).
Model the leaves, leave to dry in a natural shape and colour in autumn colours. Form the earthworms one by one from a rolled marzipan strip. Use an M 1 to apply an even texture to their bodies. Form one end of the worm into a head by rounding it off. Use an M 1 to score the eyes and mouth. | 1 |
Immediately proceed to give the figure the required shape and arrange between the supporting blocks. | 2 |
Later on it is nearly impossible to correct the shape since the marzipan will dry out very quickly and would break where it has been scored. Put the two worms together to make a heart shape and attach immediately. | 3 |
Apply white base coat and lightly spray with red. Roll out the base slab from a marzipan ball, apply the colouring, arrange the mushrooms, leaves and heart-shaped worms and finish off with the sign.

PROFI **TIPP** *Je freitragender das Exponat, desto mehr Trocknungszeit muss berücksichtigt werden. Da bei jedem Farbauftrag wieder Feuchtigkeit zugeführt wird, die erneut abtrocknen muss, sollte man diese Zeit mit einberechnen.*

The less support there is for slender objects, the more time is required for drying. As each coat of colour adds moisture, care must be taken to let the object dry before adding another coat. This drying process needs to be taken into account in the overall time planning.

Wo die Liebe hinfällt

Where love strikes

1

2

3

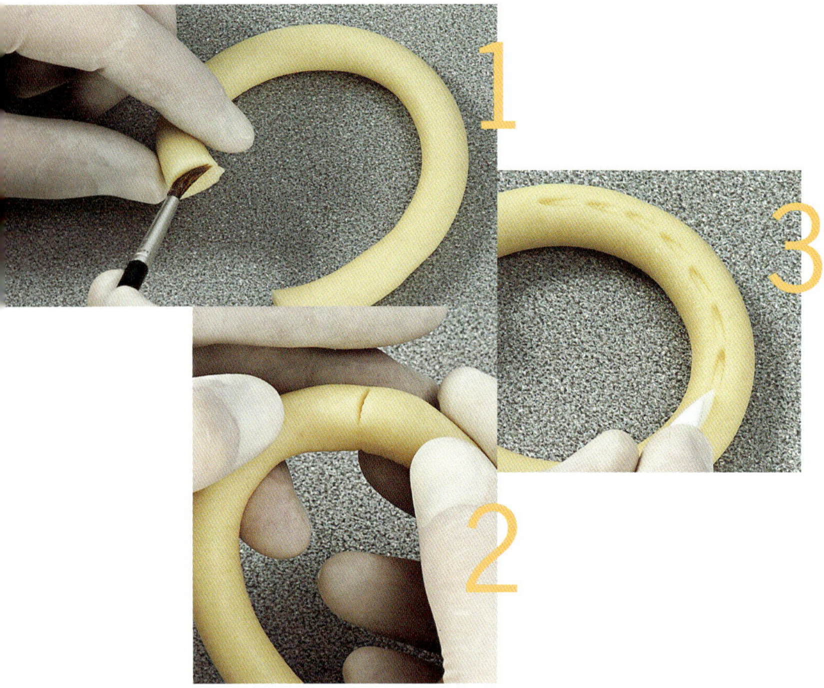

> Eine dicke Marzipanstange zwischen den Handflächen platt drücken, die Ecken herausarbeiten und eine Kissenform modellieren. Mit M 1 ein Muster eindrücken. Weiß besprühen und trocknen lassen.
Für die Ringe zwei gleichmäßige Stangen passend abschneiden und in Ringform biegen. Die beiden Endstücke jeweils mit etwas Eiweiß aneinander kleben. | 1 |
Durch Reiben und Tippen die Naht unsichtbar machen. | 2 |
Mit der gekerbten Seite des M 10 ein Muster in den Ring eindrücken. | 3 |
Ringe gelb grundieren, zart mit Rot übersprühen und mit leichtem Wassernebel die Farbe in die Vertiefungen laufen lassen. Ringe Seite an Seite auf dem Kissen platzieren.
Aus durchgefärbtem Marzipan ein Band herstellen und auf den beiden nebeneinander liegenden Ringen auflegen, den übrigen Teil des Bands geschwungen drapieren und gegebenenfalls bis zur Trocknung stützen.
Wenn das Band vollständig getrocknet ist, Zierstreifen aus Eiweißspritzglasur aufbringen und Schildchen auflegen.

> Take a thick bar of marzipan between both hands and press until flat; shape the corners until the form of a cushion has been modelled. Use an M 1 to score a pattern. Spray on white colouring and leave to dry.
To make the rings, cut a suitable length of two rolled strips and bend into the shape of rings. Attach the two ends to each other with a little egg white. | 1 |
Tap and rub the join until it disappears. | 2 |
Use the indented side of an M 10 to make a pattern in the rings. | 3 |
Apply yellow base coat to the rings and follow on with a light red spray; then spray on a light water mist so that the colour runs into the indentations. Place the rings next to each other on the cushion.
Use tinted marzipan to make the ribbon and place this onto the two rings, with the rest of the ribbon draped to suit; if necessary support the ribbon until dry.
When the ribbon has dried completely, apply a decorative stripe in royal icing and add the sign.

Zur Verlobung

... engagement

Als Geschenk oder als Tortenaufsatz ideal

Ideal as a present or to place on decorative cakes

> Für das Bett helle Kuvertüre auf Papier oder Folie streichen, riffeln und nach Schnittplan zuschneiden. Zum Zusammensetzen der Teile die Folien umdrehen und abziehen.
Die beiden Seitenwände des Bettes mit etwas Kuvertüre auf der Unterseite der Grundplatte befestigen. Nach der Aushärtung das Bett drehen, Kopf- und Fußteil sowie die vier Eckpfosten anbringen. Auf jeden Eckpfosten eine braun gefärbte Marzipankugel setzen.
Die Decken und Kissen aus durchgefärbtem weißem Marzipan herstellen. Aus zwei Stangensegmenten die Kissen formen. Bettlaken und Kissen auf dem Bett befestigen.
Köpfe und Hände des Pärchens wie im Grundlagenkapitel „Modelliertechniken“ (ab Seite 232) beschrieben herstellen und auf das Bett andrücken. Die jeweiligen Körper aus kurzen Stangen andeuten und später unter der Bettdecke kaschieren. Kleine, zylinderförmige Marzipanabschnitte für die Füße abrunden und im 90°-Winkel knicken. Mit Daumen und Zeigefinger die Wölbung der Fußform zurechttippen. | 1 |
Die Zehenkante muss in ihrer Stärke von einer zur anderen Seite zunehmen. An dieser dickeren Stelle mit M 9 den großen Zehen einkerben und die weiteren anschließen lassen. | 2 |
Mit M 3 auf der Unterseite des Fußes die Zehen abgrenzend eindrücken. | 3 |
Alle Füße direkt am Bett befestigen und dabei in spielerische Form bringen. Ausgerollte Marzipandecke als Bettdecke über die Figuren legen. Ein ausgestochenes, rot-gelb geschminktes Herz auflegen. Die Namen mit Kuvertüre aufspritzen.

> To make the bed, spread light coloured couverture on paper or foil, apply texture and cut out according to the cutting plan. Take the parts off the foil and join together. Apply a little couverture to the lower edge of the sides and attach these to the base slab. Once this has dried, turn the bed and attach the two ends as well as the four corner posts. Place a brown-coloured marzipan ball onto each of the corner posts. Apply as much decoration as you like to the bed.
Make the covers and pillows from white tinted marzipan. Form the pillows from two segments cut from a roll. Attach the sheets and pillows onto the bed.
Make the heads and hands of the pair as described in the chapter on “Modelling techniques” (from page 232) and lightly press onto the bed. Cut some short pieces of roll and place these under the bed cover later on to suggest the bodies. To make the feet, use small round slices of marzipan, round off and bend at an angle of 90 degrees.
Use thumb and forefinger in a tapping motion to shape the arc of the foot. | 1 |
The row of toes should increase in thickness from one side to the other. At the thick end you can use an M 9 to score the big toe and follow on from there for the other toes. | 2 |
Use an M 3 to score the shape of the toes on the underside of the foot. | 3 |
Attach all feet directly to the bed and arrange playfully as seen in the picture. Drape the rolled-out marzipan as a bed cover over the figures. Cut out a heart shape, colour in red and yellow and place on the bed. Pipe on the names in couverture.

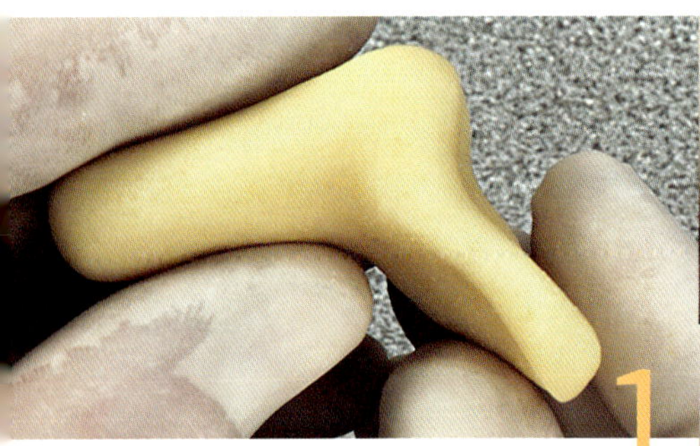
1

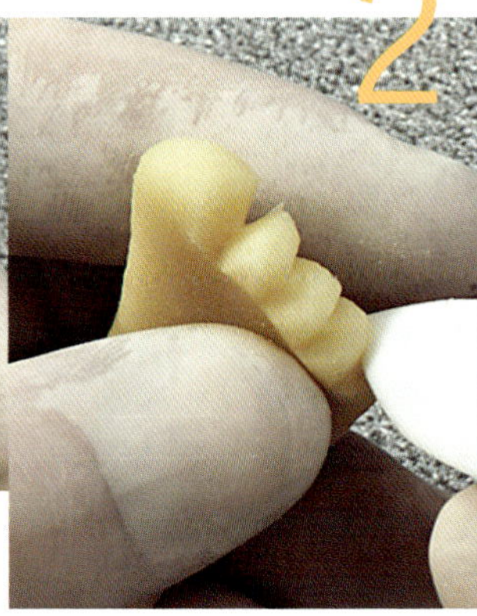
2

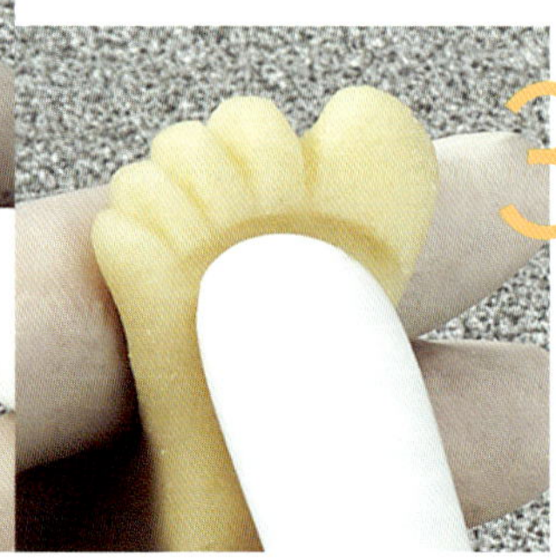
3

Hochzeitsbett

Wedding night

Lebenslänglich
ohne
Bewährung

Lebenslänglich ohne Bewährung

Life without parole

> Den Bräutigam wie im Grundlagenkapitel „Modelliertechniken“ (ab Seite 232) beschrieben herstellen.
Die Braut weitgehend gleich anfertigen. Die Ausgangsform ist ein Kegel, wobei das breitere Ende den weiten Rock des Brautkleids ergibt. Diesen platt drücken, so dass die Braut eine „kniende“ Haltung bekommt. Das aufwendige Ausformen der Beine ist nicht nötig. Die schlanke Taille wird durch ein eingearbeitetes Holzstäbchen stabiler. Das Gesicht der Braut wird im Gegensatz zum Bräutigam etwas zierlicher und runder gestaltet. Auf den noch herausstehenden Teil des Holzstäbchens den Kopf stecken. Den Ansatz am Hals kaschieren, indem eine Perlenkette aufgespritzt wird. Gegebenenfalls können auch weitere Schmuckelemente, wie zum Beispiel Ohrringe, hinzugefügt werden. Figur weiß grundieren und Hautfarbe gesondert aufsprühen. Die Farbübergänge mit dem Pinsel nacharbeiten, um scharfe Abgrenzungen zu erhalten. Die Haare ebenfalls mit dem Pinsel färben. Erst nachdem die Braut vollständig geschminkt ist, den Schleier anbringen. Figur bis zur Trocknung gut abstützen.
Braut und Bräutigam zusammenfügen und mit Schildchen fertig stellen.

> Make up the bridegroom as described in the chapter on “Modelling techniques” (from page 232).
Make the bride in much the same way. Start with a cone shape where the wider end is used to make the wide skirt of the wedding gown. Press it flat so that the bride adopts a “kneeling” position. You don’t need to apply a lot of detail for the legs. The slender waist can be strengthened by working in a small wooden stick.
The face of the bride is made a little more dainty and rounder in contrast to that of the bridegroom. Place the head onto the end of the wooden stick that is still protruding. Hide the join at the neck by piping on a chain of pearls.
You may wish to add further pieces of jewellery, for example earrings etc.
Apply a white base coat to the figure and spray on the skin colour in a separate process. Use a brush to go over the transitions in the colour in order to crisp up the contours. To colour the hair you can also use the brush. Do not attach the veil to the bride until she has been completely coloured. Support the figure well until it is dry. Join the bride and bridegroom together and complete with the sign.

PROFI **TIPP** *Schmuck wirkt besonders schön, wenn er mit Goldfarbe hervorgehoben wird. Bei diesem Exponat kann besonders gut auf individuelle Wünsche der Kundschaft eingegangen werden, indem man sich zum Beispiel Farbe und Art der Kleidung vom Besteller vorgeben lässt.*

Any jewellery looks particularly nice if it is highlighted in gold. This miniature is particularly well suited to incorporating individual requirements of customers, for example by designing the clothes in accordance with details supplied by the customers.

> Grundplatte sowie eine Säule aus weißer Schokolade herstellen. Schrift und Zierelemente mit dunkler Kuvertüre auf Folie spritzen, erstarren lassen und mit Goldfarbe überstreichen. Nach Aushärtung können die einzelnen Teile abgenommen und an der Säule sowie auf der Grundplatte mit Kuvertüre befestigt werden.
Zylinder aus einem Stangenabschnitt, ausgestochener Rundplatte und schmalem Marzipanband zusammenfügen, in Form bringen und schwarz besprühen. Das Hutband mit dem Pinsel und weißer Farbe nachziehen.
Für den Brautschleier aus einer Stange einen länglichen Tropfen formen und zwischen zwei Folien ausstreichen. Mit M 8 Muster des Schleiers eindrücken. | 1 |
Zwei dünne, zugespitzte Marzipanstangen etwas versetzt zueinander verdrehen und ringförmig zu einem Kränzchen formen. | 2 |
Aus einem kleinen Stangensegment das „Krönchen“ formen und mit M 8 sowie M 11 einkerben. | 3 |
Alle Teile in noch weichem Zustand zusammenfügen und vor dem Schminken in die endgültige Position bringen. | 4 |

> Make the base slab as well as a column from white chocolate. Pipe on the writing and decorative elements in dark couverture, leave to harden and paint with gold colouring. Once the parts have hardened, they can be taken up and attached with couverture to the column as well as the base slab.
Make up the top hat from a rolled piece, a round slab with the hole cut out and a narrow marzipan ribbon. Join these items together and spray in black. Outline the ribbon with the brush and white paint.
To make the veil for the bride, form a longish drop and roll out between two pieces of foil. Use an M 8 to score the texture of the veil. | 1 |
Twist together two thin pointed marzipan cords, slightly offset and join together to make a little wreath. | 2 |
Make the “little crown” from a small rolled segment and use an M 8 and M 11 to score the required patterns. | 3 |
Join all parts together while still soft and arrange in their final position before applying the colour. | 4 |

PROFI ***TIPP*** *Goldschriften lassen sich in nahezu perfekter Form herstellen, wenn man die Vorlage in gewünschter Schriftart direkt aus dem Computer ausdruckt. Den Vordruck in eine Schutzhülle stecken und mit Kuvertüre nachspritzen. Bevor sich die Kuvertüre löst mit Goldfarbe überpinseln.*

Golden writing can be produced in nearly perfect shape by printing out the words in the required font directly from the computer. Place this template into a protective sleeve and pipe over with couverture. Brush on gold paint before the couverture is detached.

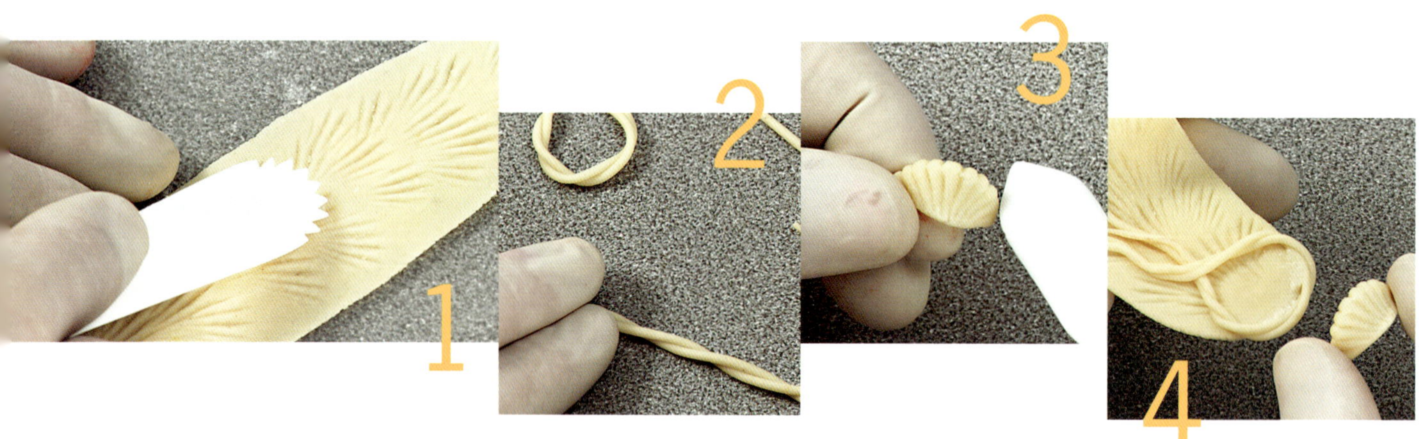

Just married

Just married

> Eine Grundplatte unregelmäßig ausschneiden, Ränder breitflächig mit Gelb grundieren und mit etwas Braun nachsprühen.
Die Eidechse aus einer Stange formen, Mund einschneiden, Nase mit M 1 eindrücken und die Gliedmaßen ansetzen. Augen aufspritzen. Die Figur hauptsächlich vom Rücken her mit den Farben Gelb, Grün und einem Hauch Braun besprühen.
Die „Klebstofftube" aus einer kurzen Marzipanstange fertigen. Ein Ende platt drücken und gerade schneiden. Die andere Seite spitz modellieren, ebenfalls abschneiden und etwas rund tippen. Ein Gewinde formen und auf der Tube anbringen. Gelb grundieren, den Rest mit dem Pinsel nachschminken.
Zur Herstellung der einzelnen Rosenblätter kleine Marzipanscheiben zwischen zwei Folien ausstreichen. Seitlich an einer dünnen Kante eine Blütenblattspitze eindrücken. | 1 |
Auf einem Schaumstoffstück die Innenseite des Blattes mit M 5 sanft kreisend vertiefen, damit durch die nachgebende Unterlage eine kleine Wölbung entsteht. | 2 |
Die dicke Kante an der Unterseite des Rosenblattes zwischen Daumen und Zeigefinger leicht herausziehen. | 3 |
Einen Rosenstiel aus einer Marzipanstange fertigen und eine Rose mit vielen Blütenblättern aufbauen. Beliebige Farbe oder Farbkombinationen aufsprühen. Die Intensität zur Unterseite hin abnehmend. Schildchen fertig stellen und mit den anderen Einzelelementen auf der Grundplatte zu einem „Gesamtbild" zusammenfügen.

> Cut out an irregular base slab, colour a wide edge in yellow base coat and follow on with a little spray of brown.
Form the lizard from a rolled strip, cut the shape of the mouth, imprint the nose using an M 1 and attach the limbs. Pipe on the eyes. Spray the figure mainly from the back with yellow, green and a touch of brown.
Make the "tube of glue" from a short marzipan roll. Press one end flat and cut off square. Shape the other end to a point, also cut off and tap until it is slightly round. Form the shape of the threaded neck and apply to the tube. Apply a yellow base coat and apply the remaining colour with the brush.
To make the individual rose petals, cut slices of marzipan and flatten out between two pieces of foil. Form a point on one side of the petal. | 1 |
Place a petal on a piece of foam rubber and make a slight indentation using an M 5 in a gently rotating movement so that an indentation is created on the flexible base of the foam rubber. | 2 |
Slightly elongate the thick edge of the petal between thumb and forefinger. | 3 |
Make a stalk from a rolled marzipan stick and build up a rose with many petals. You can add any colour or colour combinations, decreasing the intensity towards the bottom end of the petal. Make the sign and arrange with the other individual elements on the base slab to form the miniature.

PROFI ***TIPP*** *Diese Blätter lassen sich ungefärbt sehr gut vorbereiten und aufbewahren. Bei Bestellungen sind sie schnell in gewünschter Farbe geschminkt und beleben jede Freifläche auf Hochzeits- und Festtagstorten.*

It is very easy to prepare these petals and store them without colouring. They can then be used very quickly when an order comes in, coloured in the required way. They make a lively addition to any empty space on a wedding cake or festive torte.

Nichts hält ewig ...
Nothing lasts forever ...

1

2

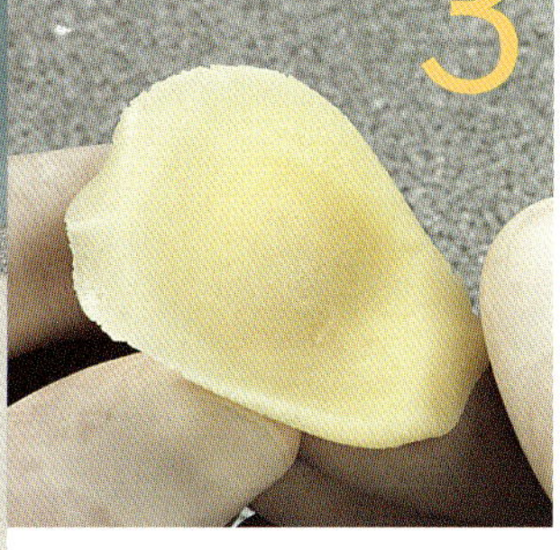
3

It all comes right

Alles wird gut

Dangerous love

Dangerous love

1

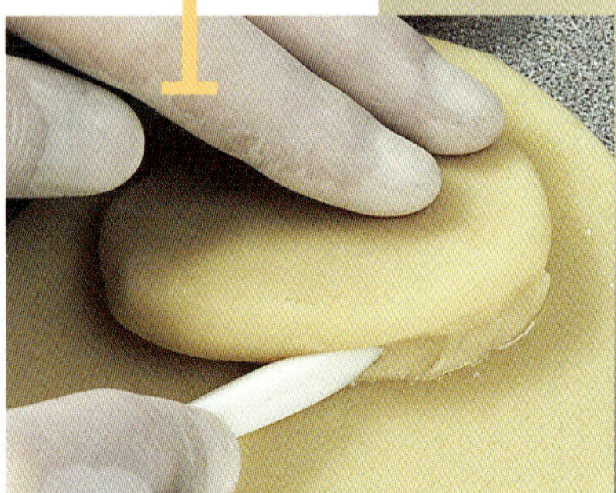

2

3

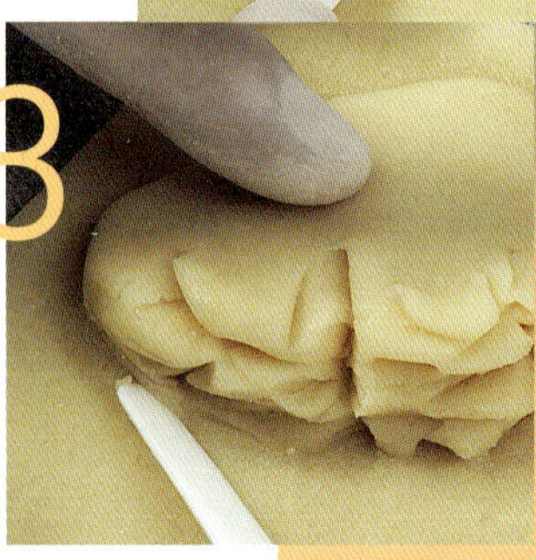

> In beliebiger Form eine Grundplatte ausschneiden, wenden und die Kanten rund tippen. Anschließend die Platte nochmals umdrehen und ein kleines Stück Marzipan für den „Fels" auflegen. Mit M 1 den kleinen Felsen an die Platte anmodellieren. | 1 |
Unter Verwendung der verschiedenen Winkel von M 1 die groben Felsstrukturen einarbeiten. | 2 |
Die Ansatzkante mit etwas Wasser benetzen und mit M 3 den Übergang glatt streichen, bis keine Trennlinien mehr zu erkennen sind. | 3 |
Der Kaktus besteht aus einer langen, etwas bauchigeren und zwei kurzen Stangen. Nach dem Zusammensetzen des Kaktus die Enden rund abmodellieren. Mit M 1 längs feine Kerben eindrücken. Mund, Nase und Augen anbringen. Kaktus auf dem Felsen drappieren. Die Stacheln mit leicht angestockter Kuvertüre horizontal rings um den Kaktus ansetzen. An der rasierten Stelle die Stacheln nach dem Schminken mit dem Skalpell wieder entfernen. Sombrero aus einer runden Platte und einer abgeschnittenen Halbkugel zusammensetzen. Übergang, wie oben beim Felsen beschrieben, kaschieren und auf dem Kopf ankleben.
Die Schlange aus einem Stück formen. Mund einschneiden und Zunge einsetzen. Die Schlange mit Augen versehen und in den Körper ein Schuppenmuster einkerben. Zum Trocknen gut abstützen und anschließend vor dem Felsen platzieren.
Von einem langen Band kleine Teilstücke abschneiden, um die Grundform der Heftpflaster zu erhalten. Die einzelnen Abschnitte durch leichte Einkerbungen und Schminken fertig stellen.
Nach Herstellen und Anbringen des Rasierapparates fehlt zur Vervollständigung der Szenerie nur noch ein kleines Schildchen.
Schminkanregungen sind ausführlich im Grundlagenkapitel „Schminktechniken" (ab Seite 238) nachzulesen.

> Cut a base of any shape, turn over and tap with your fingers until the edges are smooth. Then turn the slab again and put a small piece of marzipan onto it to represent the "rock". Use an M 1 to model the small rock onto the slab. | 1 |
Use the different angles of the M 1 to work in the different rough textures of the rock. | 2 |
Wet the join with a little water and stroke smooth using an M 3 until the line of the join can no longer be seen. | 3 |
The cactus consists of a longer, slightly bulging round piece and two shorter ones. Once you have put the cactus together, round off the ends. Use the M 1 to score fine grooves along the cactus and apply mouth, nose and eyes separately. Arrange the cactus on the rock. Fix the spikes horizontally around the cactus using slightly thickened couverture. Where the cactus has had a shave, remove the spikes again with the scalpel after applying the colour. Make up the sombrero from a round plate and a cut-off half ball. Make the join disappear as described under the rock above and attach the sombrero to the head.
Form the snake in one piece. Cut in the mouth and insert a tongue. Give eyes to the snake and score a scale pattern on the body. Support well for drying and subsequently arrange in front of the rock.
Cut small pieces from a long ribbon in order to obtain the basic shape of the fabric plasters.
Complete the individual sections with slight scoring and colouring. Once you have made and attached the razor, you only need a small sign to complete the scene.
Ideas for colouring are covered in detail in the chapter on "Colouring Techniques" (from page 238).

PROFI **TIPP** *Bei der Darstellung von Felsen muss beachtet werden, dass die meisten Gesteinsformationen in parallelen Schichten angeordnet sind. Wer sich daran orientiert, bekommt glaubwürdigere Ergebnisse.*

When making the rock one should bear in mind than most rock formations are formed in some sort of parallel layers. If you reflect this pattern your result will look authentic.

Jetzt geht's aufwärts

Up, up and away

Mit Zuversicht und guten Ideen zum Ziel

Getting ahead with ideas and optimism

1

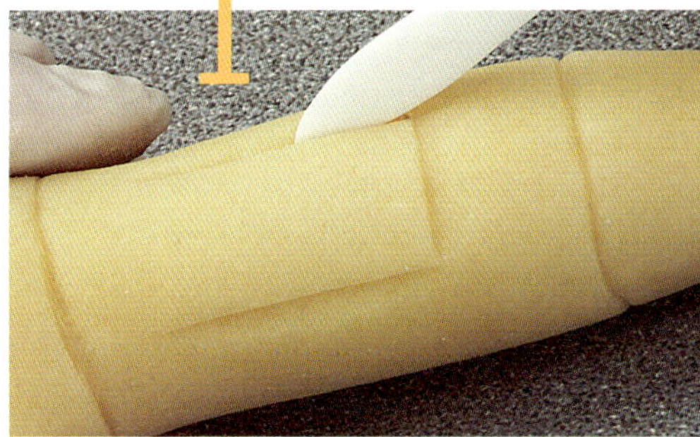

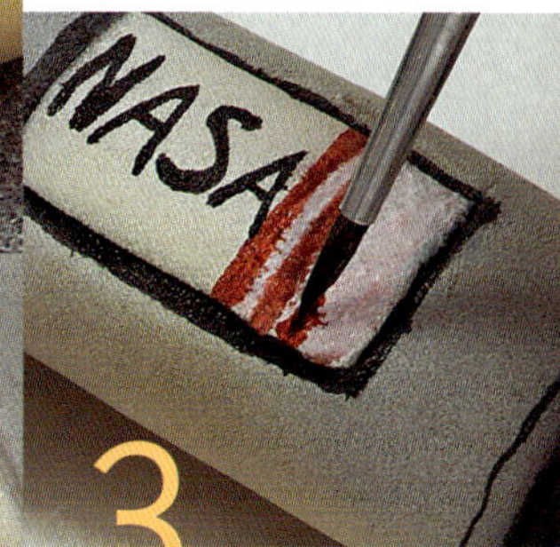

3

2

› Das Huhn aus einer lang gezogenen Birnenform modellieren. Einen Schnabel einschneiden und die Augenhöhlenpartie eindrücken. Die Flügel zwischen zwei Folien ausstreichen und mit M 11 sowie M 6 die Federn andeuten. Mit etwas Eiweiß am Körper befestigen. Hahnenkamm, Kehllappen und Füße modellieren und ansetzen. Das komplette Huhn schminken und Augen aufspritzen.
Die Rakete aus einem Stück formen und mit M 1 feine Vertiefungen für die später folgenden Farbabgrenzungen einkerben. | 1 |
Das Mittelstück großzügig mit Weiß grundieren und gut antrocknen lassen. Mit Schwarz den Raketenkopf und -fuß färben. Mit Ausnahme des Schilds vereinzelt Schattierungen aufsprühen. Mit einem Pinsel die eingekerbten feinen Linien mit Schwarz nachziehen. Schriftzug „NASA" mit dem Pinsel auftragen. | 2 |
"Stars and Stripes" der amerikanischen Flagge auf die weiße Grundierung aufbringen. Dies verhindert ein Zerfließen der feinen Linien. | 3 |
Die Halteriemen aus einer dünnen Marzipanplatte ausschneiden und sofort befestigen. Vier kleine „Beschläge" sichern den Halt der Bänder. Hier am besten durchgefärbtes Marzipan verwenden. Nach Belieben ein Schildchen auf einem Flügel des Huhns befestigen.

› Model the chicken from a long drawn-out bulb shape. Cut in to form a beak and make some hollows for the eye sockets. Make the wings by placing them between two pieces of foil and rolling them. Use an M 11 as well as an M 6 to sculpt the feathers. Use a little egg white to attach the wings to the body. Model the chicken's crest, wattle and feet and attach them to the trunk. Colour the whole chicken to your liking and pipe on the eyes.
Make the rocket from one piece and use an M 1 to score slight grooves as demarcations for the subsequent colour patterns. | 1 |
Generously apply white base coat to the middle part and leave to dry well. Use black to colour the head and the end of the rocket. Spray on some extra colour to apply some shading except in the area of the sign. Use a brush to highlight the fine lines and black colour. Write the word "NASA" with a brush. | 2 |
Apply the Stars and Stripes of the American flag to the white base coat, which stops the fine lines from running. | 3 |
Cut out the holding bolts from a thin marzipan slab and attach immediately. Four small "buckles" secure the ribbons in place. It is best to use tinted marzipan for this purpose. If you want, you can attach a small sign to one of the chicken wings.

> Den Hundekörper, bis auf den Kopf, aus einem Stück modellieren. Aus einer kleinen Birnenform den Kopf herstellen. Mit M 1 die Mundpartie gestalten, Augen aufspritzen. Ohren und hochgezogene Augenbrauen ansetzen. Um eine natürliche Körperhaltung zu erzielen, erst am fertigen Modell eine Körperdrehung vornehmen. Figur schwach mit Gelb grundieren. Kräftig mit Braun nachschminken, dabei den Bauchbereich heller lassen. Die Schnauze vornehmlich mit Weiß nachsprühen, aber auch im Arm- und Beinbereich Schattierungen setzen. Mit einem Pinsel den Mund rosa färben. Nase, Augenbrauen sowie Ohren und die Pfotenlinien mit Schwarz hervorheben.
Eine Grundplatte aus dünnem Marzipan schneiden. Mit M 1 die klare Begrenzungslinie für eine Straße einkerben und M 10 zum Einrollen des Grases verwenden. |1|
Aus einer angespitzten Stange das Hundeschwänzchen formen. Auf die Platte legen und mit M 3 in „Reifenbreite“ platt andrücken. Einen Profilabdruck eines Reifens fortlaufend von der Straße über das Schwänzchen hinweg mit M 11 einkerben. |2|
Auf der oberen Hälfte des Hundeschwänzchens mit M 11 eine buschige Struktur andeuten. |3|
Das Schwänzchen von der Grundplatte abnehmen, mit dem Hund verbinden und den Ansatz kaschieren. Die Grundplatte noch vor dem Aufsetzen der Figur schminken. Durch Übersprühen der grauen Straße mit Wasser verstärkt sich der Reifenabdruck.
Für den Straßenbegrenzungspfosten eine Marzipanstange im Dreieck zwischen Daumen, Zeige- und Mittelfinger hindurchmodellieren. Dabei entsteht die entsprechende Grundform. Den Begrenzungspfosten zuschneiden, färben und auf der bereits geschminkten Grundplatte befestigen. Das Arrangement mit einem Schildchen vervollständigen.

> Model the body of the dog, except the head, from one piece. Make the head from a small bulb shape. Use an M 1 to shape the area of the mouth and pipe on the eyes. Put on the ears and the raised eyebrows. In order to achieve a natural posture of the body it is best to finish the figure first and then turn the body. Apply a light yellow base coat and then follow up in strong brown colours, leaving the belly area lighter. Spray the snout with white and also add some white shades on the arm and leg areas. Paint the mouth pink with a brush. Highlight the nose, eyebrows as well as ears and paw lines with black.
Cut a base slab from thin marzipan. Use an M 1 to score the edge line of a road and an M 10 roller to create the texture of the grass. |1|
Use a pointed roll to form the little tail of the dog. Place it on the slab and use an M 3 to press it down equivalent to the width of a tyre. Use an M 11 to score the imprint of a tyre along the road and then across the tail. |2|
Indicate a bushy hairy texture on the top half of the dog's tail, using an M 11. |3|
Take the little tail from the base slab, attach to the dog and hide the join. Colour the base slab before placing the figure on it. By spraying the grey road with water, the pattern of the tyre profile is highlighted.
To make the post by the road, form a marzipan strip in between your thumb, forefinger and middle finger into a triangular shape. This gives the necessary basic shape. Cut the post to the required size, colour it and attach to the already coloured base slab. Complete the arrangement with a small sign.

Wow, das war knapp

Wow, that was close

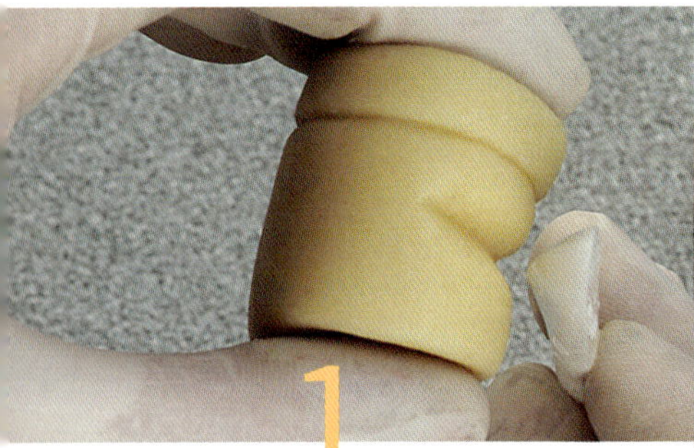

1

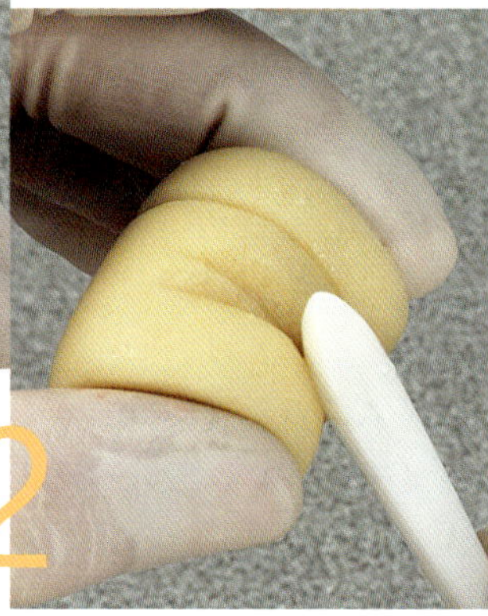

2

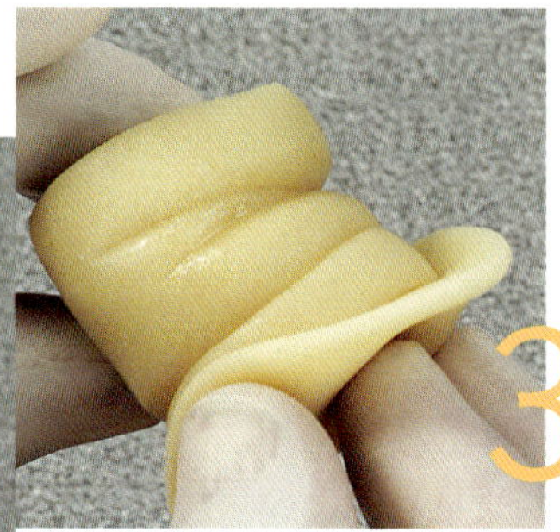

3

› Bei dieser Winterszenerie am besten mit durchgefärbtem Marzipan arbeiten. Die Wasserfläche und die Tränentröpfchen aus gefärbtem, gekochtem Zucker herstellen. Dafür ist eine Konsistenz wie beim Zuckergießen notwendig. Die Tränenpfütze auf leicht zerknitterte Alufolie gießen, um naturgetreue Wasserreflexionen hervorzurufen. Nach dem Trocknen auf einer achteckigen Grundplatte andrücken. Für die Tränentröpfchen eine Messerspitze in den flüssigen Zucker tauchen und auf einer Trennfolie abstreifen. Die Tränen trocken lagern und erst zum Schluss an dem Schneemann befestigen.
Den Schneemann selber aus drei Kugeln zusammensetzen. Arme formen und anbringen. Durch ein Gesicht das Schneemännchen „zum Leben erwecken". Die Kohlenknöpfe einzeln modellieren und färben. Eine weniger aufwendigere Alternative ist das Aufspritzen der Knöpfe mit schwarzer Eiweißspritzglasur. Den geknickten Zylinder aus einem Stangensegment herstellen. Das Hutband mit M 1 abgrenzen. Dann mittig zur Form eine größere Kerbe mit M 1 eindrücken. | 1 |
Eine zweite Vertiefung einarbeiten und den Zylinder zwischen den Fingern einseitig zusammendrücken. | 2 |
Ein rundes Marzipanplättchen als Hutkrempe ankleben. Um den typischen Zylinder zu erhalten, diese nach oben biegen. | 3 |
Den Zylinder schwarz schminken und mit Weiß das Hutband nachziehen.
Ein Schild mit der Aufschrift „ Winter ade" herstellen und an einem zurechtgeschnittenen Schaschlikspieß befestigen.
Die Grundplatte kann man mit Schokolade und kleinen Schneeglöckchen aus Marzipan verzieren.

› For this winter scene it is best to work with tinted marzipan. Prepare the water surface and the small tear drops from coloured boiled sugar. This requires a consistency as used for sugar pouring. Pour the puddle of tears onto slightly creased aluminium foil in order to create a natural impression of the reflection of water. Once it has dried, press onto an octagonal base slab. To make the tear drops, dip the tip of a knife into the liquid sugar and brush off onto a piece of foil. Keep the tears dry and wait until everything else is complete before you attach them to the snowman.
Make the snowman itself from three balls. Form arms separately and attach to the figure. Form a face to bring the snowman to life. Form individual coal buttons and colour them black. If you want to simplify the process, it is easier to pipe the buttons on with black royal icing. Make the squashed top hat from a rolled piece, marking the hat ribbon with an M 1. Then use an M 1 to press in a groove in the middle of the shape. | 1 |
Work in a second indentation and squash the top hat together on one side between your fingers. | 2 |
Attach a little round plate of marzipan as the rim of the hat. In order to achieve the typical top hat look, bend the rim upwards. | 3 |
Colour the top hat with black paint, outlining the ribbon in white.
Make a sign with the inscription "Goodbye winter" and attach to a wooden skewer, cut to size.
The base slab can be decorated with chocolate and small marzipan snowflakes.

Winter ade

Goodbye winter

Frühlingsgefühle kontra Winterspaß

Spring in the air?

Hals- + Beinbruch

Break a leg

> Die Wollmütze entsteht aus einer Tropfenform, bei der man die Rundungen kappt. Mit M 11 das Strickmuster einkerben. Bommel und Mützenumschlag modellieren und mit M 10 ein Muster einkerben. Mütze gelb grundieren, grün auftragen und mit Wasser nachsprühen. Umschlag sowie Bommel weiß färben und dann anbringen. Als Schal ein einfaches Marzipanband verwenden. Mit M 10 die Fransen einrollen. Den Schal mit Gelb grundieren und mit Rot schattieren. Noch in weichem Zustand in die endgültige Form legen.
Aus einer Marzipanplatte die Skier herausschneiden und in Form bringen. | 1 |
Die Skischaufel nach oben biegen, etwas dünner modellieren und gut abstützen. | 2 |
Aus einer stärkeren Platte die Bindung herausschneiden. Die Haltebacken mit M 1 andeuten. | 3 |
Mit etwas Eiweiß oder Wasser die Halterung an die jeweiligen Skier fixieren. | 4 |
Nach ausreichender Trocknung mit beliebigen Farben schminken und weitere Halterungen zwischen den Haltebacken aufspritzen.
Die Einzelteile zu einem kleinen Arrangement zusammensetzen und mit einem Schildchen fertig stellen.

> The woolly hat is made from a drop shape with the round ends cut off. Use an M 11 to create the knitting pattern. Model the pompon and turn-up of the cap and use an M 10 to make the pattern. Apply a yellow base coat, then spray with green and follow up with water. Colour the pompon and the turn-up white and fix into place. The scarf is made from a simple marzipan ribbon. Roll in the fringes with an M 10. Apply a yellow base coat to the scarf and follow up with red shading. Form into the desired shape while still soft.
Cut the skis from a marzipan slab. | 1 |
Bend the tip of the skis upwards, thin out a little and support well. | 2 |
Cut the binding from a thicker slab. Use an M 1 to lightly mark the outlines of the holding jaws. | 3 |
Use a little egg white or water to attach the bindings to each ski. | 4 |
Once they have dried sufficiently, apply any colour of your liking and pipe on any extra detail required. Place all the individual parts into the desired arrangement and add the small sign plate to complete.

PROFI **TIPP** *Um eine zarte Gewebestruktur, wie zum Beispiel beim Schal, sichtbar nachzuahmen, benutzt man eine feine Gewindestange. Die gleichmäßigen Rillen entstehen durch einmaliges längs und quer rollen, wie mit einem Riefenholz.*

In order to achieve a subtle fabric texture as in the scarf, it is best to use a metal rod with a fine thread. The even grooves are made by rolling the threaded rod once along and once across just like a textured roller.

1

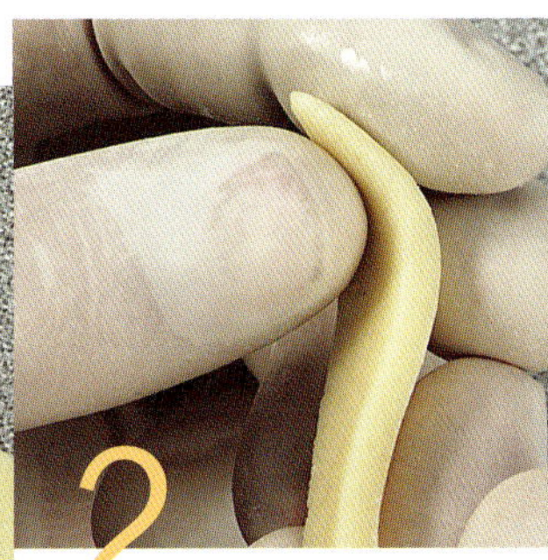
2

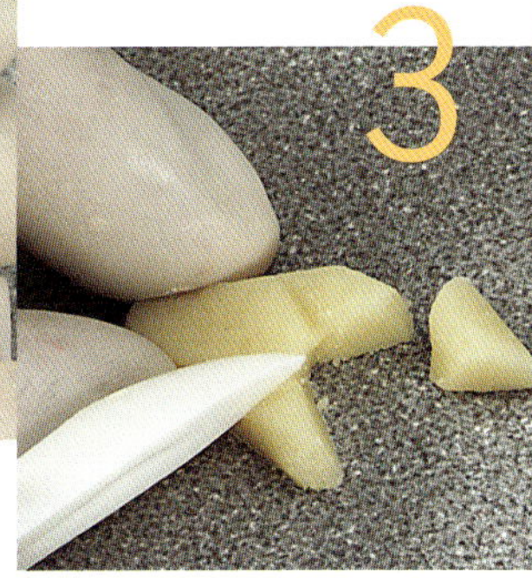
3

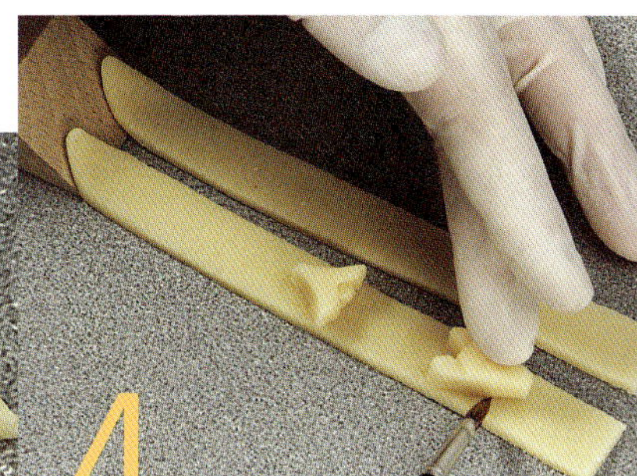
4

Aller Anfang ist schwer

All beginnings are hard

> Eine Grundplatte auswellen und unregelmäßig ringsum abreißen. Gelb grundieren und den Rand braun nachsprühen.
Ein Häschen, außer dem Rüssel, wie gewohnt (Beispiel hierzu auf Seite 84 bei "Sorry boy ... too late again") modellieren.
Die Figur des Zauberers setzt sich aus drei Teilen zusammen. Das erste Teilstück besteht aus Körper, Armen und Händen. Um die Stabilität des Magiers zu gewährleisten, ein Holzstäbchen mit einarbeiten. Bis zur vollständigen Trocknung der Arme die ganze Figur gut abstützen. Die Falten des Zauberumhangs mit M 1 eindrücken. Kopf und Hut aus einer Grundform modellieren. Erst nach ausreichender Trocknung diesen zweiten Bestandteil der Zaubererfigur mit dem ersten verbinden. Den Übergang vom Haar zur Kopfbedeckung durch Einkerben mit M 1 entstehen lassen. Die Haare selbst mit M 10 anfertigen. Das Gesicht gestaltet sich wie im Grundlagenkapitel „Modelliertechniken" (ab Seite 232) beschrieben. Zusätzlich noch einen Oberlippenbart aus zwei Tropfen mit dem dicken Ende unter der Nase ansetzen. Für den weißen, langen Bart eine Marzipanstange, die an beiden Enden konisch ausläuft, platt drücken und mit M 10 einkerben. Der weite Stehkragen entsteht aus einer dünnen Marzipanplatte, die am Rücken angeklebt wird. Danach so verstreichen, dass kein Übergang mehr sichtbar ist. Die endgültige Kragenform mit der Schere direkt korrigieren.
Mit dem Airbrush alle blauen Teile besprühen. Im Übergangsbereich den Pinsel benutzen.
Die Sterne nach Trocknung aller Farben mit gelber Eiweißspritzglasur aufspritzen.
Zauberer, Häschen und ein kleines Schild auf der Grundplatte zu einem „magischen Ganzen" zusammenfügen.

> Roll out a base slab and tear bits off irregularly all round. Apply yellow base coat and then spray the edge in brown.
Make a rabbit in the usual way except for the trunk (see example on page 84 under "Sorry boy ... too late again").
The figure of the magician is composed of three pieces. The first piece consists of the body, arms and hands. In order to ensure adequate stability of the magician, it is best to work around a wooden stick as reinforcement. Until the arms have dried completely, the whole figure must be supported well. Shape the folds of the magician's cloak with an M 1. Model the head and hat from one basic shape. Do not connect this second component with the figure of the magician until it has dried sufficiently. Create the transition from the hair to the hat by scoring with an M 1. Make the hair itself with an M 10. The face is modelled as described in the basics chapter "Modelling Techniques" (from page 232). Also add a moustache made from two drops with a thick end under the nose. To make the long white beard, take a rolled piece of marzipan that is tapered at both ends, press it flat and score with an M 10. The wide stand-up collar is made from a thin marzipan slab attached to the back of the figure. The join is then smoothed down so that it is no longer visible. Trim the shape of the collar with scissors to give it the final shape. Use an airbrush to spray all blue parts. Use a brush at the transitions to other colours in order to avoid any mixing/bleeding.
Pipe on stars after all the colours have dried using yellow royal icing.
Arrange the magician, the rabbit and the small sign on the base slab to form a complete "magical whole".

ALLER ANFANG
IST SCHWER

> Marzipan ausrollen, eine runde Grundplatte ausstechen und grau besprühen.
Flasche und Korken aus zwei Marzipanstangen formen und gelb grundieren. Die Flasche mit Grün komplett nachsprühen. Den unteren Teil mit Braun oder Rot nachdunkeln. Den Korken mit Braun und im Anschluss mit Wasser nachsprühen.
Die Etiketten sowie deren Beschriftung mit dem Pinsel auf weiß grundiertem Marzipan aufmalen, ausschneiden und auf der Flasche platzieren.
Für die Grundform der Fliege eine kleine Marzipanbirne herstellen. Das schmale Ende lang modellieren und über die Fingerkuppe umbiegen. | 1 |
Mit jeweils beiden Daumen und Zeigefingern das Gesicht formen. | 2 |
Mit M 1 den Mund in Form bringen. Schmale Kügelchen als Augen einsetzen. Aus kleinen, platt gedrückten Tropfen die Flügel modellieren. Diese leicht ausgestellt am Rücken ankleben. Kleine Löcher für die Fliegenbeinchen vorstechen. | 3 |
Die Beinchen aus dünnen Stangen zurechtbiegen und gut trocknen lassen. Anschließend in die dafür vorgesehenen Vertiefungen stecken. | 4 |
Fliege mit Gelb grundieren. Den Körper mit Schwarz und Braun nachschminken. Lippen und Saugrüssel rosa färben. Flügel mit Hellgrau/-blau nacharbeiten. Die Augen mit Weiß und Schwarz vervollständigen. Mit Spritzglasur oder dunkler Kuvertüre die Fliege auf dem Flaschenkopf fixieren. Die Flasche auf der Grundplatte anordnen. Auf der übrigen Fläche Ornamente mit Glasur aufspritzen. Mit einem passenden Schild und dem Flaschenkorken das Szenarium fertig stellen.

> Roll out the marzipan, cut out a round base slab and spray in grey colour.
Form the bottle and cork from two rolled pieces of marzipan and apply a yellow base coat. Spray the bottle completely with green, then darken the lower part with brown or red. Spray the cork in brown and then with water. Use a brush to paint the labels as well as the writing after applying a white base coat. Cut out and attach to the bottle.
For the basic shape of the fly, make a small marzipan bulb. Form the narrow end into a longish shape and bend over the tip of your finger. | 1 |
Shape the face of the fly with both thumbs and forefingers. | 2 |
Use an M 1 to form the mouth and add small balls as eyes. Model the wings from small drops that have been pressed flat. Attach these on the back, slightly turning outwards. Make small holes in which to attach the legs of the fly. | 3 |
Use thin sticks to cut the legs and bend them into shape before letting them dry completely. Then place them into the holes made previously. | 4 |
Apply a yellow base coat to the fly, then colour the body with black and brown. Colour the lips and the proboscis in pink. Work over the wings in light grey/blue. Complete the eyes with white and black.
Attach the fly on the top of the bottle using icing or dark couverture. Arrange the bottle on the base slab and pipe the icing ornaments on the rest of the area. Complete the scenario with a suitable sign and the cork of the bottle.

PROFI **TIPP** *Um das umständliche, nachträgliche Schminken der Augen zu umgehen, kann man gleich mit durchgefärbtem Marzipan arbeiten.*

In order to avoid having to colour the eyes one can work with tinted marzipan.

Happy birthday!

Happy birthday!

1

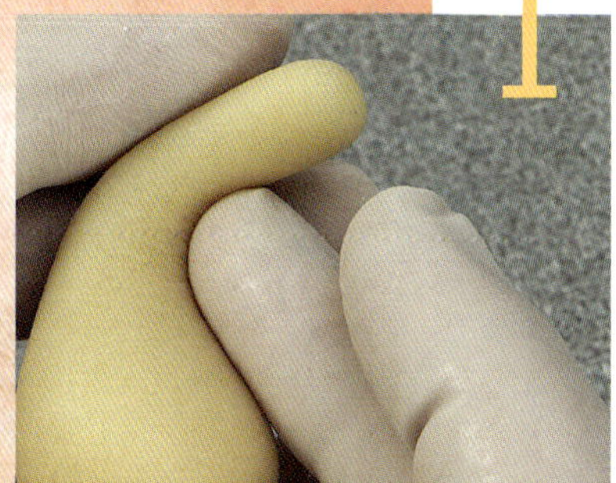

2

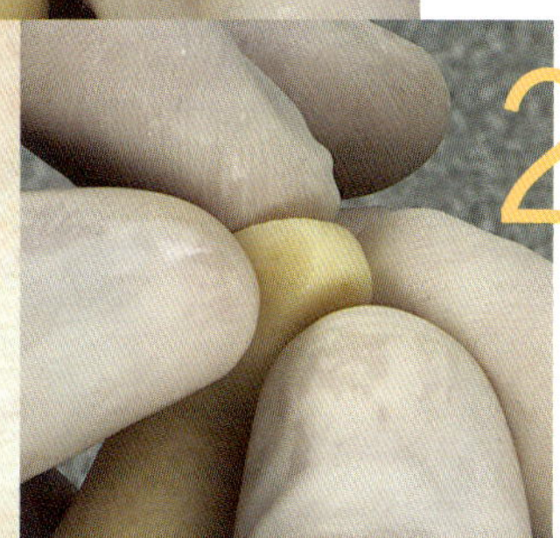

3

4

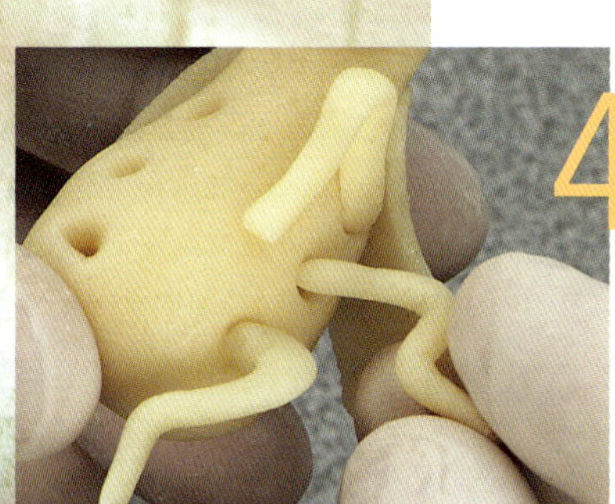

> Eine Grundplatte grau besprühen und mit Ornamenten am Rand verzieren.
Den Gipsfuß aus einer kurzen Stange formen. Mittig einkerben und im 90°-Winkel knicken. Die Zehenöffnung mit M 3 vertiefen und mit M 1 die Bandagen anlegen. | 1 |
Für den Einstieg mit M 5 eine Wölbung eindrücken. Aus kleiner werdenden Kügelchen die Fußzehen einsetzen. | 2 |
Das Bein, ein kleiner Zylinder, in der Wölbung befestigen. Mit M 7 die Zehennägel andeuten. | 3 |
Den Skischuh ebenfalls aus einer kurzen Stange formen und zurechtbiegen. Bein wie beim Gipsfuß beschrieben anbringen. Mit M 1 die Bindungen und die Schuhpolsterung abgrenzen. Aus kleinen Stangenteilen die Schnallen und Ösen herstellen und ankleben.
Die Grundfarbe des Schuhs und die weiße Farbe des Gipsbeins werden mit dem Airbrush gefärbt. Die restlichen Bestandteile, um saubere Abgrenzungen zu erhalten, mit dem Pinsel schminken. Feine schwarze Linien unterstützen die Wirkung der Bandage. Beschriftung auf dem Gipsfuß mittig anbringen.
Beide Füße auf die getrocknete Grundplatte stellen.

> Spray a base slab in grey and embellish with ornaments around the edge.
Make the foot in plaster from a short rolled piece, insert a groove in the middle and bend to an angle of 90 degrees. Use an M 3 to hollow out the space for the toes and score the lines with an M 1 to indicate the bandage. | 1 |
Make a hollow at the top with an M 5. Insert the toes which you have made from balls of different sizes. | 2 |
Attach the leg, in the shape of a small cylinder, in the hollow. Use an M 7 to score the toe nails. | 3 |
Make the ski boot also from a short rolled piece and bend into shape. Attach the leg in the same way as on the foot in plaster. Use an M 1 to delineate the bindings and the padding of the boots. Make the straps and eyelets from small rolled sections and stick into place.
The basic colour of the boot and the white colour of the plastered foot are sprayed on by airbrush. Colour the other parts with a brush in order to obtain clear demarcations. Fine black lines underline the effect of the bandage. Apply the writing on the plastered foot in the middle.
Arrange both feet on the dry base slab.

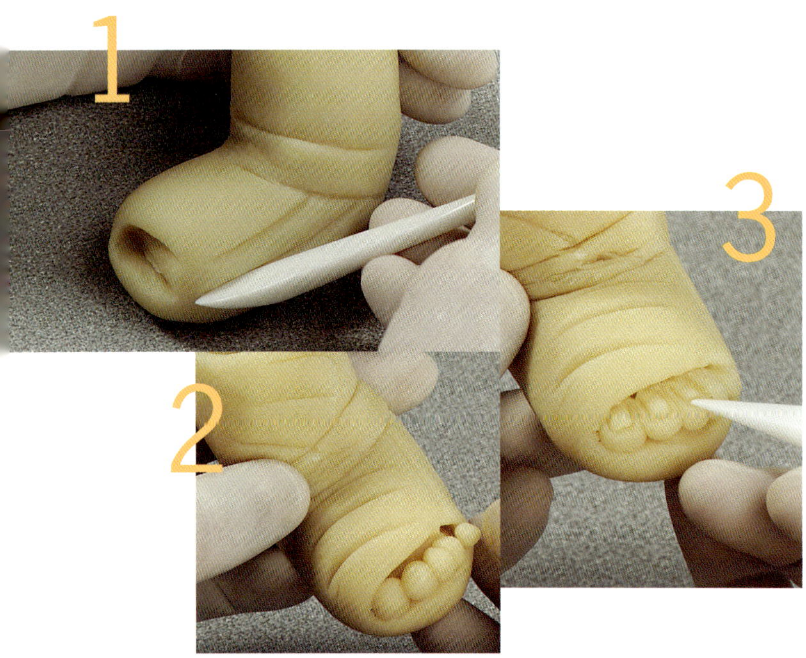

PROFI **TIPP** *Kontrastarme Exponate, wie hier zum Beispiel der Gipsfuß, erhalten mehr Leben, wenn die Vertiefungen mit dünnen Pinselstrichen nachgezogen werden. Dabei muss nicht immer wie in diesem Beispiel schwarz auf weiß treffen. Es genügt oft schon, mit derselben Farbe – nur ein paar Nuancen dunkler – einzelne Stellen nachzuziehen, um eine schöne Wirkung zu erzielen.*

Items with little contrast such as the plastered foot in this example become more vivid if the scoring is highlighted with thin brush strokes. That does not always have to be black on white as in this example. Often it is sufficient to retrace a few areas in the same colour – just a few shades darker – in order to achieve a nice effect.

Gute Besserung

Get well soon

Au Backe!

Ouch!

› Den hohlen Baumstamm aus einer Stange formen. Mit M 6 den Stamm von beiden Seiten her bis etwa zu einem Drittel aushöhlen. Das Frontloch ebenfalls mit M 6 einarbeiten. Mit der gekerbten Seite des M 1 die Rinde einkerben. Mit einem Messer und/oder einer Schere die Ränder ausfransen. Nach guter Trocknung mit Gelb grundieren. Die Rinde dunkel mit Braun nachfärben. Die Tiefenwirkung durch das Aufbringen von Schwarz in der vorderen Vertiefung sowie an den Borkenrändern verstärken.
Den Tigerkörper aus einer lang gezogenen Birne formen. Durch Spalten der dünnen Birnenhälfte die Vorderpfoten einteilen. Die Hinterläufe durch Einkerben mit M 1 und M 2 andeuten. Einen Schwanz gesondert formen und ankleben. Den Ansatz so verstreichen, dass er nicht mehr erkennbar ist. Den Körper über ein Rundholz legen, das denselben Durchmesser aufweist wie der Stamm. Die Vorderpfoten auf den vorher rund modellierten Seiten mit M 1 doppelt einkerben und zurechtbiegen. Die Hinterläufe fertig gestalten. Den Kopf aus einer gedrungenen Birne formen. Die Ohren aus der Kopfform herausmodellieren und mit M 1 in Form bringen. Aus der Mitte mit M 7 nach rechts und links je einen Halbkreis für die Schnauze einschneiden. Mit M 3 den Unterkiefer herunterdrücken und gleichzeitig die fransige Schnittkante glätten. Zwei Zähne formen und ansetzen. Nase und Augenhöhlen mit M 1 einkerben. Den fertigen Kopf mit einem Holzstäbchen am Körper befestigen. Aus einer dünnen, langen Marzipanplatte das Tuch formen und anlegen. Mit einer Schere das Tuch an den Enden spitz zuschneiden. Figur gut trocknen lassen. Die Grundierung erfolgt von zwei Seiten. Die untere Körperseite des Tigers mit Weiß grundieren, den übrigen Teil mit Gelb. Auf gelb folgen vorsichtig braun und rot. Mit dem Pinsel – nach erneuter Trocknung – rosa und schwarz auftragen.

› Form the hollow tree trunk from a marzipan roll. Use an M 6 to hollow the trunk from both sides about one third of the way down. Make the front hole also with an M 6. Use the notched side of the M 1 to score grooves for the bark. Use a knife and/or scissors to "fray" the edges. After it has dried out well apply a yellow base coat and then follow on with dark brown for the bark. Increase the sculptural effect by applying black in the front indentation as well as at the edges of the bark.
Form the body of the tiger from a long drawn out bulb. By splitting the thin end of the bulb you separate the front paws. The rear legs are just outlined by scoring with an M 1 and an M 2. Shape the tail separately and attach. Smooth out the join so that it can no longer be seen. Drape the body round a circular piece of wood with the same diameter as the tree trunk. Model the front paws into a round shape and then use an M 1 to score the grooves and bend them into the required position. Complete the rear legs. Make the head from a squat bulb and model the ears from the shape of the head, using an M 1 to make the final shape. Use an M 7 to cut a semi-circle from the middle to the right and to the left to make the snout. Use an M 3 to press down the lower jaw and at the same time smooth out the frayed edge. Form two teeth and insert them into the jaw. Make grooves for the nose and the eye sockets using an M 1. Attach the completed head with a wooden stick to the body. Shape the cloth from a thin long marzipan slab and colour to suit. Use scissors to cut the pointed ends of the cloth. Allow the figure to dry well. Apply the base coat from two sides. Coat the lower part of the body of the tiger in white and the rest of the body in yellow. Follow the yellow carefully with brown and red. Once the figure has dried apply the pink and black marking with a brush.

Au Backe !

Die gute Planung zählt!

Putt for dough!

Für Hobby-Golfer und andere Sportskanonen

For golfers and other sportsmen

> Den liegenden Golfspieler weitgehend wie im Grundlagenkapitel „Modelliertechniken“ (ab Seite 232) beschrieben herstellen. Ein Auge mit einer kleinen Marzipankugel verschließen und anmodellieren. Die Figur vor dem Schminken gut gestützt trocknen lassen und schminken.
Die Golftasche aus einem Zylinder formen. Mit M 1 die Fronttasche einkerben. Mit der Kugel des M 5 auf einer Seite des Zylinders eine kleine Vertiefung schaffen. In die nach innen gehende Wölbung mit M 4 Löcher für die Golfschläger einarbeiten. Golfschläger für die Tasche und die Figur modellieren und gut trocknen lassen. Einzelteile schminken und zusammenfügen.
Für die Grundplatte ein Stück Marzipan mit einem kleinen Rundholz bearbeiten. Eine Seite dabei etwas dicker als die andere auswellen. Mit M 5 die Abgrenzung eines Sandbunkers einkerben. | 1 |
Die Struktur des sandigen Untergrunds mit M 12 nachahmen. Mit M 10 durch sanftes Rollen den Rasen auf der Platte kennzeichnen. | 2 |
Das kurz geschnittene Green filigran mit M 11 gestalten. | 3 |
Mit Hilfe einer scharfen Rundklinge die gewünschte Form der Grundplatte zurechtschneiden. Die Grundplatte mit Gelb grundieren, braun und grün aufbringen und mit Wasser nachsprühen, um die Vertiefungen hervorzuheben. Ein Golfloch ausstechen. Nach dem Anbringen der einzelnen Bestandteile auf der Platte kleine Golfbälle und ein Schildchen hinzufügen. Als zusätzliches Detail einen kleinen Maulwurf in den Sandbunker setzen.

> Make the golf player largely as in the chapter on “Modelling Techniques” (from page 232). “Close” one eye by inserting a small marzipan ball. Support the figure well and allow to dry before colouring.
Shape the golf bag from a cylinder. Use an M 1 to apply the grooves of the front pocket. Use the round shape of the M 5 to work in a small indentation on one side of the cylinder. Use an M 4 to push in the holes for the golf clubs on the inside of the bag. Model golf clubs for the bag and the figure and leave to dry well. Apply colour to all parts and join together.
To make the base slab, work a piece of marzipan with a small rolling pin. Make sure that one side is a little thicker than the other. Use an M 5 to score the edge of the sand bunker. | 1 |
Imitate the texture of the sandy ground using an M 12. Use an M 10 in a gentle rolling motion to mark the lawn on the slab. | 2 |
Apply the texture of the closely mown green with an M 11. | 3 |
Use a sharp rolling knife to cut the desired shape of the base slab. Apply a yellow base coat to the base slab, then follow with brown and green and finally with a spray of water in order to accentuate the texture. Cut out a hole for the target. Once you have assembled the individual components on the slab, add small golf balls and a sign. You can add more detail such as the small mole in the sand bunker.

> Aus einer Kugel die grobe Tiergestalt vormodellieren. Mit M 2 die Konturen der Beine vorgeben. | 1 |
Die entstandenen Kanten mit M 3 glätten und die Form ebenfalls mit M 3 weiter abrunden. Mit Daumen und Zeigefinger die Hufe formen. | 2 |
Saubere Kanten und Vertiefungen mit M 1 in den Körper einarbeiten. | 3 |
Den Kopf modellieren. Nackenfalten, Backen und Nase mit M 1 kennzeichnen. Maul mit M 3 eindrücken und seitlich kerben, um die Figur lächeln zu lassen. Die Ohren mit M 1 kerben und extra ansetzen. Augenpartie gestalten. Aus einem kleinen Tropfen das Schwänzchen formen und den Ansatz kaschieren. Beide Hörner über Nacht vor dem Befestigen trocknen lassen. Figur gelb grundieren, mit Braun kräftig nachfärben und zum Schluss nur senkrecht von oben mit etwas Schwarz nachsprühen. Mit schwarzem Pinselstrich Hörner und Mundpartie aufwerten.
Felsen wie bei "Dangerous love" (Seite 62) beschrieben herstellen und schminken. Mit etwas durchgefärbtem Marzipan kleine Grasbüschel durch ein Sieb drücken und anbringen. Die Figur mit einem Holzstäbchen befestigen.

> Make a rough model of the animal shape from a ball. Use an M 2 to outline the contours of the legs. | 1 |
Smooth the edges with an M 3 and use this tool to further round off the form. Shape the hooves with thumb and forefinger. | 2 |
Use an M 1 to work neat edges and indentations into the body. | 3 |
Model the head. Mark the folds at the neck, the cheeks and the nose with an M 1. Indent the mouth with an M 3 and add grooves on the side in order to indicate a smile. Score the ears with an M 1 and attach to the figure. Shape the area around the eyes. Form the little tail from a small drop, attach and smooth out the join. The two horns should dry out overnight before attaching them to the figure. Apply a yellow base coat followed by dark brown and finally from the top vertically down a little black spray. Use a brush to highlight the horns and area around the mouth in black.
Make the rock as described in "Dangerous love" (page 62) and colour it. Use some tinted marzipan pushed through a strainer to represent tufts of grass and attach these to the ground. Fix the figure with a wooden stick.

PROFI **TIPP** *Statisch derart gewagte Exponate nur unter Zuhilfenahme von Holzstäbchen wagen. Hier verläuft ein Stab von ganz unten bis weit in die Figur hinein. Nur so kann auch ein problemloser Transport gewährleistet werden. Unbedingt auf das Verhältnis von Grundplatte zur Figur achten. Die Grundplatte sollte dabei immer dominieren.*

From a structural point of view the above example is quite risky and should not be attempted without the help of wooden sticks. In this case a wooden stick runs from below right into the figure. This is also the only way in which the item can be transported without any problems. It is imperative to ensure the right proportion between the base slab and the figure. The base slab should always be somewhat heavier than the figure.

It’s lonely at the top

It's lonely at the top

Sorry boy ... too late again

Sorry boy ...

1

2

3

> Hasenkörper aus einer Birnenform modellieren. Die obere Birnenhälfte spalten, um die Arme einzuteilen, anschließend die Hinterläufe einkerben. Ein Schwänzchen ankleben und Kopf aus einer Tropfenform modellieren. Den Tropfen in der Mitte stumpf einkerben und die Spitze teilen, mit M 1 jeweils eindrücken, um die Ohren zu formen. Augen eindrücken und aus zwei platt gedrückten Kügelchen die Backen herstellen. Nase anbringen, trocknen lassen und schminken.
Aus einer leicht konisch verlaufenden Stange den Körper des Nikolaus formen. Oben abrunden und mit M 1 Falten und Gürtelkerbe einbringen. Für die Frontpartie eine schmale Marzipanstange ankleben und mit M 1 segmentieren. | 1 |
Unteren Saum anmodellieren und mit den Fingern leichten Schwung in den Mantel bringen. | 2 |
Eine Marzipankordel um die Hüfte legen. Ärmel und Handschuhe aus einem Stück herstellen. Aus einer Stange erst die Hand herausbilden und für den Ärmel Material zurücklassen. Ärmel leicht spitz abmodellieren und mit M 1 zur Hand hin abgrenzen. Armbeuge eindrücken und am Körper befestigen. | 3 |
Den Kopf wie bei "Good old days" (Seite 86) geschildert modellieren. Mütze, Sack und Rute formen und ankleben. Mit Rot vorsichtig grundieren. Dabei die andersfarbigen Teile abdecken, um Farbvermischungen vorzubeugen. Den Rest mit dem Pinsel schminken.
Den Nikolaus zusammen mit einem Schild auf einer Grundplatte arrangieren. Bunte Ostereier und das Häschen hinzufügen.

> Model the body of the rabbit from a bulb shape. Split the top half of the bulb to separate the arms and then score the shape of the hind legs. Attach a little tail and model the head from a drop shape. Make an indentation in the middle of the drop and separate the pointed end, using an M 1 to shape the ears. Push in the eyes and make the cheeks from two flattened little balls. Attach the nose, leave to dry and apply the colour.
Make the body of Father Christmas from a slightly tapered roll. Round off at the top and use an M 1 to score the folds and the belt. Attach a thin rolled strip for the ruff down the front of the coat and use an M 1 to score the segments. | 1 |
Attach the lower seam and use your fingers to mould a slight curve into the coat. | 2 |
Place a marzipan string around the waist. Make the sleeves and gloves from one piece. Use a rolled piece to first model the hand while leaving some material for the sleeve. Form the sleeve with a slight point and use an M 1 to accommodate the hand. Shape the elbow part and then attach this part to the body. | 3 |
Model the head as described in "Good old days" (page 86). Form and attach the hat, sack and whip. Carefully apply a base coat in red whilst covering up parts of a different colour in order to prevent any mixing of colours. Colour the remaining parts with a brush.
Arrange Father Christmas together with a sign on a base slab. Add coloured Easter eggs and the rabbit.

PROFI **TIPP** *Hier wäre es eine große Zeitersparnis, die Figur mit bereits gefärbtem Marzipan zu produzieren. Farbreflexionen können nachträglich mit dem Airbrush aufgetragen werden.*

You can save a lot of time by making the figure with ready-tinted marzipan. Any colour shading can be applied subsequently with an airbrush.

Good old days

Good old days

Die gute alte Zeit – wäre es doch wieder wie einst!

The good old days – if only we could go back to it!

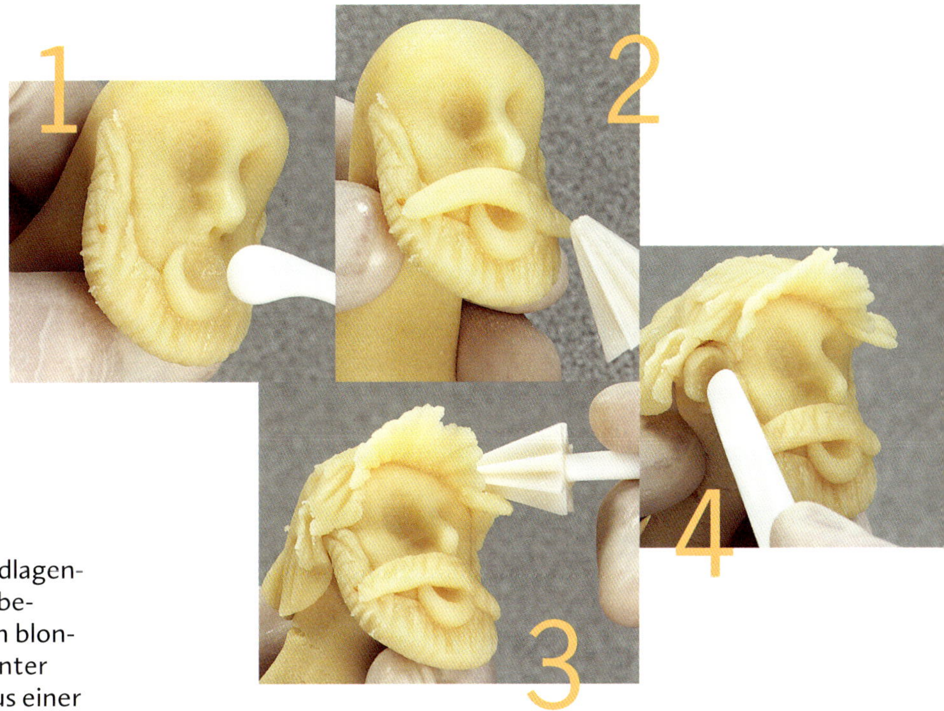

› Das Urzeitpärchen wie im Grundlagenkapitel „Modelliertechniken“ (ab Seite 232) beschrieben weitgehend gleich herstellen. Den blonden Zopf der Frau gesondert flechten und unter der Haarplatte ansetzen. Für das Röckchen aus einer dünnen Marzipanplatte mit M 7 eine Fransenbordüre produzieren. Das Oberteil aus zwei kleinen Dreiecken herstellen.
Die Fellbekleidung des Urmenschen durch Einschneiden eines weiteren Marzipandreiecks mit einer Nagelschere profilieren. Einen Bart an das Kinn ansetzen, in Form bringen und mit M 10 die Haarstruktur einrollen. Für den Mund eine kleine Kugel ankleben und mit M 2 eindrücken. | 1 |
Eine schmale Marzipanrolle zum Oberlippenbart ausformen. | 2 |
Vorsichtig eine runde Marzipanplatte für die Haare auf dem Kopf befestigen. Schließlich mit M 10 die wild zerzauste Frisur einkerben. | 3 |
Mit einer kleinen Kugel ein Ohr anbringen und mit M 3 festdrücken. | 4 |
Nach Belieben ein zweites Ohr anbringen (oder weglassen) und die Haare darüber modellieren. Figuren mit Hautfarbe grundieren. Restliche Farbgebung mit dem Pinsel ausführen.
Auf einer Grundplatte das Urzeitpärchen und ein Schildchen befestigen. Mit etwas durchgefärbtem Marzipan kleine Grasbüschel durch ein Sieb drücken und auf der Platte verteilt anbringen.

› Prepare the couple from prehistoric times much as described in the chapter “Modelling Techniques” (from page 232). Make the blond plait of the lady separately and attach underneath the small plate of marzipan used for the hair. Use a thin marzipan slab and an M 7 to produce a fringe for the skirt. Make the top from two small triangles.
Make the fur clothing of the prehistoric man by cutting a rough edge to a further marzipan triangle, using small scissors. Attach a beard to the chin, form into shape and roll the hair structure with an M 10. Attach a small ball for the mouth and use an M 2 to sculpt the shape. | 1 |
Use a narrow marzipan roll to form the moustache. | 2 |
Carefully attach a round marzipan plate to the head to represent the hair. Use an M 10 to sculpt the wild and unkempt hair. | 3 |
Make a small ball and attach as an ear; use an M 3 to press it into place. | 4 |
You can also attach a second ear or instead model the hair in such a way that it covers the ear. Apply basic skin colour to the figures. The rest of the colouring should be carried out with a brush.
Arrange the prehistoric couple on the base slab and attach a sign. Squeeze some tinted marzipan through a strainer to make tufts of grass and fix these to the base slab.

Angeln verboten

No fishing

› Aus einer Marzipanstange einen Baumstamm formen. Die Borke mit M 3 abgrenzen und die Rinde mit M 1 einkerben. Mit einem Schneiderad eine Grundplatte gestalten. Den Baumstumpf schminken und anbringen.
Kleine Äste aus dünnen Marzipanrollen herstellen und neben dem Baumstumpf drappieren.
Die Flamme aus einem Stück modellieren und unten abschneiden. Die Steine der Feuerstelle grob gestalten und um die Flammen legen. Die Feuerstelle schminken und auf der Grundplatte platzieren.
Ein Schild mit der Aufschrift „Angeln verboten“ herstellen. In den Pfosten einen Holzstab einarbeiten und hinter dem Baumstamm aufstellen.
Den Körper des Anglers wie im Grundlagenkapitel „Modelliertechniken“ (ab Seite 232) beschrieben modellieren. Den Rollkragen durch eine aufgesetzte Kugel mit der Spitze von M 5 eindrücken und dann mit M 7 einkerben. In das Gesicht des Anglers mit M 3 beherzt ein breites Grinsen einarbeiten.
Für den Haarkranz eine kurze Marzipanstange um den Kopf legen und mit M 10 strukturieren. | 1 |
Den Schnauzbart auf gleiche Weise wie den Haarkranz herstellen. | 2 |
Mit M 11 einige Falten auf der Stirn und Lachfalten um die Augenpartie einkerben. | 3 |
Ein Fischchen modellieren und auf einem mit Marzipan ummantelten Edelstahldrahtstück aufspießen. Den Drahtabschnitt etwas länger belassen als nötig, um das untere Ende in die Figur stecken zu können. Somit wird die Angelrute zusätzlich stabilisiert.
Die Einzelteile gut trocknen lassen und getrennt voneinander besprühen, um Farbüberlagerungen zu vermeiden.

› Form a tree log from a marzipan roll. Mark the end of the log, using an M 3 and score the bark texture with an M 1. Shape a base slab with a cutting wheel and then colour the log and fix to the slab.
Make small branches from thin rolled marzipan sticks and arrange next to the log.
Model the flame from one piece and cut off at the bottom. Shape the stones around the camp fire in uneven sizes and rough shapes and place around the fireplace. Colour the camp fire and place on the base slab.
Make a sign with the inscription “No fishing”. Work a wooden stick into the post and put it up behind the log.
Model the body of the angler very much as described in the chapter “Modelling Techniques” (from page 232). Make the roll-neck by indenting a ball with the point of an M 5 and then scoring the pattern with an M 7. Give the fisherman a broad grin, using an M 3 firmly. To make the hair, place a short rolled piece of marzipan around the head and work in the texture using an M 10. | 1 |
Make the moustache in the same way as the hair. | 2 |
Use an M 11 to score a few wrinkles on the forehead and laugh lines around the eyes. | 3 |
Model a little fish and spike it onto a length of stainless steel wire encased in some marzipan. Allow the wire to protrude a little so that the bottom end can be stuck into the figure. This gives extra stability to the fishing rod.
Allow all parts to dry well and spray with colour separately in order to prevent the colours mixing.

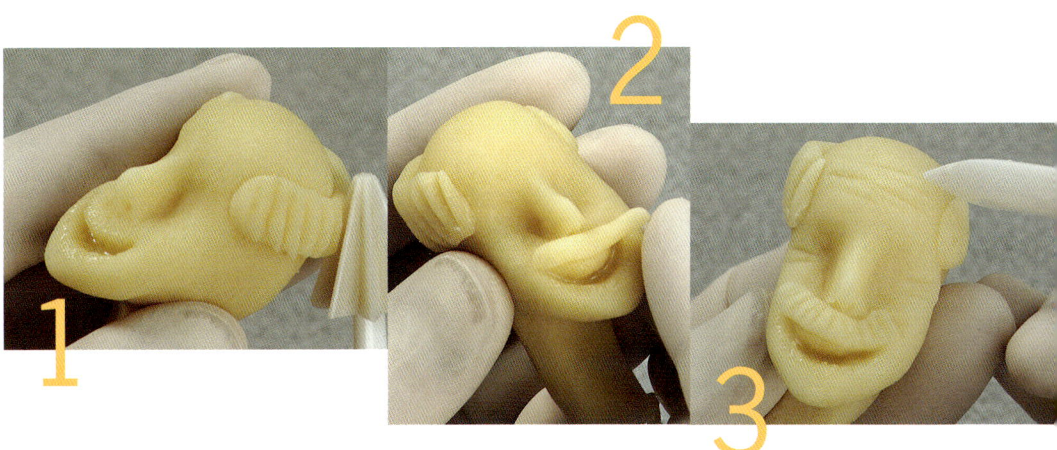

> Einen Gipssack aus einem Teilstück einer Marzipanstange durch leichtes Plattdrücken herstellen. Mit M 11 die Öffnung eindrücken und die Frontwand einreißen. Die Schrift mit M 7 eingravieren. Mit Weiß grundieren und durch unregelmäßigen Farbnebel das Gipssäckchen von außen einfärben. Das Innere des Sacks und den Schriftzug mit einem Pinsel schminken. Nach guter Trocknung mit Puderzucker oder süßem Schnee füllen.
Die Grundplatte aus einem Stück grob auswellen, um gerissene Ränder zu erhalten. Mit der Doppelkerbung des M 10 mit Hilfe eines Lineals die Fliesen einkerben. Gelb zum Grundieren der Fliesen benutzen und mit Rot nachsprühen. Weiße Lebensmittelfarbe aus nächster Nähe zügig entlang den Fugen aufspritzen. Bei zu starker Farbüberdeckung der Fliesen mit Wasser nachsprühen.
Die Kelle aus einem Stück erstellen und dabei die ungefähre Form des Griffs festlegen. Mit den Fingern die Kelle grob plätten. | 1 |
Zum sauberen Glätten M 7 verwenden. | 2 |
Wenn die Kelle ausreichend bearbeitet ist, mit M 7 die scharfen Konturen schneiden. Abschließend den hinteren Rand der Kelle begradigen. | 3 |
Das entstandene Werkzeug mit Weiß grundieren und leicht mit Schwarz nachsprühen. Den Griff mit dem Pinsel schminken.
Um das Arrangement fertig zu stellen, kleine Details, wie zum Beispiel Schwämmchen, Eimer, Lappen, Spatel, modellieren und hinzufügen.

> Make a bag of plaster from a rolled piece of marzipan by squashing it slightly. Use an M 11 to insert the opening and the tear in the front. Use an M 7 to engrave the writing. Apply a white base coat and use an irregular colour mist to colour the bag of plaster from the outside. Use a brush to colour the inside of the bag and the writing. After it has dried, fill the bag with icing sugar or moisture resistant sugar.
Roll out the base slab from one piece in a rough fashion in order to obtain frayed edges. Use the double scoring point of the M 10 and a ruler to mark the tiles. Apply a yellow base coat to the tiles and follow up with red spray. Use white food colouring to spray along the joints from very close proximity. If too much paint gets onto the tiles, spray with water. Make the trowel from one piece and give the handle its shape. Use your fingers to smooth the trowel roughly. | 1 |
Use an M 7 to give it the final smooth finish. | 2 |
To complete the trowel, use an M 7 to cut the sharp edges. Finally cut the rear edge of the trowel to make it straight. | 3 |
Apply a white base coat to the tool and follow up with a slight spray of black. Use the brush to touch up the handle.
To complete the arrangement, add small details such as e.g. sponges, bucket, rag, spatula, and add these on.

PROFI **TIPP** *Mit etwas Übung auf neutralem Untergrund lassen sich mit dem Airbrush feine Linien, wie hier in den Fugen, ziehen. Diese Technik erfolgt mit nur zaghaft gezogenem Farbmengenregler an der Spritzpistole. Die Bewegungen müssen hingegen sehr zügig und zielgerichtet ausgeführt werden.*

With a little practice it is possible to draw fine lines with an airbrush on a neutral background as can be seen in the example here for the joins between the tiles. For this technique, the trigger on the airbrush must only be lightly pressed. The movements must be relatively swift and focussed.

Super Arbeit, Leute

Well done everybody

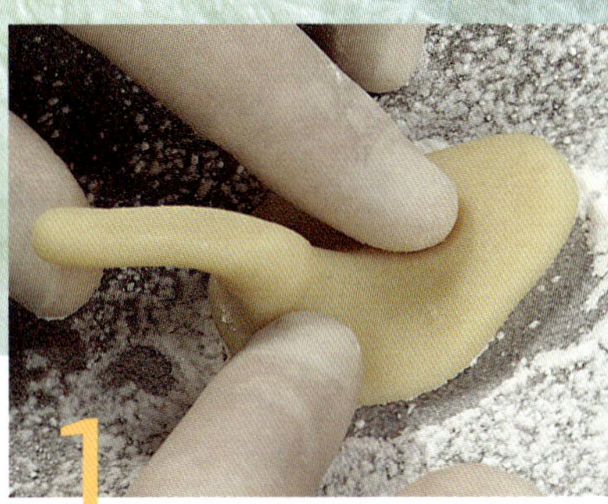

1

2

3

Just in case

Für alle Fälle

1

2

3

› PC-Tower aus einer dicken Marzipanplatte schneiden. Ränder glätten und mit M 7 die Komponenteneinschübe einkerben. Die Gehäuseteile gegeneinander abgrenzen und mit M 3 die Zierkanten der Front eindrücken. PC-Tower schminken und auf einer runden Grundplatte ankleben.
Den Monitor aus einer dünneren Platte schneiden und den Bildschirm mit M 3 nach innen abgrenzen. Aus drei kleinen Quadern die Lautsprecher und den Untersatz des Monitors formen und ansetzen. Mit dem Airbrush komplett einfärben und neben dem Tower anbringen.
Für die Tastatur ebenfalls aus einer dünnen Platte ein Rechteck ausschneiden. Mit M 7 parallele Längsstreifen einkerben. Anschließend die Tasten vervollständigen. | 1 |
Mit Schwarz leicht grundieren und mit Wasser nachsprühen. | 2 |
So lange Wasser und Luft sprühen, bis sich die Farbe in die Ritzen gezogen hat. | 3 |
Die CDs durch Ausstechen mit der Lochtülle anfertigen und das Mittelloch mit M 4 eindrücken. Silberne Lebensmittelfarbe mit dem Pinsel auftragen.
Eine Maus und ein PC-Pad modellieren und zusammen mit einem Schildchen vor der Tastatur auf der Grundplatte anbringen.

› Cut the PC tower from a thick marzipan slab. Smooth the edges and use an M 7 to score the drawers for the components. Score a demarcation line between the parts of the housing and use an M 3 to make the decorative pattern at the front. Colour the PC tower and attach to a round base slab.
Cut the monitor from a thinner slab and use an M 3 to delineate the screen towards the inside. Form the loudspeakers and the base of the monitor from three small cubes and put into place. Colour completely with the airbrush and set up next to the tower.
To make the keyboard, also cut a rectangle from a thin slab. Use an M 7 to score lines in parallel to the long edge. Then complete the keys. | 1 |
Apply a light base colouring of black and follow on with a spray of water. | 2 |
Keep spraying water and air until the colour has run into the grooves. | 3 |
Make the CDs by cutting them out with a round piping point and punching the centre hole with the M 4. Apply silver food colouring with a brush.
Model a mouse and a mouse pad and assemble together with a sign in front of the keyboard on the base slab.

Gefährliches Suchtmittel

Caution – addictive

Surfen auf allen Wellen

Surfing on all waves

Bavarian Aborigine

Bavarian Aborigine

> Die Figur wie im Grundlagenkapitel „Modelliertechniken“ (ab Seite 232) beschrieben herstellen. Die Träger der Lederhose einkerben und mit dem Pinsel die Konturen schwarz nachziehen. Um die Farben insgesamt beim übrigen Teil besser gegeneinander abzugrenzen, am besten nur mit dem Pinsel arbeiten. Jeden Farbauftrag vollständig trocknen lassen, bevor der nächste aufgetragen wird.
Aus einer kurzen Marzipanrolle den Maßkrug modellieren. Mit M 2 die Seiten symmetrisch eindrücken und den Boden mit M 7 einkerben. Den Henkel ankleben und das Ganze mit dem Airbrush schminken. Den Schaum aus Eiweißspritzglasur aufspritzen.
Für Tisch und Bank aus einer Marzipanplatte Streifen in unterschiedlicher Länge schneiden. Länge der beiden „Tisch- und Bankbeine“ abschneiden. | 1 |
Aus einem Reststück die Verstärkungen abschneiden und an den Seitenteilen ankleben. | 2 |
Beide Stücke auf die Unterseite der jeweiligen Platte kleben. | 3 |
So gestaltet, braucht die Garnitur einen oder mehrere Tage, bis sie fest ist.
Beim Zusammensetzen der gesamten Komposition darauf achten, dass die Figur möglichst über einem „Stuhlbein“ zu sitzen kommt, um die Stabilität zu erhöhen. Mit einem Schildchen und einer bayerischen Tischdecke das Arrangement fertig stellen.

> Make the figure as described in the chapter “Modelling Techniques” (from page 232). Score the braces for the lederhosen and use the brush to highlight the contours in black. For the rest of the colour scheme, in order to contrast the colours better with those in the other parts, it is best to work only with a brush. Allow each coating of colour to dry out completely before applying the next coat.
Model the beer jar from a short roll of marzipan. Use an M 2 to mark the sides symmetrically and an M 7 to score the bottom. Attach the handle and colour the whole jar using an airbrush. Pipe on the foam in royal icing.
To make the table and the bench, cut strips from a marzipan slab in different lengths. Cut the length of the two legs for the table and the benches. | 1 |
Cut the reinforcements from an off-cut and attach these to the sides. | 2 |
Stick both parts on the underside of the respective slab. | 3 |
When constructed in this way, the set will take one or several days until it is firm.
When assembling the set, make sure that the figure comes to sit above a “leg” of the bench in order to give greater stability. Complete the arrangement with a small sign and a Bavarian-style tablecloth.

PROFI **TIPP** *Die bayerische Tischdecke kann man sich mit dem Lebensmittelfarbdrucker auf Zuckerfolie drucken.*

Accessories with delicate detail can easily be produced with the food colour printer on sugar paper.

> Aus einem Quader einen Strohballen formen. Mit M 7 die Längsriffelung und mit M 8 das gepunktete Relief des Strohs herstellen. Gelb grundieren, leicht mit Braun und dann mit Wasser nachsprühen.
Die Gerte aus einem einfachen Marzipanstab durch schräges Profilieren mit M 7 anfertigen.
Zaumzeug und Hufeisen aus dünnen Marzipansträngen modellieren. Alle Einzelteile gesondert schminken und trocknen lassen.
Den Sattel auf einer Unterlage modellieren, die den Abmessungen des Strohballens entspricht. Die Rückenauflage in Form einer abgerundeten ovalen Platte vorbereiten. Aus feinen Streifen mit M 4 Halteriemchen herstellen. | 1 |
Zwei davon auf der Sattelunterlage anbringen und kleine Löcher einstechen. Mit M 3 aus einer Kugel einen Steigbügel zurechtbiegen und ihn an einem Riemen befestigen. | 2 |
Diesen wiederum an entsprechender Stelle ankleben. Aus einem Tropfen den Sattel formen. Einen kleinen Tropfen in eine Vertiefung am Vorderteil des Sattels einstecken. Mit einer eingerollten Marzipandecke den Westernsattel vervollständigen. | 3 |
Den Sattel schminken und auf dem Strohballen positionieren.
Alle Komponenten erst nach guter Trocknung mit einem Schildchen auf einer vorbereiteten Grundplatte zusammenfügen.

> Form a straw bale starting from a basic cube shape. Use an M 7 to mark the pattern of the straw on the side and an M 8 to produce the relief of the pointed ends of the straw. Apply a yellow base coat, follow on with a light brown spray and then with water spray. Make the whip from a simple marzipan stick, using an M 7 to give it the appropriate profile. Model the harness and horseshoes from thin strands of marzipan. Colour all parts individually and leave to dry.
Model the saddle on a suitable base that corresponds with the dimensions of the straw bale. Prepare the backrest in the shape of a rounded oval plate. Use an M 4 to shape little straps from fine strips of marzipan. | 1 |
Attach two of these onto the saddle base and puncture with small holes. Use an M 3 to shape a stirrup from a ball and attach it to one of the straps. | 2 |
Attach this at the appropriate place. Shape the saddle from a drop. Place a small drop into an indentation in the front of the saddle. Roll a small slab of marzipan to resemble a rolled-up blanket and complete the western-style saddle. | 3 |
Colour the saddle and position on the straw bale.
Join up all components after they are well dried and complete with a little sign on the prepared base slab.

PROFI **TIPP** *Feine Einzelteile, die sich schlecht mit Schokolade oder Spritzglasur ankleben lassen, ohne dass man es sehen würde, einfach auf einen frisch mit Lebensmittellack besprühten Untergrund legen. Der trocknende Lack fixiert dann das Schmuckteil.*

Delicate parts that are not easy to attach with chocolate or icing without it being visible can be attached simply by spraying the base with food lacquer and placing the part on the fresh spray. As it dries up, the lacquer will keep the part in place.

Das Glück der Erde ...

Saddle up

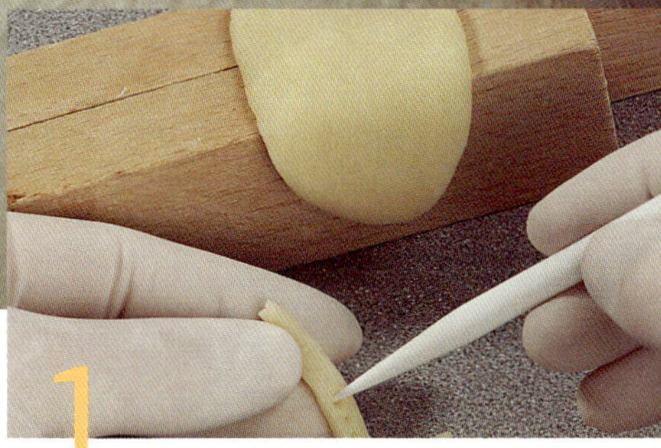

1

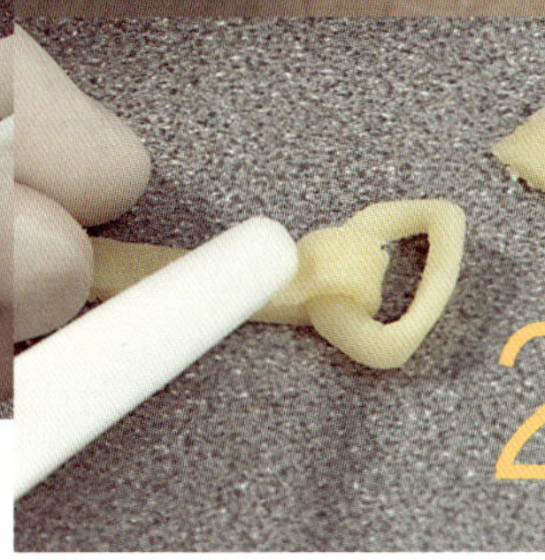

2

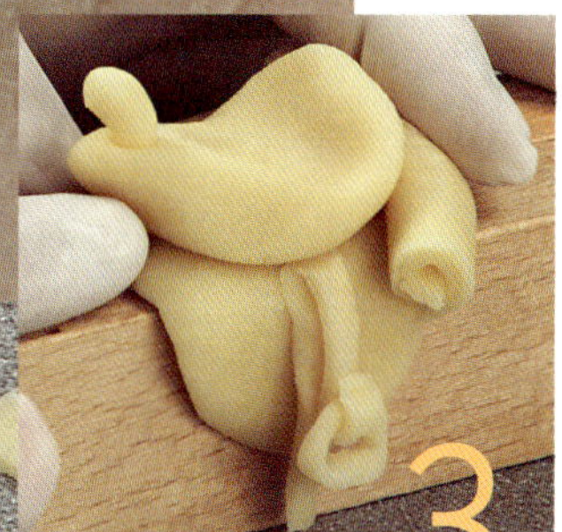

3

1

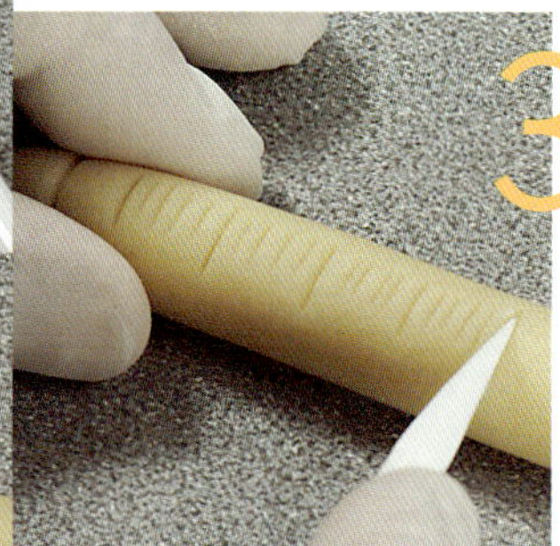
3

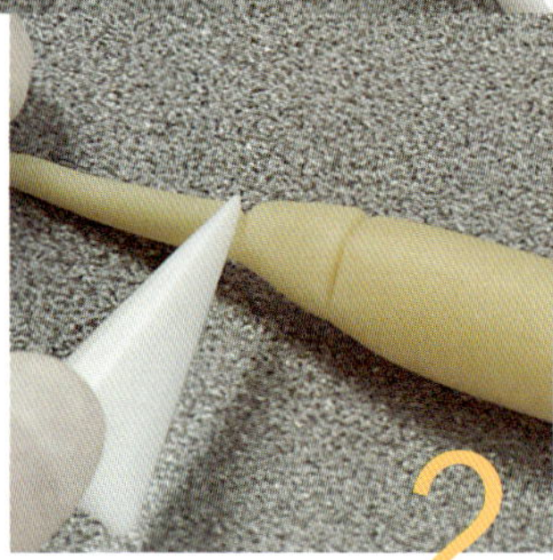
2

› Für die Grundplatte ein Kreuz zurechtschneiden und gleichmäßig mit Rot grundieren. Mit Weiß die Ränder nachziehen.
Die Tasche aus einem Marzipanrechteck formen und mit M 3 abrunden. Mit M 1 die beiden Seiten zum Klappverschluss hin vertiefen und die Metallbeschläge mit M 7 abgrenzen. Die Taschenschnalle aus einem kleinen Marzipanzylinder modellieren und ankleben. Aus zwei Marzipanstangen die Griffe zurechtbiegen und befestigen. Die Konturen für das rote Kreuz auf der Tasche mit M 11 einkerben. Die Arzttasche mit Weiß grundieren.
Restliche Farben mit dem Pinsel auftragen. Feinste schwarze Striche erhöhen die Tiefenwirkung.
Die Spritze aus einer einfachen Stange mit einem spitz ausgeformten Ende herstellen. Mit dem Rücken des M 7 vorsichtig den Stößel von der Spritze abgrenzen. | 1 |
Die einzelnen Segmente der Nadel durch leichte Vertiefungen betonen. | 2 |
Die Skaleneinteilung einkerben. | 3 |
Die gesamte Spritze mit Weiß grundieren. Die Nadel leicht mit Schwarz nachsprühen. Restliche Färbung mit dem Pinsel vornehmen.
Aus dünnen Marzipanrollen ein Stethoskop anfertigen und zusammen mit den anderen Bestandteilen sowie einem Schildchen das Arrangement vervollständigen.

› To make the base slab, cut out the shape of a cross and apply an even base coat of red. Outline the edges in white.
Form the bag from a rectangular piece of marzipan and use an M 3 to round it off. Use an M 1 to indent the two sides towards the closing flap and an M 7 to outline the metal fittings. Model the buckles from a small marzipan cylinder and attach. Take two rolled strips of marzipan to bend the handles and attach these to the bag. Use an M 11 to score the contours of the red cross on the bag. Apply a white base coat to the doctor's bag. Apply the other colours by brush. Very fine black lines will accentuate the visual depth.
Make the syringe from a simple roll with the end shaped to a point. Use the back of an M 7 to carefully delineate the plunger. | 1 |
Accentuate the individual segments of the needle through slight indentations. | 2 |
Mark the dividing lines of the scale. | 3 |
Apply a white base coat to the whole syringe and follow on with a slight black spray for the needle. Apply the other colours by brush.
Make a stethoscope from thin rolls of marzipan and complete the arrangement together with the other components and a small sign.

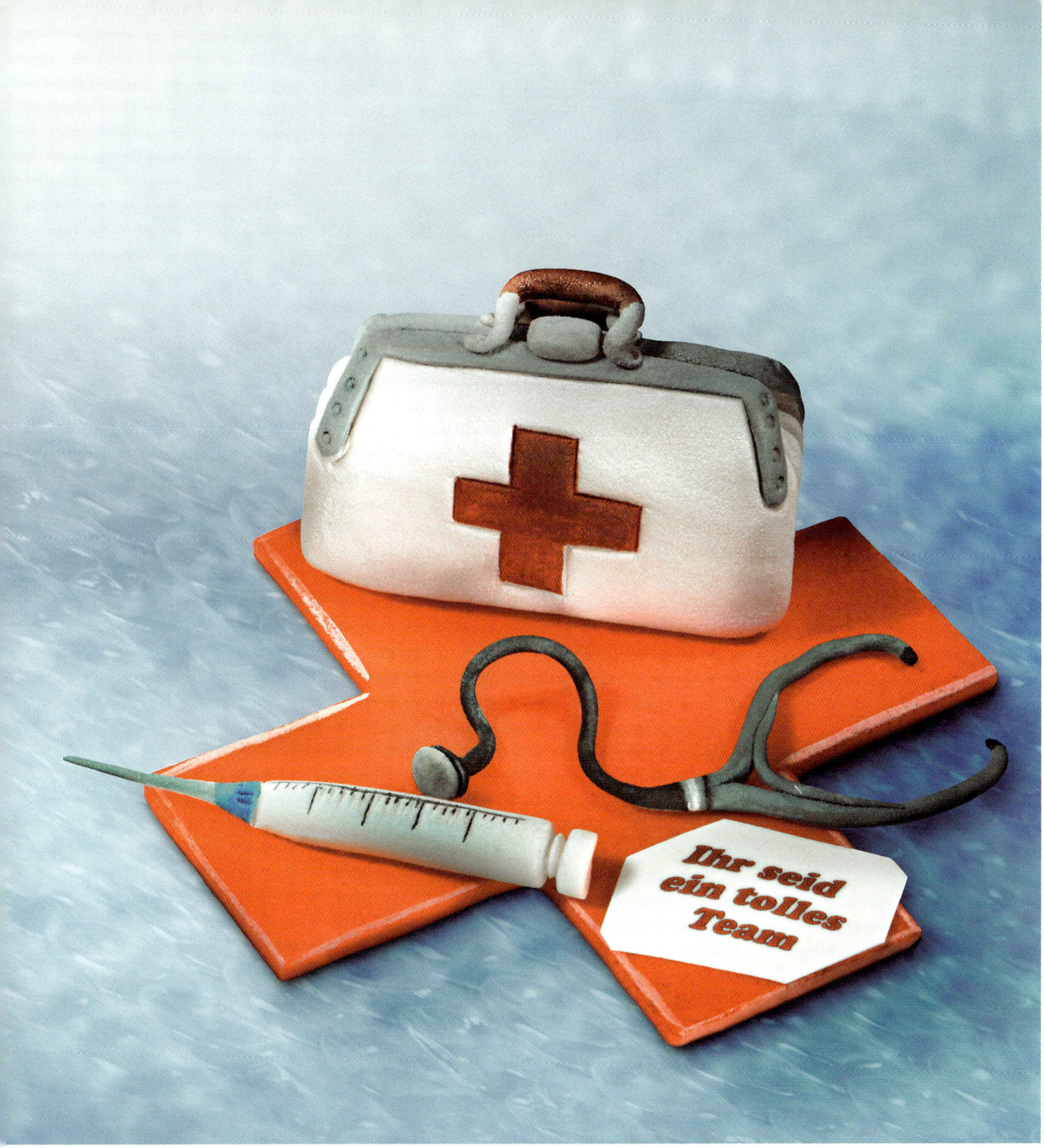

Ihr seid ein tolles Team

You're a great team

Ein süßes Dankeschön für Schwestern und Ärzte

A sweet thank you for nurses and doctors

A bad day of boarding ...

A bad day of boarding ...

› Den Snowboarder wie im Grundlagenkapitel „Modelliertechniken“ (ab Seite 232) beschrieben weitgehend gleich erstellen. Mit Holzstäbchen für Stabilität sorgen. Um den Eindruck einer fahrenden Figur zu erreichen, die Haare und Kleidungsstücke „lose“ nach hinten flattern lassen. Den Schal aus einem dünnen Streifen schneiden und auf dem Oberkörper befestigen. Die Figur sollte dabei schon etwas abgesteift sein, damit sie keine eigenen Stützen mehr benötigt. Mit M 10 die Fransen des Schals einrollen. | 1 |
Solange das Marzipan noch weich ist, zügig den Faltenwurf des wehenden Schals modellieren. | 2 |
Den Arm und die Unterseite des Handschuhs mit Eiweiß benetzen, um den Schal daran ankleben zu können. | 3 |
Diese dünnen Teile trocknen rasch durch und sind auf Grund dessen am nächsten Tag schon fest genug, um sich selbst zu tragen. Die Figur mit dem Airbrush und Pinsel schminken.
Das Snowboard ebenfalls aus einer Platte schneiden, formen und absteifen lassen. Mit Weiß grundieren und ein beliebiges Muster mit dem Pinsel aufzeichnen.
Die Figur auf dem Board anbringen und ein Schildchen hinzufügen.

› Make the snowboarder in much the same way as described in the basics chapter “Modelling Techniques” (from page 232). Use wooden sticks to ensure stability. In order to create the impression of a figure in motion, arrange the hair and items of clothing so that they appear to flap loosely towards the back. Cut the scarf from a thin strip and attach to the upper body. Before doing that, the figure should have become somewhat stiff so that it no longer requires support. Use an M 10 in a rolling motion to make the fringes of the scarf. | 1 |
While the marzipan is still soft, swiftly model the folds of the scarf as it flaps in the wind. | 2 |
Apply some egg white to the arm and the underside of the glove in order to be able to attach the scarf to them. | 3 |
These thin parts dry out quickly and therefore are already firm enough on the next day to be self-supporting. Colour the figure using an airbrush and brush.
Make the snowboard also from a slab, form into the correct shape and leave to dry. Apply a white base coat and then any pattern by brush you like on the board.
Fix the figure on the board and add a small sign.

PROFI **TIPP** *Die Farbe Lila kommt nur auf weiß grundierten Flächen richtig zur Geltung.*

The colour lilac only really has the desired effect in combination with white as a base coat.

1
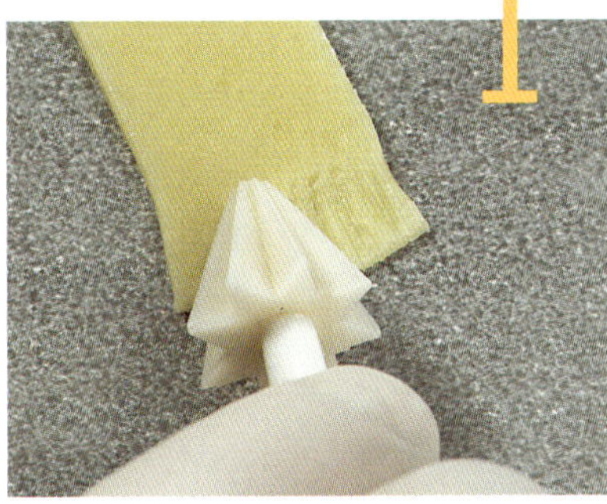
2
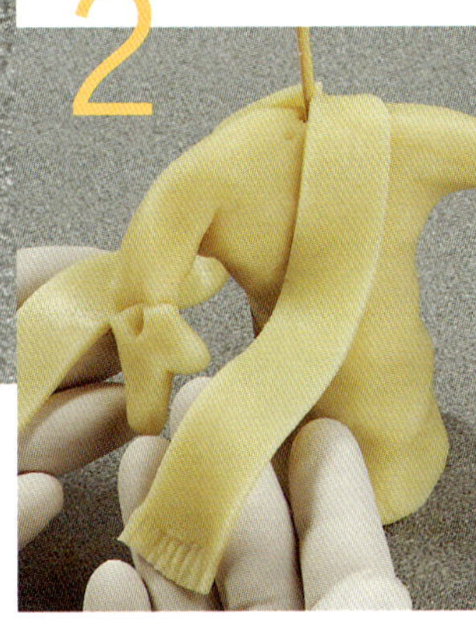
3

> Den Hobel aus einem Marzipanquader schneiden. Die Kanten mit den Fingern durch Tippen leicht abrunden und mit M 3 glätten. Die Klinge und das dazugehörende Arretierholz aus einer Platte schneiden und an den Hobel ankleben. Den Griff aus einer kurzen Stange zurechtbiegen und befestigen. Gelb grundieren und mit Braun nachsprühen. Die Klinge grau einfärben. Eine dünne Marzipanrolle für das Sägeblatt anfertigen und einseitig mit einem Backhorn glätten. | 1 |
Beide Kanten parallel sauber abschneiden. Mit einem scharfen Messer erst alle Links-, dann alle Rechtsschnitte ausführen. | 2 |
Den Bügel der Säge aus einer etwas dickeren Stange formen. | 3 |
Das Sägeblatt mit wenig Eiweiß mit dem Bügel verbinden, trocknen lassen und schminken.
Aus Schokolade eine Grundplatte gestalten. Falls vorhanden, mit einem speziellen „Gummikamm“ eine Holzmaserung einarbeiten. Die Hobelspäne aus aufgestrichener Kuvertüre herstellen. Diese temperiert auf eine Marmorplatte streichen, kurz warten, bis sie beginnt anzuziehen, und dann zügig mit dem Metallspatel Streifen abschaben. Die einzelnen Bestandteile auf der Schokoladenplatte platzieren. Mit einem modellierten Hämmerchen, einem Schild und den Hobelspänen das Exponat dekorieren.

> Cut the shape of the plane out of a cube of marzipan. Slightly round the edges by tapping with the fingers – use an M 3 to smooth off. Cut the blade and clamping block from a slab and attach to the plane. Bend the handle into shape, using a short marzipan roll, and attach this to the plane. Apply a yellow base coat and follow on with a brown spray. Use grey to colour the blade. Make a thin marzipan roll for the saw blade. Smooth this on one side with a dough scraper. | 1 |
Cut both edges neatly in parallel. Use a sharp knife to first make all left-hand cuts and then all right-hand cuts. | 2 |
Make the bow of the saw from a slightly thicker roll. | 3 |
Connect the saw blade with egg white to the bow, leave to dry and colour.
Make a base plate from chocolate. If you have a special “rubber comb”, use this to create the impression of the wood grain. Make the wood shavings from couverture that has been tempered and spread out on a marble slab. Wait for a short while until it begins to set and then swiftly scrape strips off with a metal spatula. Place all components on the chocolate slab. Model a little hammer and use this, the wood shavings and a small sign to decorate the item.

PROFI **TIPP** *Manche Marzipanteile sind so filigran, dass sie in frisch modelliertem Zustand nicht zu verwenden sind. Solche Teile am besten auf Backfolie oder einer anderen, nicht klebenden Unterlage herstellen. Dort vollständig trocknen lassen, bis alles stabil genug ist. Danach können die Einzelteile ohne Schaden zu nehmen abgelöst werden, um sie in ein Arrangement zu integrieren.*

Some marzipan parts are so delicate that they cannot be used in their freshly modelled state. It is best to make these parts on baking foil or another base material that does not stick. Leave the item there to dry completely until everything is rigid enough. Then the parts can be taken off, without the risk of damage, and fitted into the ensemble.

Dem süßen Heimwerker

For the sweet DIYer

1 2 3

Zum Fest des Kegelbruders oder für besonders Standhafte!
Happy bowling – but don't "throw a wobbly"!

Alle Neune
Strike!

> Eine Grundplatte ausschneiden und mit einem seitlich angeklebten dickeren Marzipanstreifen die Bande der Kegelbahn darstellen. Mit M 3 daran anschließend den Kugelablauf eindrücken. Alles gelb grundieren und mit Grün nachsprühen. Den Kugelablauf braun einfärben und die Bande oben mit Weiß nachziehen.
Aus lang gezogenen Birnenformen die Kegel modellieren. Um einen einheitlichen Eindruck zu vermitteln, die einzelnen Kegel in Größe und Form ähnlich gestalten. Mit M 2 die Augenhöhlen eindrücken. Für die verschiedenen Mundformen mit M 3 und M 7 arbeiten. Alle Kegel weiß grundieren und gut trocknen lassen. Die Zierstreifen mit dem Pinsel anbringen und die Augen aufspritzen.
Die Bowling- oder Kegelkugel formen und mit entsprechenden Grifflöchern versehen. Die Augenhöhlen einkerben und einen zwiespältigen Gesichtsausdruck durch einen wellenförmigen Mund einritzen. Mit Gelb und Braun besprühen und Augen sowie Mund mit Schwarz nachziehen.
Die abgesteiften Teile gut fixieren, um sie leicht schräg zu arrangieren. Mit einem Schild das Szenario fertig stellen.

> Cut out a base slab and attach a thicker marzipan strip on the side to represent the sides of the bowling lane. Then use an M 3 to shape the side of the bowling lane. Apply a yellow base coat to everything and follow up with green. Colour the side in brown and outline the edge with white. Shape the pins from elongated bulb-shaped pieces of marzipan. It is important here to give the pins an equal shape and size to convey an impression of uniformity. Use an M 2 to make the eye sockets. Use an M 3 and an M 7 to shape the different forms of the mouths. Apply white base coat to all pins and leave to dry well. Apply the decorative strips by brush and pipe on the eyes. Shape the bowl and put in the appropriate finger holes. Make the eye sockets and create an ambiguous facial expression by giving the mouth a wavy shape. Spray on yellow and brown and add a black outline to the eyes and the mouth.
Once the parts have become rigid, fix them well and arrange in a slightly slanting position. Complete the scenario with a sign.

PROFI **TIPP** *Ein solches Arrangement bietet eine witzige Alternative zur normalen Gratulationskarte. Anlass oder Name des Gratulanten können leicht variiert und aufgetragen werden. Hier zum Beispiel bietet sich vornehmlich der vordere Kegel für eine Beschriftung an. Der weiße Untergrund macht ein Beschreiben mit dem Pinsel möglich, ohne dass die Farben ausfließen.*

This type of arrangement represents a humorous alternative to a normal greeting card. It is easy to vary the occasion and the name of the recipient. One option is to apply the writing to the front pin. The white base coat ensures that the brush writing won't run.

Motivationstraining

Motivational training

> Eine Grundplatte mit einem Schneiderad anfertigen. Das Gras mit M 10 einrollen und eine Sandfläche mit M 11 aufrauen.
Die Bauernfigur wie im Grundlagenkapitel „Modelliertechniken“ (ab Seite 232) beschrieben herstellen und gut gestützt auf entsprechender Unterlage trocknen lassen.
Aus einer Marzipanstange einen Strohballen herstellen, indem man mit einem Backhorn die Stange zum Quader formt. Dabei die vorgesehene Höhe einhalten, welche die sitzende Figur vorgibt.
Mit einer Messerklinge die Längsriffelung eindrücken. | 1 |
Beide Stirnseiten werden mit M 12 aufgeraut. | 2 |
Die doppelte Kante des M 10 ermöglicht das Einkerben der Schnur in einem Handgriff. | 3 |
Den Strohballen gelb grundieren und zart mit Braun und schließlich mit Wasser nachsprühen.
Die Hühner aus einer fertigen Form drücken (wenn vorhanden). Ansonsten von Hand modellieren. Die Hühnerschar mit Weiß grundieren, gut trocknen lassen und mit dem Pinsel Kamm, Schnabel sowie Augen schminken.
Einen kleinen Koffer modellieren, schminken und zwei unterschiedlich große Eier mit Untersetzer darauf setzen.
Auf der vorbereiteten Grundplatte die Einzelteile mit einem Schildchen ankleben.

> Use the cutting wheel to prepare a base slab. Roll in the grass pattern with an M 10 and use and M 11 to apply roughness to the surface to represent sand.
Make the figure of the farmer as described in the chapter “Modelling Techniques” (from page 232) and leave to dry whilst well propped up on an appropriate support.
Make a bale of straw from a marzipan roll by shaping it into a cube, using a dough scraper. Make sure to model the height such that the figure can sit comfortably on it. Use a knife to score the straw pattern on the side. | 1 |
Use an M 12 to roughen the surface of the front and rear end of the bale to resemble the straw ends. | 2 |
The double edge of the M 10 makes it easy to score the string with just one movement. | 3 |
Apply a yellow base coat to the straw bale and spray with a touch of brown and finally water. The chickens can be cut out with a ready-made shape. If this is not available they can be modelled by hand. Apply a white base coat to the flock of chickens, leave to dry well and colour the crest, the beak as well as the eyes, using a brush.
Model a small briefcase, colour it and place two different sized eggs in eggcups on it.
Fix the components on the prepared base slab, together with the sign.

PROFI **TIPP** *Wenn viele identische Teile benötigt werden lohnt es sich, über die Herstellung einer Silikonform nachzudenken. Das entsprechende Silikon ist im Fachhandel erhältlich.*

When many identical parts are needed it is worth thinking about producing a silicone mould. The silicone needed to make such moulds can be purchased in specialist shops.

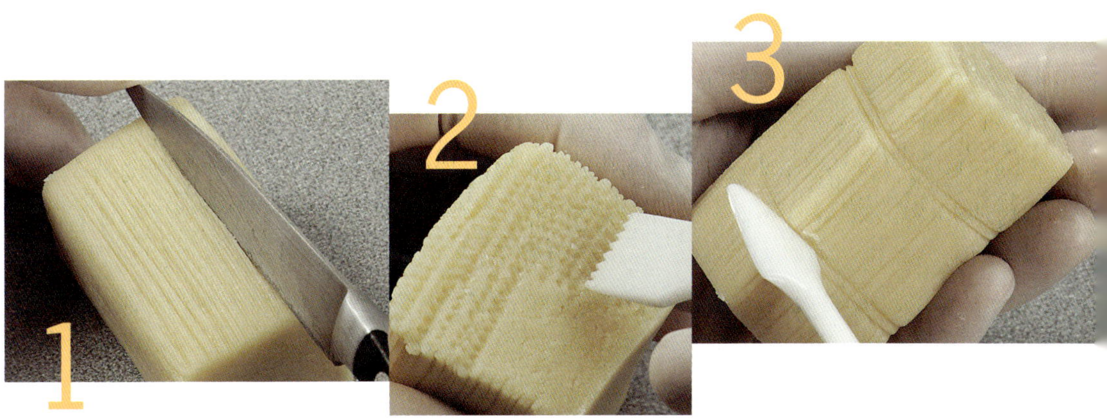

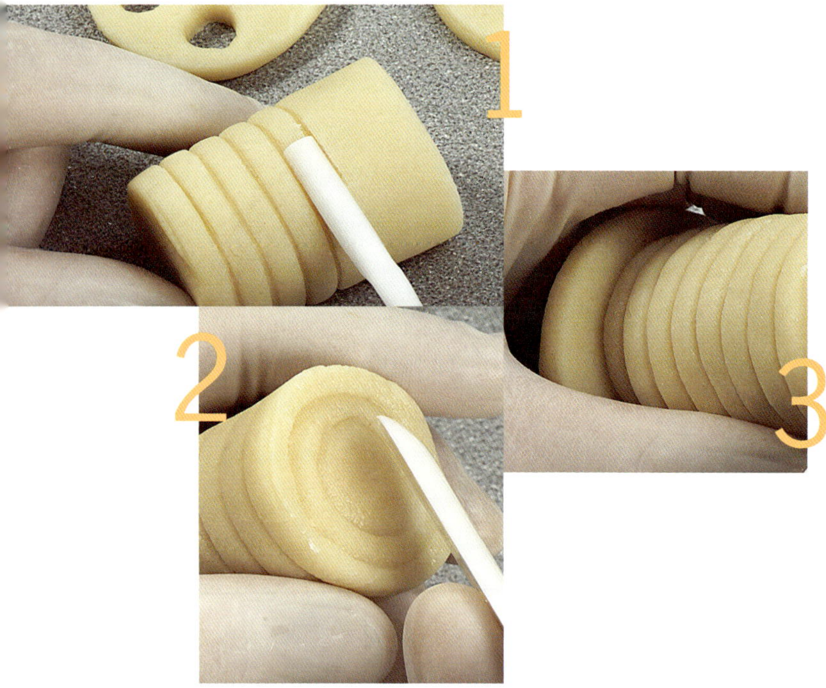

> Die kleinen Details wie die Axt, einen Feuerwehrhelm und eine Bierflasche modellieren. Gut trocknen lassen und schminken.
Aus einer Marzipanplatte zwei runde Scheiben ausstechen. Mit einer Lochtülle das entsprechende Muster der Stellage für den Feuerwehrschlauch ausstanzen. Einen kurzen Marzipanzylinder mit etwas geringerem Durchmesser wie die Scheiben zurechtschneiden. Mit M 6 die gleichmäßigen „Schlauchreihen" eindrücken. | 1 |
Das Seitenteil der Schlauchrolle mit M 3 spiralförmig einkerben. | 2 |
Die Schlauchrolle auf einen kleinen Quader setzen und ankleben. Mit Weiß grundieren und leicht mit Schwarz nachsprühen. Beide Seitenteile des Gestells rot schminken und an den Schlauch ansetzen. | 3 |
Aus jeweils einer dünnen Stange einen Schlauchanfang und ein Endstück herstellen und ankleben. Auf einer mit dem Schneiderad gefertigten Grundplatte den Schriftzug aufbringen und die Einzelteile, gut miteinander verklebt, befestigen.

> Model the small details such as the axe, the fireman's helmet and the beer bottle. Allow to dry well and colour.
Cut out two round discs from a marzipan slab. Use a round piping nozzle to cut out the appropriate pattern of a reel for a firefighting hose. Cut a short marzipan cylinder with a slightly smaller diameter than the discs. Use an M 6 in order to score the regular rolled-up hose pattern. | 1 |
Use an M 3 to score a spiral shape into the sides. | 2 |
Place the hose roll on a small cube and attach. Apply a white base coat and follow on with a light black spray. Colour both sides of the reel in red and fix to the hose. | 3 |
Use a thin rolled strip to make the end pieces of the hose and attach these to the reel. Use the cutting wheel to cut out a board and apply the writing; fix the components together and attach them to the base.

Lösch-Geräte

Quenching ...

Für jeden Notfall das geeignete Lösch-Gerät
What to quench first?

Nicht aufregen ...

Keep cool ...

Wenn man wieder mal rotsieht!

Don't let things get on top of you!

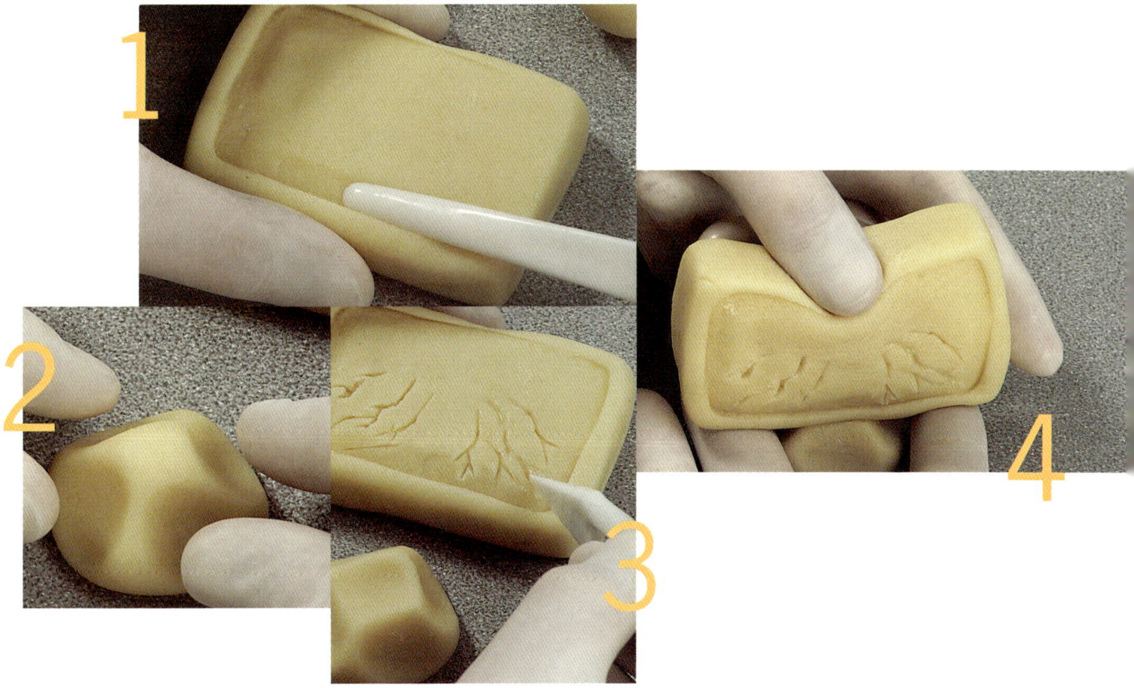

› Eine Tastatur wie unter „Gefährliches Suchtmittel“ (Seite 94) beschrieben herstellen.
Für den Monitor ein Rechteck vorbereiten. Mit M 3 eine Trennlinie ziehen, um die Scheibe vom Gehäuse abzugrenzen. | 1 |
Eine kleine Kugel für den Sockel mit Daumen und Zeigefinger beider Hände auf jeder Seite eindrücken. | 2 |
Die Risse auf dem Bildschirm mit M 7 einritzen. | 3 |
Mit dem Daumen eine großflächige Delle auf dem oberen Monitorrand eindrücken. | 4 |
Den Bildschirm leicht schwarz grundieren. Die „Glasfläche“ mit Wasser nachsprühen, so dass die schwarze Farbe vornehmlich in die Ritzen fließt. Nach der Trocknung mit Blau nachsprühen.
Aus einer lang gezogenen Birnenform die Keule formen. Mit M 1 an der dicken Seite einkerben und kleine Marzipankügelchen als Steine ankleben. Die Keule schminken und in die Mitte der Kuhle anbringen.
Die Grundplatte in Blitzform ausschneiden, gelb grundieren und mit Rot nachsprühen. Monitor und Tastatur sowie ein Schildchen aufsetzen.

› Make a keyboard as described under the item “Caution – addictive” (page 94).
Prepare a rectangular shape for the monitor. Use an M 3 to draw the line that separates the screen from the housing. | 1 |
Make the plinth by squaring off a small ball with the thumb and forefinger of both hands, pressing on the four sides. | 2 |
Score the cracks on the screen with an M 7. | 3 |
Use your thumb to push in a large dent on the top of the monitor. | 4 |
Apply a light black base coat to the screen. Spray water onto the screen surface so that the black colour runs mostly into the cracks. Once dry, apply a spray with blue colour.
Shape the club from a long drawn out bulb shape. Use an M 1 to score the thicker side and attach small marzipan balls to resemble stones. Colour the club and place it on the middle of the dent.
Cut out the base slab in zigzag shape, apply a yellow base coat and follow on with red spray. Place the monitor and the keyboard on the base plate and finish off with a small sign.

> Als Grundkörper für das Auto eine Halbkugel anfertigen. Mit den Fingern die grobe Kontur der Motorhaube und der Frontscheibe vormodellieren, dann die beiden Seiten mit den Kotflügeln. Überschüssiges Marzipan mit einem scharfen Messer abtrennen. Mit M 3 und M 9 die Flächen gut glätten. Mit einem Ausstecher die Radkästen aushöhlen. Dazu die Karosserie mit der entsprechenden Seite ein Stück über die Tischkante hinausschieben. Ausstecher drehend in das Marzipan treiben und nach unten abziehen.
Zum Ausformen der Kanten eignet sich M 1. Mit M 7 und M 11 werden Motorhaube, Scheiben und Türen eingeritzt. Die Stoßstangen aus Marzipanstreifen gesondert herstellen und ankleben. Die Lampen aus zwei platt gedrückten Kugeln formen und ansetzen. Um die Schräglage des Autos zu erreichen, die Karosserie auf einen Keil stellen. Beim Schminken darauf achten, dass die Wagenfarbe nicht auf die Fenster kommt. Diese nur im Randbereich leicht mit Blau besprühen. In die Frontscheibe mit dem Airbrush Lenkrad und Rückspiegel einsprühen. Alle Spalten und Dichtungen mit Schwarz nachziehen.
Die Reifen einzeln ausstechen oder von einer Marzipanrolle abschneiden. | 1 |
In die Reifen mit M 10 ein Profil einrollen. | 2 |
Mit M 3 die Abgrenzung zwischen Felge und Reifen einarbeiten. Die Durchbrüche der Felge mit M 1 profilieren. | 3 |
Für die Schraubenlöcher mit M 4 kleine Vertiefungen einstechen. Die Felgen mit Weiß komplett einfärben. Mit Schwarz und ausreichend Wasser nachsprühen. Nach der Trocknung die Reifen mit dem Pinsel schwärzen.
Für den „Schrauber-König" nur die Beine und einen Arm anfertigen. Eine Grundplatte herstellen und die Gliedmaßen unterhalb der Karosserie platzieren. Nach Belieben das Szenario durch Details wie Wagenheber und Schildchen vervollständigen.

> Cut a ball in half as a starting shape for the car. Use your fingers to roughly model the contour of the bonnet and the windscreen, followed by the two sides with the wings. Use a sharp knife to cut off any excess marzipan. Use an M 3 and M 9 to smooth the surfaces well. The wheel arches can be cut out with a cutting tool. To do this, it is best to move the side of the car body a little distance beyond the edge of the table. Drive the cutting tool with a turning motion into the marzipan and then pull downwards.
To give the edges their final shape, the M 1 is a suitable tool. Use an M 7 and M 11 to score the bonnet, the windscreens and the doors. Make the bumpers separately from strips of marzipan and attach to the body. Make the headlights from two flattened balls and also attach to the body. In order to achieve the tilted position of the car, place the body onto a wedge. When colouring the body, ensure that the paint for the car does not get onto the windscreen or windows. Spray these around the edges lightly with blue. Spray the contours of the steering wheel and rear-view mirror onto the front windscreen, using an airbrush. Accentuate all joins and seals in black.
Cut out the tyres individually or cut them from a marzipan roll. | 1 |
Use an M 10 to roll a profile into the tyres. | 2 |
Use the M 3 to work in the separating line between wheel and tyre. Use the M 1 to sculpt the profile of the wheel. | 3 |
Use an M 4 to make small indentations for the boltholes. Colour the wheels completely in white. Follow on with a black spray and sufficient water. Once dry, use a brush to paint the tyres black.
To make the "mechanical whizz kid" you only need to make the legs and one arm. Prepare a base slab and place the limbs underneath the car body. You can add further details such as a car jack etc. Complete the arrangement with a small sign.

PROFI **TIPP** *Kleine Details, wie hier zum Beispiel die Reifen, Schraubenschlüssel und Wagenheber, beleben jedes Arrangement. Mit wenig Aufwand kann man eine große Wirkung erzielen.*

Small details such as the tyres, the spanners and the jack in this example make an arrangement come to life.

Dem Schrauber-König

Happy motoring

> Zwei unterschiedlich große Blöcke an den Kanten abrunden und aufeinander zu einem Motor zusammensetzen. Aus sechs Stangensegmenten abgerundete Zylinder formen und befestigen. | 1 |
Kleine platt gedrückte Kugeln als Deckel auf den Zylindern andrücken und mit M 4 Schraubenlöcher in den oberen Motorblock einstechen. | 2 |
Dünne „Leitungen" aus Marzipanröllchen von den Deckeln ausgehend in den unteren Vertiefungen befestigen und drei weitere Scheibchen an der Vorderseite des Motors ankleben. Ein Lüfterrad gesondert modellieren, trocknen lassen und anschließend mittig auf der Frontseite platzieren. | 3 |
Den Keilriemen aus dünner Marzipanschnur um die drei Scheiben der Vorderseite legen. Eine dreigespaltene Stange für das jeweilige Abgasrohr formen und am unteren Motorblock befestigen. Den fertigen Motor weiß grundieren und mit etwas Schwarz nachsprühen. Schraubenlöcher und Kanten mit feinem Pinselstrich nachziehen. Ebenso den Keilriemen und das Lüfterrad nachfärben.
Eine dicke, quadratische Grundplatte sowie zwei schmale Streifen für die „Kanthölzer" zurechtschneiden, schminken und zusammenfügen. Den Motor auf den Kanthölzern befestigen.
Für die Lupe ein Marzipanband um einen Ausstecher legen und trocknen lassen. Einen stabilen Griff modellieren und mit dem oberen Lupenteil verbinden. Nach dem Schminken an der Grundplatte angelehnt aufstellen.
Um das Szenario zu vervollkommnen, eine kleine Schraube herstellen, hinter die Lupe setzen und ein Schildchen platzieren.

> Take two blocks of different sizes and round off at the edges, then place on top of each other to represent an engine. Make rounded cylinders from six roll segments and attach. | 1 |
Place small flattened balls as covers onto the cylinders and use an M 4 to push boltholes into the top part of the engine block. | 2 |
Make thin "pipelines" from small rolled marzipan strips and attach these to the cylinder covers and the other end to the indentations in the engine block; attach three further discs at the front of the engine. Model a fan, leave to dry and then attach to the centre of the front of the engine. | 3 |
Place the V-belt around the three discs at the front, using a thin rolled marzipan strip. Shape a manifold exhaust pipe for each side, with three inlets each, and attach to the lower part of the engine. Apply a white base coat to the completed engine and follow up with a little black spray. Accentuate the boltholes and edges with a fine stroke of the brush. Likewise, outline the V-belt and the fan wheel. Cut out a thick square base slab as well as two narrow strips to resemble the timber sections, apply the colour and join together. Attach the engine to the timber sections. To make the magnifying glass, place a marzipan ribbon around a cutting tool and leave to dry. Model a sturdy handle and connect to the upper part of the magnifying glass. Once you have coloured it, place the item upright leaning against the base slab.
To finish off the scenario, make a small bolt, place behind the magnifying glass and attach a small sign.

PROFI **TIPP** *Um die Illusion der Vergrößerung zu unterstreichen, wird der Zierstrich hinter der Lupe verbreitert aufgemalt.*

In order to accentuate the magnifying effect, paint the section of the line that is behind the magnifying glass somewhat wider.

Eine Schraube bleibt immer übrig

Where did this go?

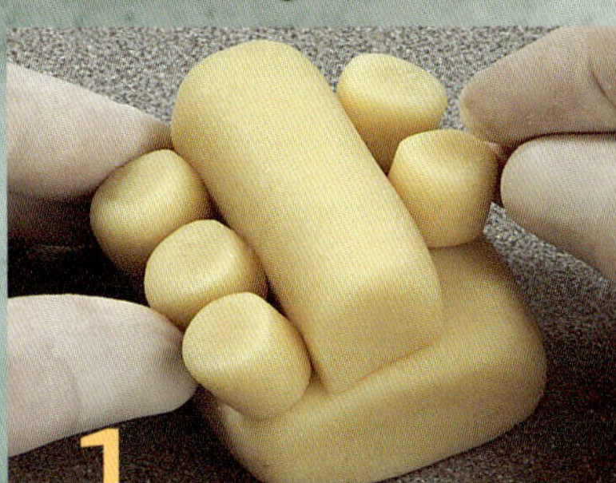
1

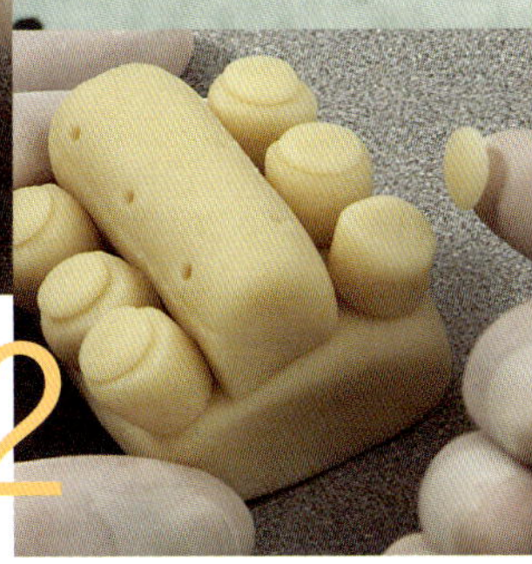
2

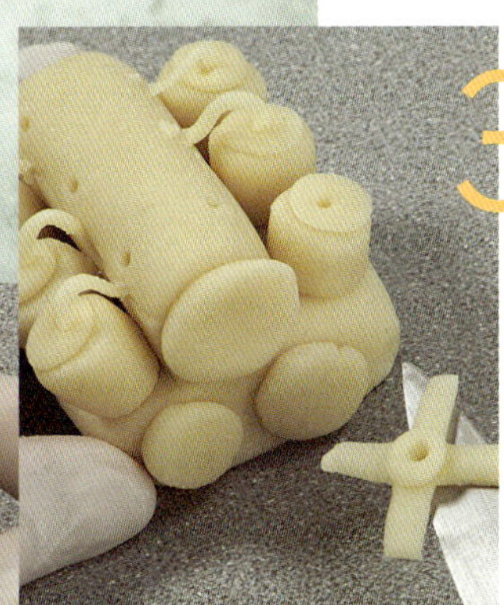
3

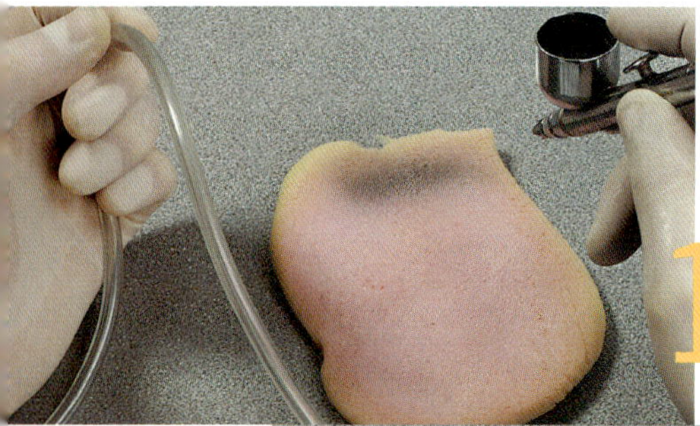

1

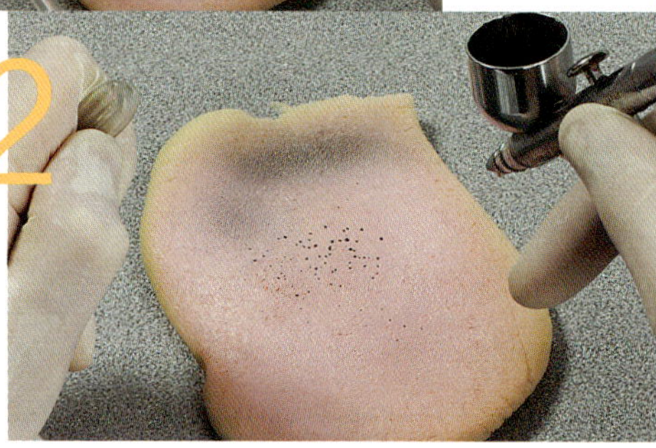

2

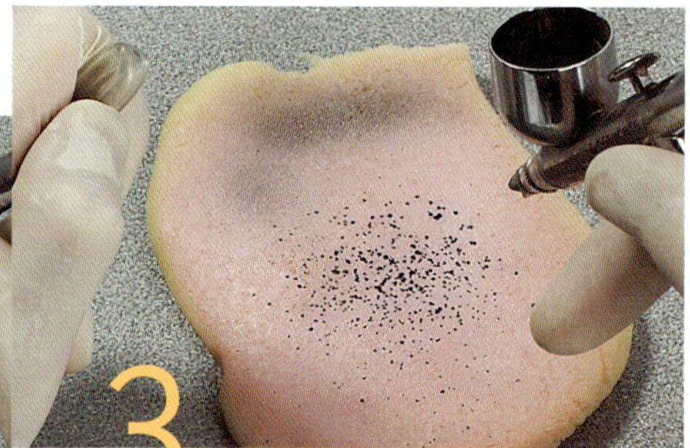

3

> Figur wie im Grundlagenkapitel „Modelliertechniken“ (ab Seite 232) beschrieben herstellen.
Alle Gliedmaßen gut stützen und ausreichende Trockenzeit einplanen. Die stabile Figur vollständig mit Hautfarbe grundieren. |1|
Haare, Hose und Schuhe mit dem Pinsel nachschminken. Das zarte Brusthaar mit dem Airbrush andeuten, indem man durch Knicken des Schlauchs die Luftzufuhr etwas verringert. |2|
Ein kurzes Antippen des Abzugs verursacht größere Farbtröpfchen, mehrfaches schnelles Antippen dagegen eine feine Sprenkeloptik. |3|
Eine Grundplatte nur am Rand mit Gelb und mit Rot besprühen. Den Rand mit dem Pinsel verzieren. Kleine Gewichte herstellen und auf der Grundplatte anbringen.
Den Schriftbogen aus einer Platte schneiden und liegend um eine runde Form biegen, gut trocknen lassen. Die Buchstaben mit Hilfe eines Ausstechers anfertigen und auf den noch liegenden Bogen ankleben. Die Punkte des Bogens aus Eiweißspritzglasur anbringen. Nach der Trocknung den Bogen aufstellen und den Adonis mittig auf die Platte setzen.

> Make the figure as described in the chapter “Modelling Techniques” (from page 232). Support all limbs well and allow for sufficient drying time. Once the figure has become stable, completely cover in skin colour as a base coat. |1|
Paint the hair, trunks and shoes by brush. Use the airbrush to very lightly spray on the hair on the chest, which can be achieved by reducing the air supply by squeezing the hose. |2|
When tapping the trigger briefly one achieves larger drops of paint whereas tapping the trigger fast will achieve a more finely speckled effect. |3|
Spray a base slab with yellow and red, but only at the edge. Embellish the edge with the brush. Make small weights and place on the base slab.
Cut the strip for the letter arch from a slab, place flat on a board and bend around a round form; leave to dry well. Make the letters with the help of a cutting tool and attach to the arch while this is still lying on the board. Pipe the dots on the arch with royal icing. Once dry, set up the arch and place the Adonis centrally on the slab.

Adonis

Adonis

Der Traum aller Frauen – zum Vernaschen!

Sweet toy boy – have him for dessert!

Non-smoker's matches

Non-smoker's matches

> Die Pfeife aus einem Stück formen und das Mundstück mit M 1 abgrenzen. Mit M 3 die Vertiefung für den Tabak eindrücken und die Asche mit M 8 imitieren. Die Pfeife fertig schminken und trocknen lassen.
Die Zigaretten aus Marzipanrollen modellieren. M 3 und M 8 auf gleiche Weise wie bei der Herstellung der Pfeife zur Fertigstellung einsetzen. Mit Weiß grundieren, Filter und Tabak mit dem Pinsel schminken. Die Zierstreifen auf die getrocknete Grundierung aufzeichnen.
Die kopflosen Streichhölzer aus einer dünnen Platte schneiden. Gut trocknen lassen, gelb grundieren und mit Braun ein wenig nachsprühen. Nach kurzer Antrocknung die „Hölzchen“ wenden und noch mal schminken.
Als Grundform für die Streichholzschachtel ein Rechteck fertigen und mit einem scharfen Messer die Frontöffnung einschneiden. | 1 |
Mit einem Längsschnitt das überschüssige Marzipan entfernen. Die Schachtel mit einer dünnen Marzipanplatte unterlegen und ein Rechteck ausschneiden. Durch Ausschneiden zweier Quadrate die Knickkanten festlegen. | 2 |
Alle drei Seiten hochklappen und verkleben. | 3 |
Beide Teile getrennt voneinander schminken. Den Einschub rein weiß, die Schachtel weiß grundieren und mit Blau nachsprühen. Mit einem Pinsel die Verzierungen aufmalen.
Eine runde Grundplatte ausstechen, rot färben. Nach ausreichender Trocknung darauf ein Schildchen zusammen mit den anderen Einzelteilen drapieren.

> Form the pipe out of one piece and delineate the mouthpiece with an M 1. Use an M 3 to push in the hole for the tobacco and use an M 8 to imitate the ash. Colour the pipe and leave to dry.
Model the cigarettes from marzipan rolls. Use an M 3 and an M 8 in the same way as when making the pipe. Apply a white base coat and paint the filter and tobacco with a brush. Paint on the decorative strips once the base coat has dried. Cut the matches, without the heads, from a thin slab. Leave to dry well, apply yellow base coat and follow up with a little brown spray. Leave to dry for a short while and then turn over to repeat the colouring.
The basic shape of the matchbox is made from a rectangular block into which the front opening is cut with a sharp knife. | 1 |
Cut off any excess marzipan. Place thin marzipan slab underneath the box and cut out a rectangular shape. Cut out two squares, which determines where the sides are folded up. | 2 |
Fold all three sides upwards and attach. | 3 |
Colour the two parts separately. Colour the “drawer” in pure white, while applying white base coat to the box, followed with blue spray. Use a brush to paint on the embellishments.
Cut out a round base slab and colour red. Once this has dried sufficiently, arrange all components and complete with a small sign.

1

2

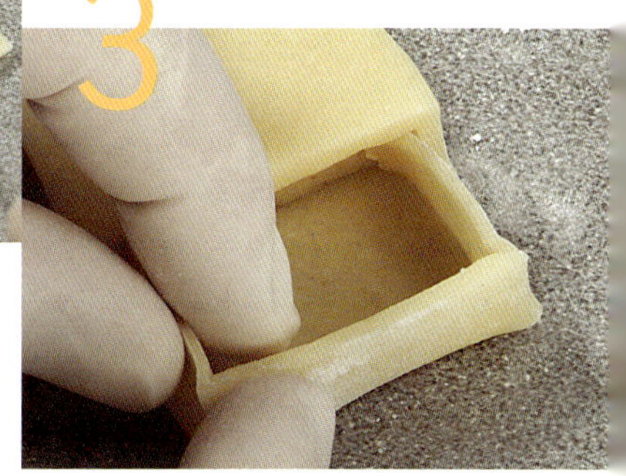
3

Wo geht's zur Milchstraße?

Catch a falling star …

› Eine Grundplatte ausschneiden. Mit Förmchen Sternchen ausstechen und gelb besprühen. Die Platte mit Blau und Schwarz besprühen und mit gelbem Esspapier unterlegen.
Mutter- und Babystern aus Marzipan ausstechen und zusammenfügen. Mit M 2 und M 3 die Mund- und Augenpartie eindrücken. Die Sterne gelb grundieren und die Ränder leicht mit Rot nachsprühen. Die Augen aufspritzen und schwarze Augenbrauen aufzeichnen. Die Vertiefungen für die Mundpartien mit Schwarz ausmalen. Eine Nuckelflasche formen, schminken und am großen Stern ankleben.
Die Wegschilder herstellen und nach Trocknung an einem mit Schokolade überzogenen Holzstab befestigen.
Eine Halbkugel für den Planeten anfertigen und vereinzelt unterschiedlich große Kugeln darauf befestigen. | 1 |
Mit M 2 die Kugeln jeweils mittig eindrücken. | 2 |
Die Kraterränder so verarbeiten, bis kein Ansatz mehr zu sehen ist. | 3 |
Das Kraterinnere noch mal kreisförmig nacharbeiten.
Den Planeten gesondert schminken und die Krater etwas dunkler gestalten. Die einzelnen Bestandteile zusammenfügen und den Übergang vom Planeten zur Platte noch einmal dunkel nachschminken.

› Cut out a base slab with the help of a cutting wheel. Use form cutters to punch out individual stars and spray in yellow paint. Spray blue and black onto the partially cut-out slab and underlay with yellow edible paper.
Cut out the mother and baby stars from marzipan and join together. Use an M 2 and M 3 to sculpt the mouth and eye areas. Apply a yellow base coat to the stars and follow up with a touch of red spray to the edges. Pipe on the eyes and draw on black eyebrows. Highlight the indentations around the mouth in black. Form a baby's drinking bottle out of one piece, colour it and attach it to the large star.
Make the signposts and, once dried out, attach to a wooden stick that has been coated with chocolate.
Cut a ball in half to make the planet and attach balls of different sizes on to it for the craters. | 1 |
Use an M 2 to press down the balls in the centre. | 2 |
Work in the crater edges so that these are completely smooth. | 3 |
Again work the inside of the craters in a circular fashion.
Colour the planet separately and keep the crater somewhat darker. Join the individual parts together and again apply some darker colour to the transition from the planet to the slab.

PROFI **TIPP** *Um Kosten und Gewicht einzusparen sind Halbkugeln aus Kuvertüre für den Planeten ebenso nützlich. Diese mit Marzipan überziehen und als Grundkörper verwenden.*

In order to save cost and weight, it is just as practical to use a hemisphere from couverture for the planet. Cover this with marzipan and use as a basic shape.

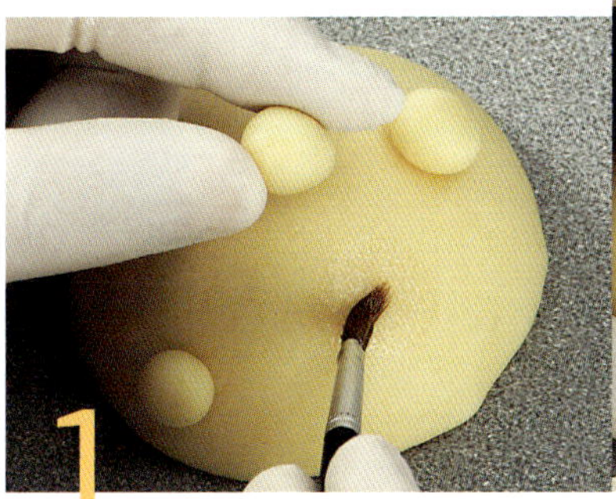
1

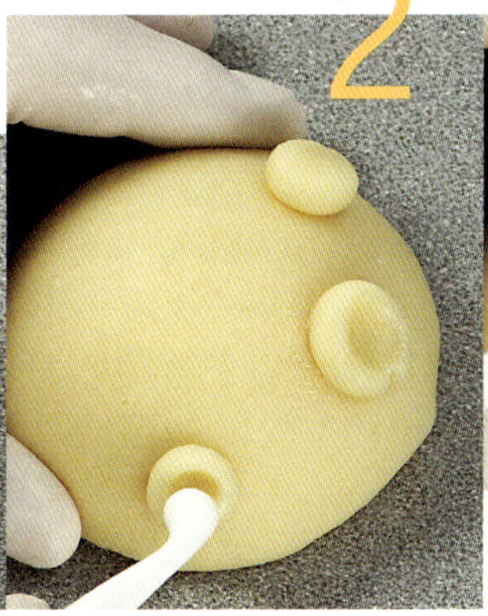
2

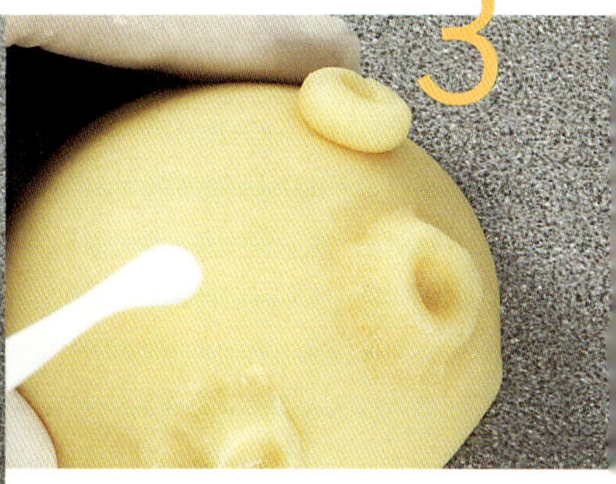
3

Animal crackers

Tierischer Ernst

Kalkuliertes Risiko

A calculated risk

> Ein kleines Mäuschen, außer Nase, Zähne und Schwänzchen, aus einem Stück modellieren. Aus einer runden Platte den Helm formen und anbringen. Die Figur grau grundieren. Schnauze, Schwanz sowie die Beine rosa nachsprühen. Mit dem Pinsel den Helm einfärben und die restlichen Konturen nachziehen. Auf einer vorbereiteten Grundplatte das Mäuschen sowie ein Schild platzieren.
Aus der Grundform der Mausefalle an einer schmaleren Seite ein kleines Rechteck herausschneiden und mit einer runden Tülle mittig eindrücken. | 1 |
Eine kurze Marzipanrolle anfertigen und mit M 7 schräg einkerben. Das bearbeitete Röllchen oberhalb des Fallenauslösers anbringen. Einen kleinen Bügel auf den Auslöser ankleben und mit einer Kugel unterlegen, damit er in Schräglage versetzt wird. | 2 |
Für den noch ausstehenden Bügel und dessen Halterung zwei weitere Marzipanstangen in Form bringen und befestigen. | 3 |
Die Mausefalle gelb grundieren und braun nachsprühen. Alle „Metallteile" mit dem Pinsel grau färben. Mit Schwarz die Federkerben nachziehen. Nach ausreichender Trocknung die Falle auf die Grundplatte setzen. Ein Stück Marzipankäse, mit Gelb besprüht, vervollständigt die Szene.

> Model a small mouse from one piece, except for the nose, teeth and the little tail. Form the helmet from a round disc and fit it around the head. Apply a grey base coat to the figure. Spray pink paint onto the snout, the tail as well as the legs. Use a brush to paint the helmet and to highlight the other contours. Place the mouse as well as a sign on a prepared base slab.
Cut a small rectangle from the shorter side of the basic shape of a mousetrap and indent in the centre with a round piping tip. | 1 |
Roll a short piece of marzipan and score it diagonally with an M 7. Fix the small roll above the trigger for the mousetrap. Attach a small loop on the trigger, with a ball underneath it so that it remains in an inclined position. | 2 |
To make the jaws of the trap and the holding wire, roll two marzipan strips, form into the required shape and attach in the appropriate place. | 3 |
Apply a yellow base coat to the mousetrap and then spray with brown. Paint all "metal parts" with a brush in grey colour. Accentuate the grooves of the spring with black. Once it has dried out sufficiently, place the trap onto the base slab. Add a piece of marzipan cheese, coloured yellow, to complete the scenario.

PROFI **TIPP** *Teile, die in Schräglage versetzt werden, wie hier der Auslöser der Falle, können auch mit Marzipankeilen gegen ein Absinken gesichert werden.*

Parts that need to be positioned with one end raised, such as the trigger of the mousetrap in this example, can also be supported with marzipan wedges.

1

2
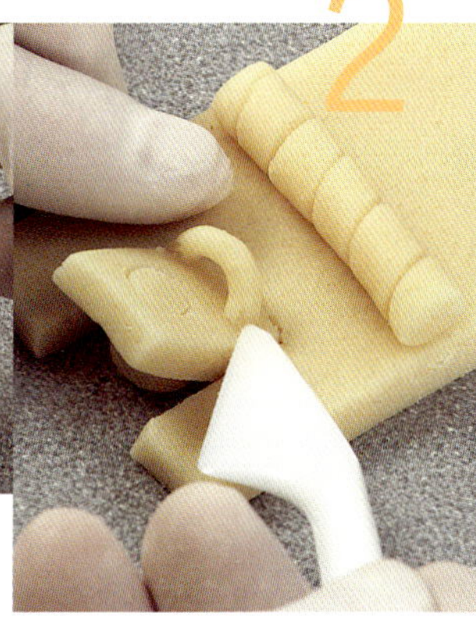

3

Vegetarier leben besser?

Vegetarians live longer?

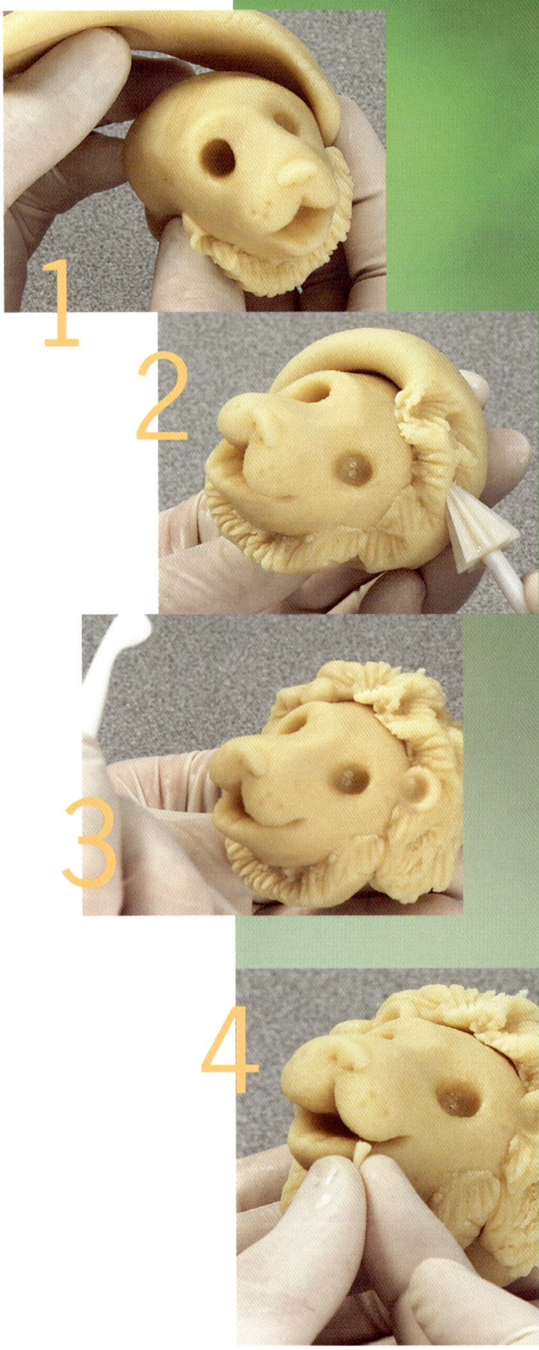

› Den Löwen, außer Schwanz und Kopf, aus einem Stück modellieren. Das Schwänzchen extra anfertigen und ansetzen. Den Kopf aus der Grundform einer Birne gestalten. Mit M 1 und M 3 Augenhöhlen, Maul und Schnauze des Tiers eindrücken. Eine kurze Marzipanrolle für den Kinnbart ansetzen. Mit M 10 die Kinnhaare einrollen und eine platt gedrückte Stange für die Mähne befestigen. | 1 |
Die zottelige Haarpracht ebenfalls mit M 10 einarbeiten. | 2 |
Zwei kleine Kugeln für die Ohren anbringen und mittig vertiefen. | 3 |
Schmale Marzipankegel als Reißzähne an der Schnauze ankleben. | 4 |
Die Kralle in gleicher Form aufsetzen. Die zusammengesetzte Figur gelb grundieren, mit Braun nachsprühen. Mähne und Schwanz ein wenig kräftiger mit dem Pinsel nacharbeiten. Eventuell mit Wasser besprenkeln, um die Farben besser in die Ritzen fließen zu lassen. Mit Rosa das Maul einfärben und Lippenkanten sowie die Schnauze leicht weiß vorgrundieren. Farben nach jedem Auftrag trocknen lassen. Die einzelnen Gesichtskonturen mit Schwarz nachziehen und die Augen aufspritzen. Die Kralle und Zähne mit Weiß bestreichen.
In weitgehend gleicher Vorgehensweise wie bei der Herstellung einer einfachen Rose einen Kohlkopf anfertigen. Um die Struktur einer Kohlart zu erhalten, jedes Blatt mit M 1 mehrfach einkerben. Den gesamten Kohlkopf aus mindestens acht Blättern zusammensetzen. Weitere Einzelblätter formen und trocknen. Mit gelber Farbe grundieren, grün und Wasser nachsprühen.
Auf einer kleinen Grundplatte den Kohl mit einem Schild befestigen.

› Model the lion from one piece except for the tail and head. Make the tail separately and attach to the body. Model the head from a basic bulb shape. Use an M 1 and M 3 to sculpt the eye sockets, the mouth and the snout of the animal. Attach a short marzipan roll for the beard. Use an M 10 to give texture to the beard and fix a flattened roll for the mane. | 1 |
Again use an M 10 to work in the appropriate shaggy texture for the hair. | 2 |
Stick on two balls for the ears and hollow out in the middle. | 3 |
Attach two small marzipan cones at the upper jaw to resemble the canine teeth. | 4 |
Attach the claws in the same way. Once the figure has been put together, apply a yellow base coat and follow on with brown spray. Use a brush to highlight the mane and tail in slightly darker colour. It may be a good idea to sprinkle a little water on it so that the paint runs better into the grooves and cracks. Colour the mouth pink and apply a slight base coat of white to the edges of the lips and the snout. Allow the paint to dry after each coat. Outline the facial contours in black and pipe on the eyes. Brush the claw and teeth with white.
Proceed in much the same way as for making a simple rose when you prepare this round cabbage. In order to create the texture of a cabbage, each leaf should be scored several times with an M 1. The whole cabbage should be made up of at least eight leaves. Form additional single leaves and leave to dry. Apply a yellow base coat and follow on with green colour and water sprayed on.
Fix the cabbage with the sign to a small base plate.

PROFI **TIPP** *Spitz zulaufende kleine Teile, wie hier die Zähne und Kralle des Löwen, lassen sich auch mit Hilfe von Eiweißspritzglasur mit einer Spritztüte anbringen.*

Small pointed parts such as the teeth and the claw of the lion can also be made with the help of an icing bag and royal icing.

Sweet things are hard to get

Sweet things ...

› Zehn stetig größer werdende Marzipanringe nach kurzer Trocknung übereinander zum Bienenkorb stapeln und eine Öffnung in den Korb schneiden. Mit Weiß grundieren sowie zart gelb und braun nachsprühen. Kleine Bienchen aus einzelnen Teilchen zusammenkleben, gelb einfärben und noch auf die feuchte Farbe des Korbs setzen. Mit dem Pinsel feine schwarze Strukturen auf den Bienenkorb auftragen.
Den Bärenkörper aus einem Stück formen. Die einzelnen Finger mit M 1 gegeneinander abgrenzen und den „Zeigefinger" etwas hervorstehen lassen. Nach dem Schminken ein Bienchen aufsetzen. Aus der Grundform einer gedrungenen Birne den Bärenkopf herstellen. Augen, Schnauze sowie den Mund mit M 1 und M 3 einarbeiten. Ohren und Nase aus drei kleinen Kugeln gestalten. Mit dem Daumen und Zeigefinger ein Stück Hals zur besseren Anbringung des Kopfs anfertigen. Die Figur schminken und das Näschen rötlich färben, um den Eindruck zu verstärken, der Bär wäre gestochen worden. Mit dem Pinsel Augen- und Mundpartie fertig stellen. Auf dem Bauch des geschminkten Bären ein Schildchen mit Aufschrift platzieren.

› Make ten rings of marzipan in slightly increasing size, leave to dry, and stack on top of each other in order to make the beehive. Cut an opening into the hive. Apply white base colouring and then follow on with a little yellow and brown spray. Stick together small bees made up from individual parts, colour yellow and stick to the hive while the paint is still sticky. Use the brush to apply delicate black patterns to the beehive.
Form the body of the bear from one piece. Use an M 1 to shape the individual fingers and leave the forefinger to protrude a little. Colour the animal and then place one bee on its finger. Make the bear's head from the basic shape of a squat bulb. Work in the eyes, snout and the mouth with an M 1 and M 3. Design the ears and nose from three little balls. Make a short neck by modelling it between your thumb and forefinger – this will help to attach the head to the trunk. Colour the figure and paint the nose a reddish colour in order to accentuate the idea that the bear has been stung. Complete the eye and mouth areas with a brush. Make a small sign with the caption and attach it to the bear's belly.

PROFI **TIPP** *Bei diesem Exponat ist die Wirkung der Augen sehr deutlich. Im Zusammenspiel mit den Augenbrauen ergibt sich der bestimmte Gemütsausdruck, der die Figur zum Leben erweckt.*

In this model, the effect of the eyes is very clear. Together with the eyebrows the eyes bring the figure to life to express a particular mood.

Sweet things are hard to get

Hello stranger

Hello stranger

› Den Kängurukörper aus einer Stange mit zulaufender Spitze für den Schwanz modellieren. Den Körper relativ schlank halten, da die Beine noch sehr auftragen. Hinterbeine anfertigen und ansetzen. Mit M 1 den Kopf abgrenzen und nach unten biegen. Die Augenhöhlen eindrücken und mit M 6 die Schnauze ausformen. | 1 |
Zwei längliche Tropfen als Ohren ankleben. Mit M 4 die Ohrmuscheln gestalten. | 2 |
Für die scharfen Kanten die Ohren mit M 1 nacharbeiten. | 3 |
Die Arme und Sprungbeine aus länglichen platt gedrückten Birnenformen herstellen.
Ein Nashornköpfchen und zwei Beinchen formen und unter einer dünnen Marzipanplatte anbringen, die den Beutel des Kängurus ergibt. Auf dem Bauch des Tiers festmachen, Nahtstelle feucht mit M 3 im Ansatz verstreichen. Das Känguru gelb grundieren, mit Rot und wenig Braun nachsprühen. Vereinzelt mit Weiß kleine Lichtreflexe anbringen und die Augen aufspritzen. Das Nashornbaby und die Feinheiten des Kängurus mit dem Pinsel schminken. Zwischen den Beinen des Tiers ein Schild mit dem Schriftzug "Hello stranger" befestigen.

› Model the body of the kangaroo from a roll with a tapered point for the tail. Keep the body relatively slim since the legs will add a lot of bulk. Prepare the hind legs and attach to the body. Use an M 1 to sculpt the head and bend downwards. Press in the eye sockets and form the snout with an M 6. | 1 |
Attach two longish drops as ears. Shape the ears using an M 4. | 2 |
Use an M1 to rework the sharp edges inside the ears. | 3 |
Make the arms and jumping legs from oblong flattened bulb shapes.
Form the head and two legs of a rhinoceros and attach to the kangaroo under the cover of a thin marzipan slab which represents the kangaroo's pouch. Smooth over the join with an M 3 and a little moisture. Apply a yellow base coat to the kangaroo and follow up with red and a little brown spray. Apply some white light effects and pipe on the eyes. Use the brush to colour the rhinoceros baby and the details of the kangaroo. Attach a sign with the caption "Hello stranger" between the legs of the animal.

PROFI **TIPP** *Die Ansätze bei zusammengefügten Teilen lassen sich angefeuchtet besser kaschieren, indem man sie mit einem glatten Modellierholz großflächig verstreicht.*

A smooth modelling tool makes it easier to smooth out the wetted joins between joined-up parts.

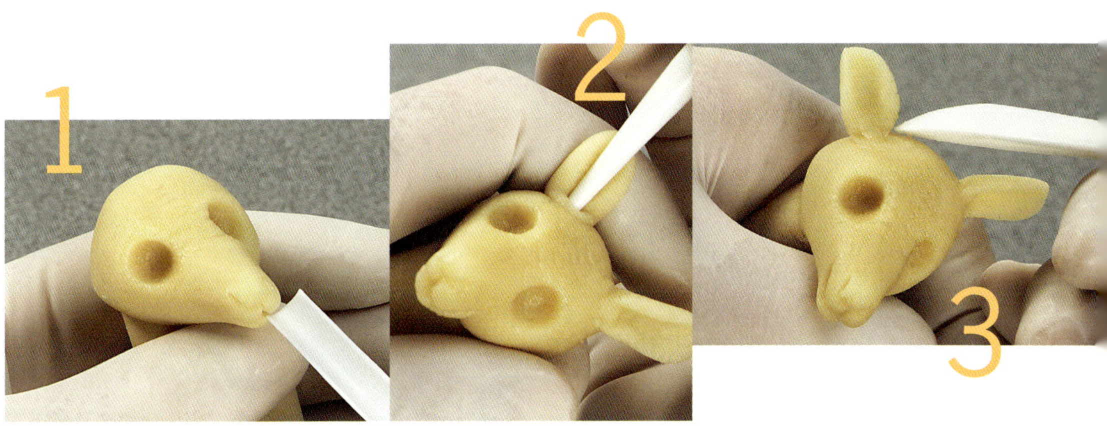

> Ein vollständig ausmodelliertes Schweinchen herstellen. Mit einem scharfen Messer das Hinterteil abtrennen und den Oberkörper nach hinten hin dünn auslaufen lassen. Beide Teile rosa schminken. Die Augen aufspritzen und trocknen lassen.
Aus einer stumpfen Birnenform den Grundkörper des Sacks mit M 5 herstellen. Mit M 1 die Falten an der Außenseite einkerben. | 1 |
Die Falten von innen nach außen durch sanftes Drücken in Form bringen. | 2 |
Für den Bindestrick eine Kerbe rund um den Geldsack einarbeiten. Einen Strick aus einem dünnen Marzipanstrang um die Kerbe legen und befestigen. | 3 |
Die Sacköffnung mit dem Schweinchenhinterteil sowie Münzen, die aus einer Marzipanplatte ausgestochen wurden, befüllen und komplett gelb grundieren. Um ein tiefes Eintauchen der Münzen vorzutäuschen, diese zum Teil halbieren. Den Sack stellenweise mit Braun nachsprühen, die Öffnung dabei dunkler halten. Die Kordel mit dem Pinsel einfärben und einen Geldbetrag auf der Sackmitte aufbringen. Das Münzgeld am Rand leicht mit Rot schattieren. Den Oberkörper des Schweinchens seitlich um den Sack legen und ankleben. Mit dem Pinsel rote Backen auf das Gesicht aufzeichnen. Nach Belieben Münzen befestigen und das Arrangement mit einem Schild vervollständigen.

> Produce a little piglet in full detail. Cut off the rear part with a sharp knife and let the front part of the body taper out to a thin end. Colour both parts in pink. Pipe on the eyes and leave to dry.
Produce the basic shape of the sack with an M 5 from a blunt shape of a bulb. Use an M 1 to score the folds on the outside. | 1 |
Gently widen out the top of the sack by pushing from the inside outwards. | 2 |
Work in a groove around the money bag for the tie rope. Make a rope from a thin marzipan strand, place into the groove and attach. | 3 |
Cut out several coins from a marzipan slab and cut some of them in half; cover completely with a yellow base coat. Fill the opening of the sack with the rear part of the piglet and several coins and half coins to give the impression that they reach deep into the sack. Spray some areas of the sack with brown, keeping the opening darker. Colour the string with a brush and paint on the figures for a sum of money on the centre of the bag. Apply a little red to the edge of the coins. Drape the top half of the piglet's body over the side of the sack and attach. Use the brush to paint red cheeks onto the face. Spread several coins around the set and complete with a sign.

PROFI **TIPP** *Einzelteile, die gut verklebt sind, halten ein Abheben vom Untergrund aus, ohne zu brechen. Auf Grund dessen ist es nicht immer notwendig, eine Grundplatte anzufertigen.*

When individual parts have been well glued together they can be lifted without breaking. For this reason it is not always necessary to prepare a base slab.

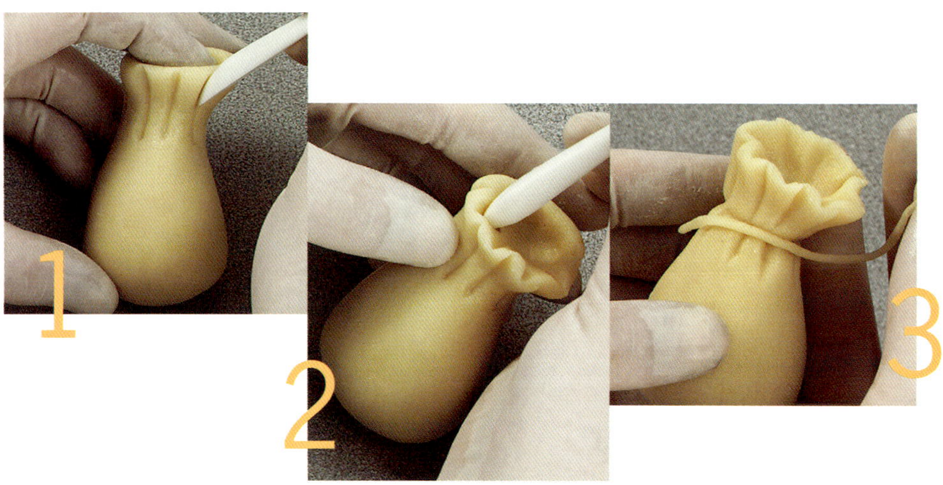

You're a winner

You're a winner

Frech kommt weiter!

Cheek wins the day!

> Eine Grundplatte aus einer ausgewellten Marzipanfläche reißen. Komplett mit Gelb grundieren und die Ränder braun und schwarz nachsprühen. Eine Efeuranke modellieren, färben und ankleben.
Das Mäuschen, außer Ohren, Nase, Schwanz und Zunge, aus einem Stück modellieren. Zur Grundierung graue Farbe verwenden. Pfoten, Schwänzchen, Ohren sowie die Schnauze mit Hautfarbe nachsprühen. Bartstoppeln mit dem Pinsel auftupfen und die Nase schwarz einfärben. Die Figur leicht nach vorne biegen und gut abgestützt trocknen lassen.
Das Gespenst aus dem Abschnitt einer Marzipanstange herstellen. Das Kopfende rund formen und das untere Ende mit Daumen und Zeigefinger trichterförmig eindrücken. Mit M 3 den Mund und die Augenhöhlen einkerben. | 1 |
Die Arme separat anfertigen und den Daumen mit M 1 abgrenzen. Für einen besseren Ansatz die Arme hinten stumpf modellieren. | 2 |
Beide Arme mit Eiweiß ankleben. | 3 |
Die Nahtstellen mit M 3 gut verstreichen, um den Ansatz unkenntlich zu machen. Die ganze Figur so weit nach hinten neigen, bis sich ein Gleichgewicht ergibt und das Gespenst in der Schräglage stehen bleibt. Den Saum des Gespenstertuchs wellig ausformen und gestützt trocknen lassen. Weiß grundieren und anschließend zaghaft mit Schwarz Lichtreflexionen aufsprühen. Schwarze Kugeln in die Augenhöhlen einsetzen und den Mund mit dem Pinsel schwarz schminken.
Das Gespenst mit einem Schild und dem Mäuschen auf der Grundplatte in Szene setzen.

> Tear off a base slab from some rolled-out marzipan. Cover completely in yellow base coat and go over the edges in brown and black spray. Model a branch of trailing ivy, apply colour and attach. Model the mouse from one piece, except for its ears, nose, tail and tongue. Use grey paint as a base coat. Apply skin colour to the paws, the little tail, the ears and the mouth. Use the brush to dab on the dots for the whiskers and colour the nose in black. Bend the figure slightly forward and support well whilst leaving to dry.
Make the ghost from a marzipan roll, with the head shaped round and using thumb and forefinger to hollow out the lower end in a funnel shape. Use an M 3 to score the mouth and the eye sockets. | 1 |
Make the arms separately and delineate the thumb using an M 1. To make it easier to attach the arms, make them flat at the back. | 2 |
Attach both arms with egg white. | 3 |
Use an M 3 to smooth out the joins in order to make them invisible. Bend the whole figure far enough back so that the ghost appears at a slant but still maintains its balance. Shape the seam of the ghostly sheet in a wavy shape and leave to dry while supported. Apply white base coat and then gently spray on black light reflections. Insert black balls into the eye sockets and paint the mouth black, using a brush. Arrange the ghost with the sign and the little mouse on the base slab.

PROFI **TIPP** *Augenbrauen haben eine nicht zu unterschätzende Wirkung. Bereits durch wenige Handgriffe ergibt sich, wie hier mit leicht nach außen gestellten Brauen, ein verunsicherter Blick, der sich auch gut für andere Figuren verwenden lässt.*

The eyebrows have an effect which should not be underestimated. It is quite easy to create a somewhat unsure expression with the eyebrows slightly turned outward as in the example here. This feature can equally be applied to other figures in different arrangements.

1

2

3

› Eine Grundplatte aus ausgewelltem Marzipan Stück für Stück in Form zupfen. | 1 |
Mit Hilfe eines Lineals und der Doppelkerbe des M 10 drei Viertel der Fläche mit Längsfugen einkerben. Im 90°-Winkel die Querfugen einritzen. | 2 |
Aus einer dickeren Marzipanplatte eine Wand herstellen. Diese nach dem Schminken so platzieren, dass sie die bearbeitete Grundfläche abgrenzt. Mit M 6 eine Stoßleiste einarbeiten. | 3 |
Mit M 7 eine schmale Trennlinie zwischen „Verputz" und Ziegelsteinen hinzufügen. Aus einem länglichen Marzipanstück ein Namensschild über der Tür ankleben. Die Wand flachliegend schminken, um die jeweilige Unterseite vom Farbauftrag freizuhalten. Die Fugen des Mauerwerks, der Fliesen und das Namensschild mit dem Pinsel nachziehen.
Eine Katze sowie ein kleines Stethoskop modellieren und in gewünschter Haltung bis zur vollständigen Trocknung abstützen. Anschließend auf der gekerbten Fläche mit einem Schildchen befestigen.
Den Wecker aus einer ausgestochenen Scheibe anfertigen. Mit M 3 das Ziffernblatt nach innen drücken. Die anderen Bestandteile des Weckers individuell formen und ansetzen. Das Verwenden von silberner Lebensmittelfarbe beim Schminken sorgt für schöne Akzente.

› Roll out a marzipan base slab and work into shape using your fingers. | 1 |
Use a ruler and the double groove of the M 10 to score the longitudinal joints in three-quarters of the area. Score the cross joints at a 90-degree angle. | 2 |
Form a wall from a thicker marzipan slab. Colour the wall and place it so that it confines the floor area with the pattern. Use an M 6 to work in a skirting board. | 3 |
Use an M 7 to add a small separating line between the "plaster" and "bricks". Use a longish piece of marzipan to make a name plate and attach this above the door. Colour the wall while it is still horizontal in order to stop the paint from getting onto the other side. Use the brush to accentuate the joins in the brickwork, the tiles and to add the writing on the name plate.
Model a cat as well as a small stethoscope and support in the desired position until completely dry. Then attach on the grooved surface together with a small sign.
Make the alarm clock from a punched out disc, using an M 3 to push the clock face inwards. Shape the other components of the alarm clock individually and attach. Using silver food colouring ensures an appealing and realistic appearance.

Nicht neugierig, nur interessiert!

Not nosy, just interested!

Am Puls der Zeit, denn Information ist alles!

Just checking!

1

2

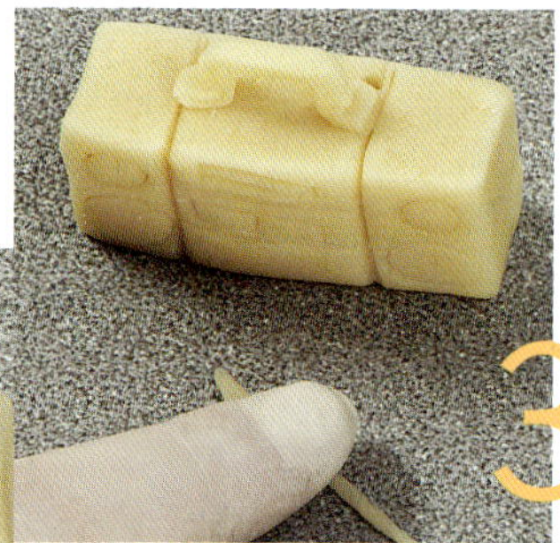

3

› Aus einer Marzipanplatte ein Rechteck für die Gymnastikmatte schneiden und blau einfärben. Die Ecken mit M 7 abgrenzen und grau nachfärben. Ein Schweinchen modellieren und auf der Matte befestigen.
Einen Expander aus dünnen Marzipansträngen anfertigen. Diesen noch im flexiblen und feuchten Zustand in geschwungener Form legen, da solche dünnen Teile sehr schnell trocknen und brüchig werden. Die Hantel aus einer kurzen Marzipanstange und vier ausgestochenen Scheiben zusammensetzen. Die Fitnessgeräte schminken und auf der Grundplatte mit einem Schildchen dekorieren.
Die Grundform des Radiogeräts aus einem Block schneiden und mit M 9 die groben Unterteilungen einkerben. Durch Abdrücke verschieden großer Lochtüllen dann die Umrisse der Lautsprecher einarbeiten. | 1 |
Die restlichen Kerben mit M 7 einbringen.
Mit einem scharfen Messer einen dünnen Strang für den Griff halbieren. Den Strang zum Griff formen und mit M 3 andrücken. | 2 |
Für die Antenne ein feines Röllchen vorbereiten und gut trocknen lassen. | 3 |
Bevor die Antenne in das mit M 4 eingebrachte Halteloch gesteckt wird, mit Schwarz leicht vorsprühen. Mit Wasser nachsprühen, bis alle Kerben deutlich hervortreten. Nach der Farbtrocknung kann das Displayfenster mit dem Pinsel nachgeschminkt werden.
Aus einer kleinen Platte ein Tischchen formen, schminken und das Radio aufsetzen.

› Cut a rectangular shape from a marzipan slab to represent the gymnastics mat and colour in blue. Use an M 7 to delineate the corners and colour in grey. Model a little piglet and attach it to the mat.
Make a chest-expander from thin strands of marzipan. Place this into a curved shape while it is still flexible and damp, since such thin parts dry out very quickly and become brittle. Make up the dumb-bells from a short marzipan bar and four cut-out discs. Colour the fitness equipment and arrange on the ground slab together with a small sign.
Cut the basic shape of the radio set from a block and use an M 9 to score the rough divisions. Use different sized round piping nozzles to mark the contours of the loudspeakers. | 1 |
For the other grooves use an M 7.
To make the handle, use a sharp knife to cut a thin roll in half. Shape the roll to make the handle and use an M 3 to press it down on the radio. | 2 |
To make the aerial, prepare a thin roll and leave to dry well. | 3 |
Before attaching the aerial into its socket, made with an M 4, apply a light spray coat with black. Follow up with a water mist until all grooves are permanently visible. Once all paint has dried, you can colour the display window using a brush.
Form a small table from a small slab, colour and then place the radio on it.

Fitness is my life

Fitness is my life

Für Fernseh-Sportler und echte Fitness-Freaks!

Happy work-out!

Spare in der Zeit ...

Start saving now ...

› Den Körper und Kopf des Eichhörnchens aus einem Stück modellieren. Mund sowie Schnauze mit M 1 und M 3 einarbeiten, dabei die Schnauze eher platt halten. Die Augenpartie gestalten. Aus kleinen Tropfen die Ohren extra ansetzen und mit M 3 nachformen. Die Arme vorbereiten, an der Figur befestigen und die Ansätze kaschieren. Aus einem an den Enden konisch zulaufenden Marzipanstrang den Eichhörnchenschwanz beginnen und in S-Form legen. Mit M 10 die Haarstruktur imitieren. Das Eichhörnchen mit Gelb grundieren und mit Braun nachsprühen. Die Rückenpartie und das Schwänzchen ein wenig dunkler färben. Um die Stabilität der Figur zu gewährleisten, sollte sie gut gestützt trocknen können.
Die Walnüsse werden separat hergestellt oder alternativ aus einem Pralinensortiment entnommen. Eine Grundplatte mit dem Schneiderad zuschneiden, schminken und mit Eiweißspritzglasur verzieren. Das Eichhörnchen auf der Platte befestigen. Die Walnüsse in Position bringen und mit einem Schild das Arrangement fertig stellen.

› Model the body and head of the squirrel from one piece. Work in the snout and the mouth with an M 1 and M 3, keeping the snout rather flat. Sculpt the area of the eyes. Attach small drops to make the ears and use an M 3 to give them the final shape. Prepare the arms, attach them to the figure and smooth over the joins. Start the squirrel's tail from a marzipan roll that tapers out at the ends and arrange it in an S-shape. Imitate the hair texture with an M 10. Apply a yellow base coat to the squirrel and follow with a brown spray, making the back and the little tail a bit darker. To ensure that the figure becomes firm it should be left to dry on an appropriate support.
The walnuts are prepared separately or, alternatively, can be taken from an assortment of pralines. Cut a base slab with the cutting wheel, paint and embellish with royal icing. Arrange the squirrel on the slab and fix. Pile up the walnuts and complete the arrangement with a sign.

PROFI **TIPP** *Die Kombination von hochwertigen Pralinen und einer Marzipanfigur fördert den Verkauf beider Produkte. Trüffel eignen sich zum Beispiel sehr gut als Spielbälle von Hunde- und Robbenfiguren. Mit etwas Phantasie beim Betrachten der Pralinenauswahl ergeben sich weitere Möglichkeiten.*

The combination of good quality pralines and a marzipan figure promotes the sale of both products; other examples are truffles, which make great balls for dogs or seals to play with. With a little imagination you can find other uses for the different kinds of pralines available.

Spare in der Zeit....

Go for gold

Go for gold

1

2

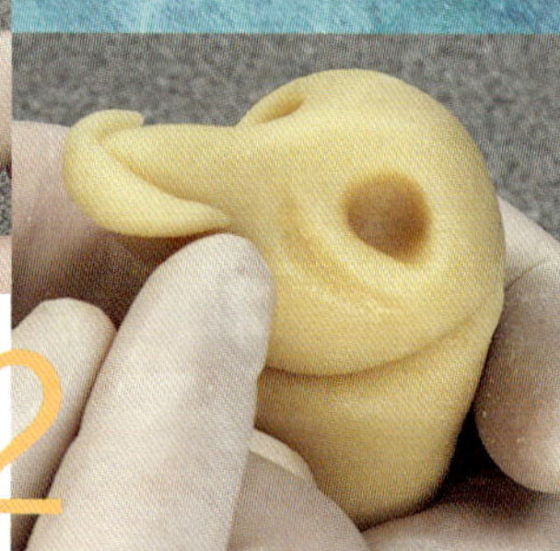

3

> Aus einem Marzipanrechteck zwei Stufen ausschneiden und weiß grundieren. Auf jeden der drei Treppenabsätze eine dünne Abdeckplatte aufkleben. Aus dünnen Marzipansträngen die Zahlen 1, 2 und 3 in Siegerpodestmanier auf der Vorderseite anbringen. Die Deckplatten und Zahlen mit dem Pinsel schminken und trocknen lassen.
Den Körper des Goldfischs aus einer Stange beginnend herstellen. Das obere Ende spitz und das untere stumpf abmodellieren. Die stumpfe Seite mit M 1 knapp spalten und platt drücken. Die entstehende Flosse etwas breit ziehen und symmetrisch formen. Mit M 9 die Lamellen einkerben. Durch Eindrücken mit M 6 den Körper ringsum mit Schuppen bedecken. Im Kiemenbereich eine tiefe Kerbe einarbeiten, damit sich der Kopf anschließend besser biegen lässt. | 1 |
Mit Daumen und Zeigefinger den Kopf in die gewünschte Position bringen. Die Augenpartie mit M 2 einhöhlen und deren Wirkung durch eine kleine darunter liegende Vertiefung verstärken. Ein beidseitig angespitztes Marzipanröllchen als Mund ankleben. | 2 |
Mit M 9 längs einkerben und mit M 1 die Lippenfalte einarbeiten. | 3 |
Die Rückenflosse für sich ansetzen oder aus dem Körper der Figur herausmodellieren. Beide Brustflossen extra formen und am Goldfisch befestigen. Eine der Flossen davon so profilieren, dass sich zwei Finger für das V-Zeichen abspreizen lassen. Gut gestützt trocknen lassen. Den gesamten Körper gelb grundieren und stärker mit Rot nachfärben. Die Augen aufspritzen und die Lippen mit dem Pinsel nachziehen. Den Goldfisch am Siegertreppchen anlehnen.
Für die Medaille eine kleine Marzipanscheibe ausstechen. Die Kanten rund tippen und mit M 10 eine Struktur am Rand aufbringen. Mit M 3 eine kleine Kerbe einritzen und die Zahl mit M 4 eingravieren. Ein schmales Band um die Figur legen und die Medaille daran ankleben. Die zusammengefügten Teile mit dem Pinsel schminken. Ein Schild mit Aufschrift zwischen Flosse und Vorderseite des Podests drapieren.

> Cut out two steps from a marzipan block and apply a white base coat. Stick a thin cover slab onto each of the three stepped platforms. Use thin marzipan rolls to form the numbers 1, 2 and 3 for the winners' platforms and attach to the front of the stand. Colour the cover slabs and the numbers by brush and leave to dry.
Make the body of the goldfish starting from a roll. Make the top bit pointed and the bottom bit more blunt. Use an M 1 to split the blunt side and press it flat. This creates a fin which needs to be broadened a little and formed symmetrically. Use an M 9 to score the texture. The scales around the body can be made by pressing in the end of an M 6. In the area of the gills, score a deep groove, which also makes it easier to bend the head. | 1 |
Use your thumb and forefinger to bring the head into the required position. Use an M 2 to hollow out the cavities for the eyes and accentuate the visual effect by a small indentation underneath. Form a small marzipan roll to a point at both ends and attach as a mouth. | 2 |
Use an M 9 to score lengthwise and an M 1 to work in the lip fold. | 3 |
Attach the dorsal fin separately or model it from the body of the fish. The two front fins are best formed separately and then attached to the goldfish. Model one of the fins in such a way that it is possible to separate out two fingers in order to show the V for Victory sign. Support well and leave to dry. Apply a yellow base coat to the whole body and then follow up with a stronger shade of red. Pipe on the eyes and outline the lips by brush. Lean the goldfish against the winners' platform.
To make the medal, cut out a marzipan disc. Tap the edges with your fingers to round them off and use an M 10 to insert a texture around the edge. Use an M 3 to score a small groove and an M 4 to engrave the number. Place a small ribbon around the figure and attach the medal to it. Use the brush to paint the ensemble. Place a sign with the caption between the fin and front of the platform.

Kleiner Glücksvorrat

A small stash of luck

Der kleine Glücksvorrat für die Theke

A small stash of luck for the counter

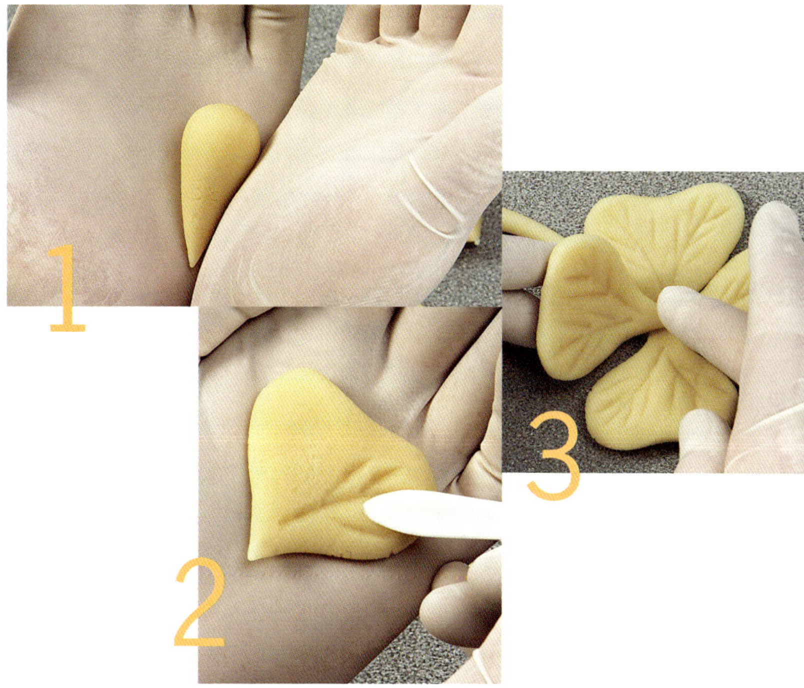

› Ein etwa 8 mm starkes Marzipanband in U-Form biegen. Die Enden gerade abschneiden und aus den Reststücken die Stollen und Nägel formen. Die Teile platzieren und weiße Grundierung auf das entstandene Hufeisen auftragen. Auf der Oberseite schwarze Farbe aufsprühen, um den gewünschten Grauton zu erzielen. Verzierungen mit Eiweißspritzglasur ausspritzen.
Den Kopf und die Vorderbeine des Glücksschweinchens herstellen und schminken.
Aus vier gleich großen Teilen kleine Tropfen für die einzelnen Glückskleeblätter anfertigen. Diese zwischen den Handballen platt drücken und in Herzform bringen. | 1 |
Die Blattadern mit stumpfem M 1 einkerben. | 2 |
Aus einer dünnen Marzipanstange den Stiel modellieren und die einzelnen Blätter mittig darauf andrücken. | 3 |
Nach ausreichender Trocknung gelb grundieren und mit Grün schattieren. Mit Wasser besprenkeln, um die Blattstruktur besser hervorzuheben. Durch dezentes, partielles Aufsprühen mit weißer Farbe vereinzelt Akzente setzen.
Mit Kuvertüre das Schweinchen und das Hufeisen auf dem Glücksklee befestigen. Mit einem Schildchen vervollständigen.

› Bend a marzipan ribbon of about 8 mm thickness into a U-shape. Cut the ends off straight and use the off-cuts to form the studs and nails. Attach the parts and apply a white base coat to the horseshoe. Spray black paint to the top side in order to achieve the desired shade of grey. Pipe on any embellishments in royal icing.
Make the head and the front legs of the lucky piglet and and colour.
Make four small drops of even size in order to make the four leaves of the lucky clover. Press them flat between the balls of your hands and form them into a heart shape. | 1 |
Use the blunt side of an M 1 to score the veins of the leaves. | 2 |
Model the stalk from a thin marzipan roll and attach the individual leaves in the style of a clover leaf. | 3 |
Once it has sufficiently dried out, apply yellow base coat and then shades of green. Sprinkle some water on it in order to highlight the texture of the leaves. Add individual accents by spraying on a little white colouring here and there.
Join all parts together with couverture and attach a small sign.

No way out !!

No way out!

No way out!

> Für die kreisförmige Grundplatte mit zwei verschieden großen Ringausstechern eine Kreisbahn herstellen. Diese gelb grundieren und am Außenrand rot besprühen.
Die Elefantenkörper weitgehend wie beim Exponat "Keep cool!" (Seite 202) beschrieben vorformen. Die Füße platt drücken und mit M 1 die Schwanzansätze und die seitlichen Bauchfalten anbringen. Aus Birnengrundformen die Köpfe modellieren. Das jeweilige obere Ende, das den Rüssel bildet, zwischen den Handflächen lang und dünner auslaufend modellieren. Mit M 5 die Rüsselspitze einkerben und die Falten auf der Oberseite mit M 1 einarbeiten. M 2 mit leichtem Schwung nach unten für die Augenpartie verwenden. Dadurch bildet sich eine kleine Wölbung, ähnlich einem Jochbein. Aus zwei kleinen Kugeln die Ohren fertigen und ankleben. Körper und Kopfteil aneinander fügen und in die gewünschte Form bringen.
Die Schwänzchen aus kurzen Marzipansträngen an die Elefantenkörper modellieren und die Ansätze verstreichen. Beim Herstellen zügig arbeiten und beachten, dass der folgende Elefant immer den Schwanz seines Vorgängers mit dem Rüssel hält. Eine ausreichende Trocknungszeit im Anschluss einplanen. Erst jetzt den fünf Elefanten Farbe verleihen. Die Augen und die Stoßzähne aufspritzen. Nach Belieben kann nach dem Befestigen der Figuren auf der Kreisbahn ein Schildchen hinzugefügt werden.

> To make the ring-shaped base slab use two circular cutters of different size to cut out the ring. Colour this in yellow base coat and spray red on the outside edge.
Shape the bodies of the elephants largely as in the item "Keep cool!" (page 202). Press the feet flat and use an M 1 to model the part for the tail and the folds on the belly on both sides. Use a bulb shape to model the heads. The top end of this, forming the trunk, can be modelled by rolling between both hands to make it long and thin. Use an M 5 to indent the point of the trunk and an M 1 to work in the folds on the top. Use an M 2 with a slight curve downwards to form the area around the eyes. This creates a slight bulge similar to a cheekbone. Make the ears from two small balls and attach. Fix the head onto the body and bring into the desired shape. Model the tails from short marzipan rolls and attach to the body, taking care to smooth out the joins. Work swiftly when producing the figures and remember that the following elephant holds the tail of the one in front with his trunk. Plan for sufficient drying time after putting it all together. Once dry, you can colour the five elephants. Pipe on the eyes and tusks.
After the figures have been arranged on the ring-shaped base you can add a small sign if required.

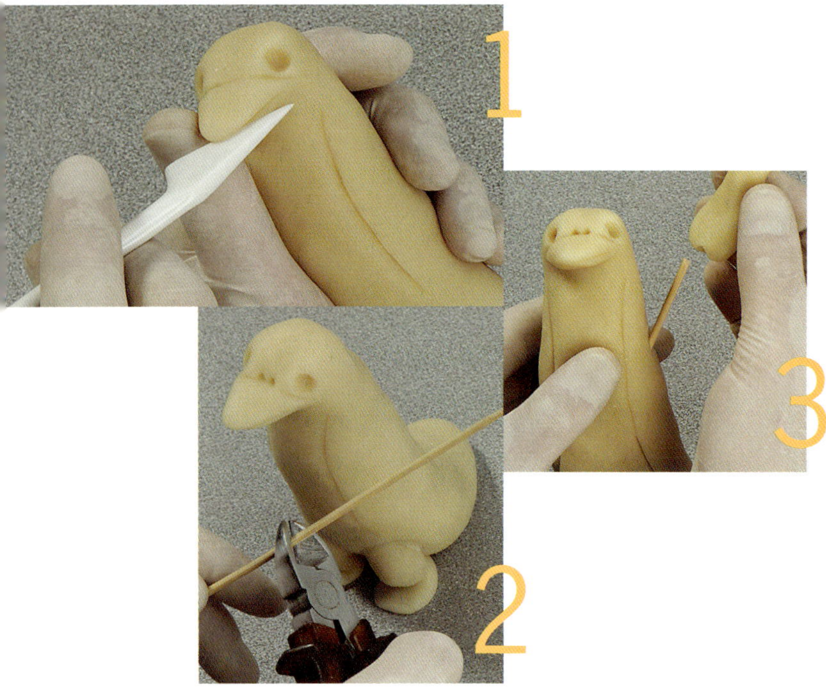

› Die Grundform des Pinguins besteht aus einer Marzipanstange mit konisch zulaufenden Enden. Durch stetiges Tippen den Kopf in die endgültige Position bringen. Die Schwimmfüße aus zwei gleichen Teilen formen und ansetzen. Schwimmhäute mit M 1 gestalten. Um den späteren Farbübergang von Weiß nach Schwarz deutlicher hervorzuheben, auf dem Körper eine sanfte Kerbe einarbeiten. Die Augenpartie einhöhlen. Mit M 3 die Schnabelkontur eindrücken und mit M 7 eine Trennlinie mittig einritzen. | 1 |
Die Nasenlöcher mit M 1 einstechen. Aus platt gedrückten Tropfen die Flügel formen. Damit der tragende Arm für das später aufgesetzte Tablett stabil genug ist, ein Holzstäbchen in passender Länge vorbereiten. | 2 |
Den tragenden Flügel auf das Stäbchen spießen und anmodellieren. | 3 |
Den anderen Flügel ebenfalls anbringen und die Ansätze verstreichen. Weiß grundieren und den restlichen Körper schwarz einfärben. Die Füße und den Schnabel mit Gelb und Rot besprühen. Die Augen aufspritzen.
Für die Servierplatte eine kleine Scheibe ausstechen. Mit M 3 einen schmalen Rand eindrücken und bläulich schminken. Nach guter Trocknung ein Fischchen anfertigen und auflegen. Das Tablett auf dem Flügel ankleben und zwischen den Schwimmfüßen ein Schildchen platzieren.

› The basic shape of the penguin consists of a marzipan roll with tapered ends. Tap gently with your fingers to model the head in the final position. Form the feet from two equal forms and attach to the body. Use an M 1 to sculpt the web of the feet. In order to accentuate the edge between white and black it is best to score a light groove on the body. Hollow out the area of the eyes. Use an M 3 to press in the contour of the beak and an M 7 to score a central separating line. | 1 |
Use an M 1 to push in the nostrils. Form the wings from drops that you have pressed flat. In order to ensure that the arm carrying the tray is strong enough, prepare a small wooden stick with the correct length. | 2 |
Push the stick into the wing and attach to the body of the bird. | 3 |
Then attach the other wing and smooth over the joins. Apply a white base coat and then black colour to the rest of the body. Spray the feet and the beak first with yellow and then with red. Pipe on the eyes.
For the serving tray, cut out a small disc. Use an M 3 to press in a small edge and colour in a bluish shade. After it has dried well, make a small fish and place onto the tray. Attach the tray to the wing carrying it and place a little sign between the feet of the penguin.

Fish, sir?

Fish, sir?

Wer würde bei dem Service nicht gerne zugreifen?

Service is everything

Doppelte Sicherheit

Safety first

Vorsicht währt länger – das wissen auch Enten

Prudence wins the day

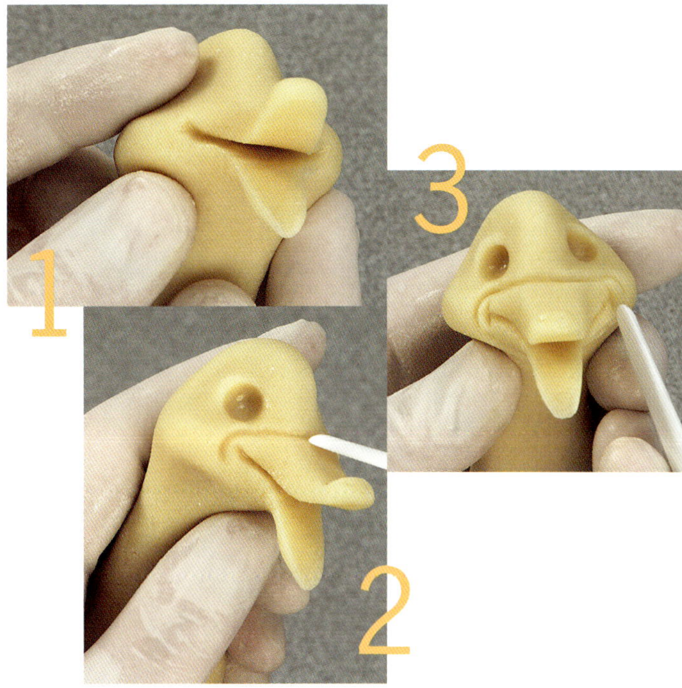

› Für die Grundplatte ein Stück Marzipan mit einem kleinen Rundholz bearbeiten. Eine Seite dabei etwas dicker als die andere auswellen. Die Wasserfläche auf der dünneren Seite mit M 1 gestalten und das Ufer mit M 10 bearbeiten.
Den Körper der Gans aus einem Stück modellieren. Aus einem birnenförmigen Ende den Kopf herstellen und platt drücken. Mit Daumen und Zeigefinger den Kopf etwas verschmälern. Die Backenpartie durch sanftes Drücken in Form bringen. Nach Einschneiden des Schnabels die symmetrische Form überprüfen. Durch ständiges Tippen die beiden Schnabelhälften abrunden und in Position bringen. | 1 |
Mit M 3 den Schnabel abgrenzen und die Augenhöhlen eindrücken. | 2 |
Durch „Grübchen" dem Gänsegesicht ein freundliches Lächeln verleihen. | 3 |
Zwei Nasenlöcher mit M 1 einstechen. Für den Schwimmreifen eine Marzipanstange um die Taille der Figur legen und an den Enden verkleben. Beide Füße und Flügel extra herstellen und ankleben. Die Naht des Schwimmreifens mit einem der Flügel kaschieren. Mit M 6 die kleineren Federn an Brust und Flügelansatz andeuten. Die Figur weiß grundieren, Schnabel, Füße und Schwimmreifen mit dem Pinsel nachschminken. Die Konturen schwarz nachziehen und die Augen aufspritzen.
Die Figur auf der Rasenfläche des Ufers befestigen und das Arrangement mit einem Schildchen vervollständigen.

› Roll out the marzipan for the base slab with a small rolling pin, leaving one side a bit thicker than the other. Use an M 1 to add water texture on the thinner side and an M 10 to make the thicker side look like the bank.
Form the body of the goose from one piece.
Make the head from a bulb-shaped piece and flatten it a little. Use your thumb and forefinger to make the head slightly narrow. Shape the area of the cheeks with your fingers. After cutting the beak, check that the form is symmetrical. Apply constant tapping with your fingers to round off the two halves of the beak and bring it into the correct position. | 1 |
Use an M 3 to delineate the beak and to press in the sockets for the eyes. | 2 |
Press in "dimples" to give the face of the goose a friendly smile. | 3 |
Use an M 1 to push in two nostrils. Make the rubber ring from a marzipan roll draped around the waist of the figure and stuck together at the ends. Make the two feet and wings separately and attach. Cover the seam of the rubber ring with one of the wings. Use an M 6 to produce a slight impression of the feathers at chest and wings. Apply a white base coat to the figure and use the brush to paint the beak, feet and the rubber ring. Accentuate the contours in black and pipe on the eyes.
Attach the figure on the lawn area of the bank and finish off by fixing a small sign.

Nicht über-gewichtig
sondern
unter-groß !!

Nicht über-gewichtig ...

Not overweight ...

› Aus einem Marzipanstrang den Körper der Raupe herstellen und mit M 1 die einzelnen Segmente gegeneinander abgrenzen. Ein Ende der Stange mit Daumen und Zeigefinger schmal zur Kopfform modellieren. Die Backen und Augenhöhlen ausformen. Mit M 3 den Mund einkerben. Die Fühler separat anfertigen und aufsetzen. Die Beinchen von kleinen Marzipanrollen abschneiden und an der Raupe befestigen. Das andere Ende jeweils plätten und zurechtbiegen. Beim Schminken die einzelnen Farben nass in nass auftragen. Vornehmlich mit Hautfarbe Bauch und Kopf besprühen. Nach der Trocknung die Konturen mit Schwarz nachziehen und die Augen aufspritzen.
Ein kleines Quadrat aus einer dicken Marzipanplatte ausschneiden. Zwischen zwei Fingern die Form leicht stauchen und abrunden. Mit M 11 eine feine Kerbe einritzen, um den späteren Mattenübergang von Schwarz nach Weiß zu kennzeichnen. Die Ziffernanzeige aus einer dünnen Platte anfertigen und die Rundung mit einer Lochtülle einstechen. Mit M 7 die Skaleneinteilung einkerben und einen kleinen Zeiger ankleben. Die Waage weiß grundieren und die Matte mit Schwarz besprühen. In den Farben Schwarz und Grau die Ziffernanzeige mit einem Pinsel schminken. Einen Herstellernachweis seitlich an der Waage aufmalen.
Nach dem Zusammensetzen von Raupe und Waage ein Schildchen mit Aufschrift hinzufügen.

› Make the body of the caterpillar from a roll of marzipan and use an M 1 to shape the individual segments. Model the end of the roll with thumb and forefinger to make a narrow head. Shape the cheeks and hollow out the eye sockets. Use an M 3 to score the mouth. Make the horns separately and attach to the body. Cut the little legs from small rolled marzipan strips and attach to the caterpillar. Press the other end flat and bend into shape. Apply the different colours wet in wet, primarily spraying skin colour to the belly and the head. Leave to dry and then accentuate the contours with black and pipe on the eyes. Cut out a small square from a thick marzipan slab. Squash the shape between two fingers and round it off. Use an M 11 to score a fine groove in order to mark the transition between black and white. Make the number display from a thin slab and cut out the round hole with a round piping nozzle. Use an M 7 to score the scale division and attach a small pointing hand. Apply white base coat to the scales and spray the mat with black. Use a brush to colour the number display in black and grey. Paint on a manufacturer's plate on the side of the scales.
Arrange the caterpillar and the scales and finish off with a small sign.

> Den gesamten Pferdekörper aus einem Stück herstellen und die Schnauze birnenförmig abmodellieren. Mit einem scharfen Messer die Mundöffnung einschneiden. Die Augen- und Nasenpartie gestalten. Zwei Ohren ansetzen und mit M 1 eindrücken. Die Mähne gesondert anbringen und mit M 10 sowie M 11 profilieren. | 1 |
Für das Gebiss mit Zahnlücke ein kurzes Marzipanröllchen zwischen zwei Folien platt drücken. M 11 zum Einritzen der einzelnen Zähne benutzen. Das gekerbte Plättchen längs teilen und oben und unten sauber abschneiden. | 2 |
Die untere Zahnreihe am Stück in das Pferdemaul einkleben und mit M 7 andrücken. | 3 |
Die obere Reihe mittig trennen und mit einer Lücke im vorderen Bereich befestigen. | 4 |
Das Pferd weiß grundieren und Ohren, Schnauze sowie das Maul partiell mit Hautfarbe besprühen. Schwarze Farbe im Maulbereich wirkt natürlich und lässt die Zähne besser zur Geltung kommen. Die Zähne mit dem Pinsel extrem weiß schminken. Mähne und Schweif ebenfalls dunkler färben und die Augen aufspritzen. Die Sprenkeloptik auf dem Pferdekörper wie bei „Adonis“ (Seite 118) beschrieben mit dem Airbrush anbringen.
Aus einer dünnen Platte die Pferdedecke ausschneiden und auflegen. Eine platt gedrückte Kugel mit M 10 zur Rosette gestalten und ankleben. Nach Belieben ein Schild platzieren.

> Make the whole body of the horse from one piece, modelling the mouth in the shape of a bulb. Cut the opening of the mouth with a sharp knife. Shape the area around the nose and eyes. Attach two ears and use an M 1 to make the indentation. Attach the mane separately and apply the appropriate texture using an M 10 and an M 11. | 1 |
To make the teeth with one missing, place a short marzipan roll between two foils and press flat. Use an M 11 to score the individual teeth. Separate the plate with the teeth scored in and cut off neatly at top and bottom. | 2 |
Attach the lower row of teeth in one piece into the mouth of the horse and use an M 7 to press it down. | 3 |
Separate the top row in the middle and attach, leaving a gap in the front part. | 4 |
Apply a white base coat to the horse and partially spray the ears, nose and the mouth with skin colour. Black colour in the mouth area looks natural and emphasises the effect of the teeth more. Use a brush to colour the teeth extremely white. Colour the mane and the tail somewhat darker and pipe on the eyes. Apply the speckling effect on the body of the horse as described under “Adonis” (page 118) using the airbrush.
Cut out the horse blanket from a thin slab and place over the horse. Use an M 10 to shape a flattened ball into the prize badge and attach. Attach a sign if required.

Nobody's perfect

Nobody's perfect

Slow food

Slow food

> Eine runde Marzipanscheibe für die Servierplatte ausstechen. Mit M 3 einen Rand einarbeiten und einfärben. Aus einer platten Kugel die beiden Burgerhälften anfertigen. Für das Salatblatt ein kleines Stück aus einer hauchdünnen Marzipanplatte reißen und auf die untere Burgerhälfte legen. Die Frikadelle, eine flach gedrückte Kugel, auf dem Salatblatt ankleben. Aus rot gefärbter Eiweißspritzglasur „Ketchup“ aufspritzen und die obere Burgerhälfte positionieren. Vereinzelt kleine Kügelchen als Sesamkörnchen befestigen. Den Burger schminken und auf dem Tablett mittig anbringen.
Aus einer Kugel zuerst die längliche Grundform für den Schildkrötenpanzer modellieren. Mit den Fingern die Seiten nach unten in eine stumpfe Kante drücken und die Kopföffnung nach oben stülpen. Mit M 11 die typische Panzerstruktur einkerben. | 1 |
Die Beinlöcher mit M 2 nach oben drücken. | 2 |
Zum Schluss die Einzelsegmente des Panzermusters mit einer Riffelung versehen. | 3 |
Aus abgerundeten Stangen die Gliedmaßen formen und befestigen. Das Köpfchen gestalten und gut trocknen lassen. Den Panzer gelb grundieren, braun und wenig schwarz nachschminken. Mit dem Aufsprühen von Wasser die Farben in die Vertiefungen fließen lassen. Konturen mit Schwarz nachziehen. Ein kleines Schildchen auf dem Tablett und ein größeres zwischen den Beinen des Tiers dekorieren.

> Cut out a round marzipan disc for the serving plate. Use an M 3 to work in an edge and colour to suit. Make the two halves of the roll from a flattened ball. To make the salad leaf, tear off a piece from a wafer-thin marzipan slab and place on the lower half of the roll. Make the burger from a flattened ball and attach on the salad leaf. Pipe on “ketchup” in red coloured royal icing and then put on the top half of the roll. Attach some tiny little balls to represent the sesame seeds. Colour the burger and attach centrally on the tray.
Use a ball to start modelling the longish base shape of the tortoise. Use your fingers to press both sides downwards to end in a blunt edge and open up the gap for the head by shaping upwards. Use an M 11 to apply the typical texture to the shell. | 1 |
Use an M 2 to push the arch over the holes for the legs upwards. | 2 |
Finally apply a ripple texture to the individual segments of the shell. | 3 |
Shape the limbs from rounded strips and attach to the body. Form the little head and leave to dry well. Apply a yellow base coat to the shell, then brush on some brown and a little black. Spray on some water to make sure the colours run into the indentations. Accentuate the contours with black. Attach a small sign on the tray and a larger one between the legs of the animal.

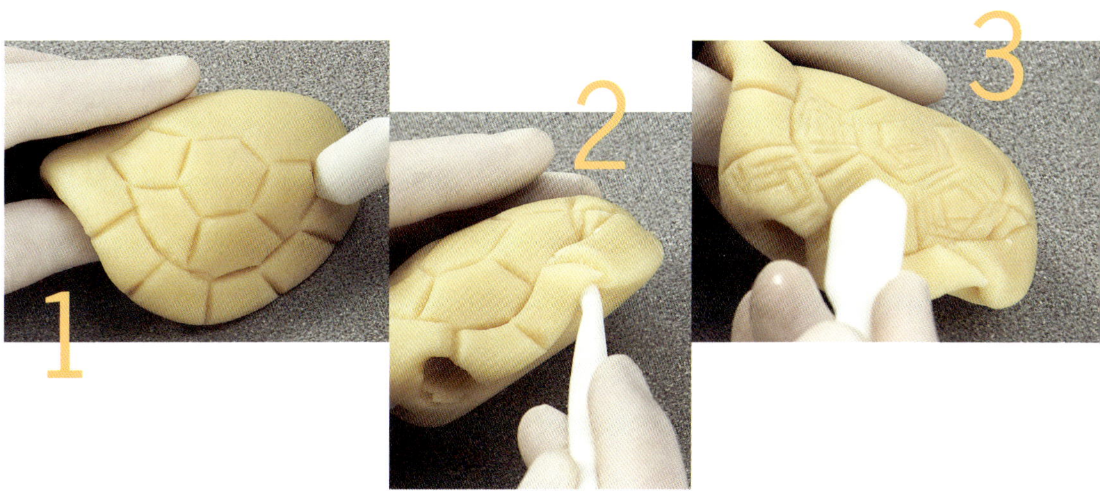

Child's play

Ihr Kinderlein kommet

Erste-Hilfe-Set für Eltern

First Aid kit

> Den Körper des Bären aus einem Stück formen und einen Kopf, bestehend aus zwei Kugeln, aufsetzen. Mit M 1 den Mund eindrücken. Die Augenpartie vertiefen. Eine Nase modellieren, ankleben und mit der Doppelseite des M 1 die Nasenlöcher einbringen. Gelb grundieren und flächig mit Braun nachsprühen. Die Augen aufspritzen. Mit dem Pinsel Ohren, Mund sowie die Nase nachziehen.
Aus einem ausgeschnittenen Stück einer Marzipanplatte die Schachtel fertigen und mit M 11 die Kerben einritzen. Mit Gelb grundieren und an den Rändern mit Braun schattieren.
Den Schnuller aus drei Teilen herstellen. Eine Marzipanscheibe aus einer Platte ausstechen und mit einer kleinen Tülle das Mittelloch ausheben. | 1 |
Aus einer Marzipanrolle den Griff in Form biegen und an den Enden abschneiden. | 2 |
Die Schnullerscheibe sowie den ringförmigen Griff zusammenfügen und mit entsprechender Farbe besprühen. Den Nuckel aus einer länglichen Tropfenform modellieren und mit gefärbter Eiweißspritzglasur in den Träger einkleben. | 3 |
Eine beliebige Grundplatte herstellen und die einzelnen Bestandteile darauf anordnen. Für die Schachtel und das gesamte Arrangement jeweils ein Schildchen gestalten und platzieren.

> Form the body of the bear from one piece and add on the head consisting of two balls. Use an M 1 to shape the mouth then hollow out the area for the eyes. Model a nose and attach it to the head, then use the double side of the M 1 to make the nostrils. Apply a yellow base coat and then spray all over with brown. Pipe on the eyes. Use a brush to accentuate the ears, the mouth and the nose.
Make the box from a piece cut out from a marzipan slab and use an M 11 to score the grooves. Apply a yellow base coat and shades of brown at the edges.
Make the dummy from three parts. Cut out the marzipan disc from a slab and punch out the central hole using a round piping nozzle. | 1 |
Take a rolled piece of marzipan, bend the shape of the handle and cut off at the ends. | 2 |
Join the disc of the dummy together with the ring-shaped handle and spray in the colour of your choice. Model the rubber part from an oblong drop shape and attach to the disc with coloured royal icing. | 3 |
Make any base slab of your choice and arrange the individual components on the slab. Design a small sign for the box and one for the whole arrangement and fix into place.

PROFI **TIPP** *Schnuller, in Rosa und Hellblau gefärbt, sind ein interessanter Blickfang auf jeder Tauftorte.*

In pink and light blue colouring the dummies make an interesting decoration for any Christening cake.

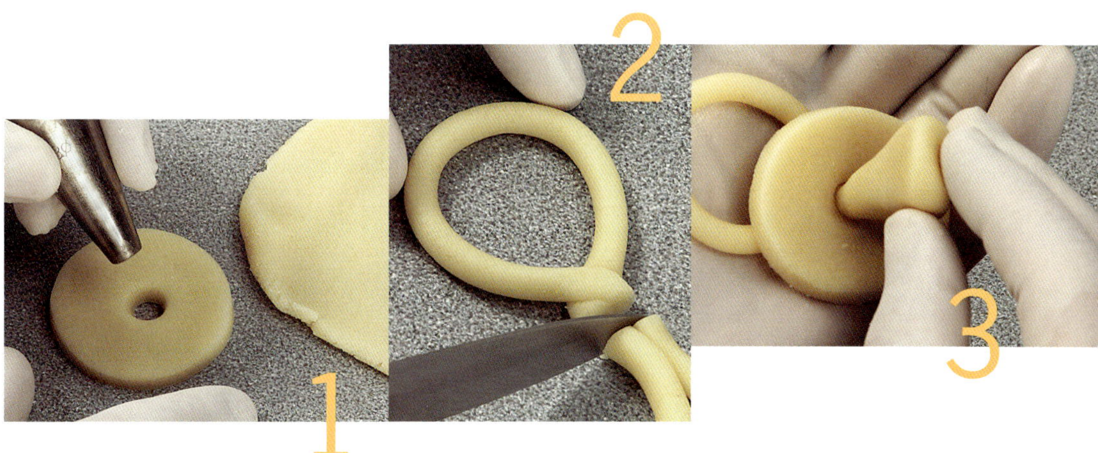

Musik beruhigt?

Music relaxes?

> Die „Super Oma“ weitgehend wie im Grundlagenkapitel „Modelliertechniken“ (ab Seite 232) beschrieben herstellen. Hier entfällt das Einschneiden der Beine, stattdessen einen Rock modellieren. Schuhe anfertigen und unter dem Rock anbringen. Die Schürze durch Einkerben mit M 1 hervorheben. An Stelle der eingespritzten Augen zwei kleine Marzipankugeln einsetzen. Mit M 7 die Stirnfalten einritzen. Auf Grund der klaren Farbübergänge die Figur am besten mit dem Pinsel schminken und auf einer Unterlage, die der Sesselhöhe entspricht, gut trocknen lassen.
Ein kleines Baby formen, schminken und mit einer Marzipandecke zugedeckt auf dem Schoß der Figur befestigen.
Die grobe Kontur eines Sessels aus einem dicken Marzipanblock schneiden, die Proportionen für die Lehne und Sitzfläche festlegen und durchtrennen. Mit einem scharfen Messer die Rückenlehne leicht abschrägen. | 1 |
Zur Stabilität einen schrägen Überhang anmodellieren und an die Sitzfläche kleben. Von einer Stange zwei Scheiben für die Seitenteile abschneiden. | 2 |
Beide Einzelteile am Sessel befestigen und mit M 3 einen sanften Schwung einarbeiten. | 3 |
Den Sessel gelb grundieren und mit Rot nachsprühen. Die Figur auf dem Sessel platzieren und ein Schildchen hinzufügen.

> Make the “Super Granny” largely as described in the chapter “Modelling Techniques” (from page 232). Of course you do not have to sculpt the legs but instead model a skirt. Make some shoes and fix them underneath the skirt. Highlight the apron by scoring the contours with an M 1. Instead of piping on the eyes, attach two small marzipan balls. Use an M 7 to score the wrinkles on the forehead. Because of the clear distinction between the colours it is best to colour the figure by brush, “sitting” it on a base that corresponds to the height of the armchair; leave to dry well.
Form a small baby, apply colour and cover with the marzipan blanket; attach onto the lap of the figure.
Cut the rough shape of an armchair from a thick marzipan block, determine the proportions for the back rest and the seat and then cut to shape. Use a sharp knife to cut the back rest to lean back at an angle. | 1 |
To give the armchair stability, attach a slanted covering and stick to the seat. Cut two discs from a roll to make the arm rests. | 2 |
Attach the two arm rests onto the armchair and use an M 3 to work in a gentle curve. | 3 |
Apply yellow base coat to the armchair and follow on with a red spray.
Place the figure onto the armchair and add a small sign.

PROFI ***TIPP*** *Wenn Pastelltöne gewünscht sind, ist die gesamte Figur weiß zu grundieren. Die folgenden Farbaufträge erscheinen dann durch das sich lösende Weiß etwas heller.*

If an item is intended to be coloured primarily in pastel colours, the whole ensemble should be covered in white base coat.

1

2

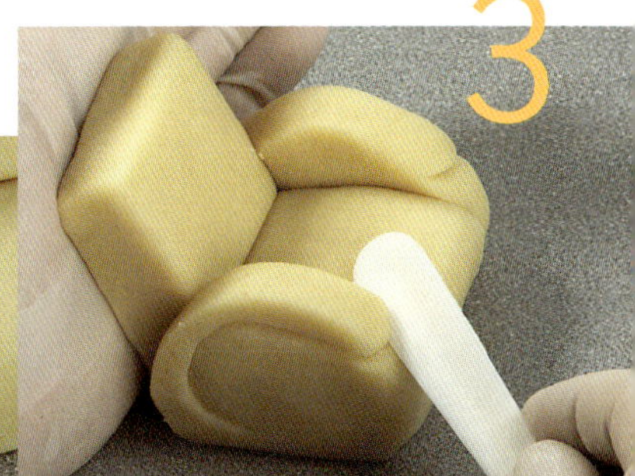
3

> In der Form einer Farbpalette eine Grundplatte herstellen und das Griffloch ausstechen. Für die Farbtöpfe kurze Stangenteile mit der Kugel des M 5 auf der Oberseite einhöhlen. Anschließend auf der Palette positionieren. Weiß grundieren und mit dem Pinsel großzügig verschiedene Farbtöne aufbringen.
Den Babykörper aus einer Eiform herausmodellieren, aus dem schmaleren Ende die Arme anfertigen und die Hände gestalten. Die Windel mit M 1 abgrenzen und den Überschlag des Tuchs andeuten. Aus einer dünnen Marzipanstange die Sicherheitsnadel formen und ankleben.
Beide Beinlöcher mit M 5 eindrücken und wie bei „Jugend forscht“ (Seite 172) beschrieben die Beine anfertigen. Einen Kopf sowie den Hals herstellen und auf den Rumpf setzen. Falls notwendig, ein Holzstäbchen einarbeiten. Den Ansatz leicht anfeuchten und mit M 3 nahtlos verstreichen.
Das Baby mit der Schminkpistole besprühen.
Nach dem Trocknen der Grundfarben vereinzelt Farbkleckse aus nächster Nähe aufspritzen.
Für den Farbpinsel eine Marzipanstange so verarbeiten, dass ein Ende dünner als das andere ausläuft. Das dickere Ende spitz modellieren. | 1 |
Mit M 7 den Schaft einkerben. | 2 |
Danach die Struktur der Borsten eindrücken. | 3 |
Griff und Schaft einfärben. Der Pinselspitze vor dem Schminken der schwarzen Borsten eine entsprechende Farbe aufmalen. Eine Einfärbung im Nachhinein würde ansonsten ein unbefriedigendes Ergebnis bringen. Nach ausreichender Trocknung den Farbpinsel an dem Baby befestigen und zusammen auf der Grundplatte mit einem Schildchen positionieren.

> Produce a base slab in the shape of a painter's palette and cut out the hole for the thumb. To make the little tubs for the paint, cut short pieces of a roll and indent at the top with the ball of the M 5. Then position on the palette. Apply a white base coat and then use the brush to colour the paint on the palette in several vivid colours.
Model the baby body from an egg shape, sculpting the arms and hands from the narrower end. Mark out the napkin with an M 1 and use this tool also to indicate the folds of the cloth. Shape the safety pin from a thin rolled strip of marzipan and attach.
Use an M 5 to push in holes for the legs and then make the legs as described in "Young researcher" (page 172). Make the head as well as the neck and place onto the trunk. If necessary, use a little wooden stick as reinforcement. Wet the joins slightly and use an M 3 to smooth them out. Spray the baby with the spray pistol. Once the basic colours have dried, add some small patches of colour from close up.
To make the painter's brush, roll a marzipan strip such that one end tapers out flatter than the other. Model the thicker end to a point. | 1 |
Use an M 7 to score the handle. | 2 |
Then mark the texture of the bristles. | 3 |
Colour both the handle and the shaft. Before painting the bristles in black, paint a colour of your choice onto the tip of the brush. Applying the colour afterwards won't give the required result. Once the brush has dried out sufficiently, attach it to the baby and position it on the base slab together with a sign.

PROFI **TIPP** *Farben, die mit weißer Lebensmittelfarbe vermischt wurden, wie hier zum Beispiel die Hautfarbe des Babys, müssen vor einem neuen Farbauftrag mit dem Airbrush vollständig abgetrocknet sein. Wird dies außer Acht gelassen, treibt der starke Luftstrom der Schminkpistole die grundierende Farbe vor sich her, und es bilden sich unschöne Farbfehler.*

Colour that has mixed with white food colouring, such as the skin colour of the baby in this example, has to dry out completely before applying a new coat by airbrush. If the colouring is not dry when applying the next coat with the airbrush, the strong airflow will dislodge the basic colour and create unsightly patterns.

Früh übt sich ...

Starting early

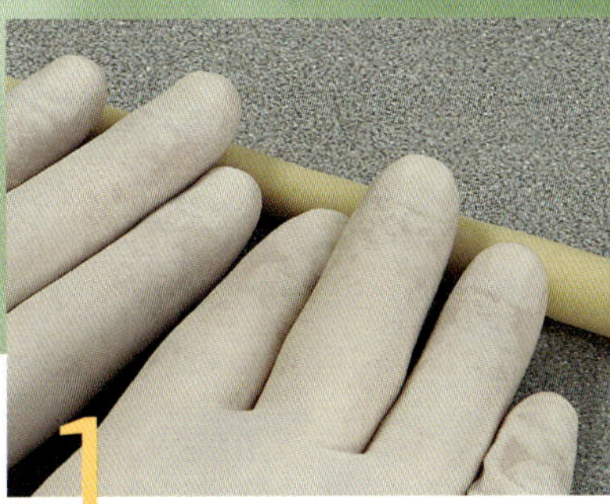
1

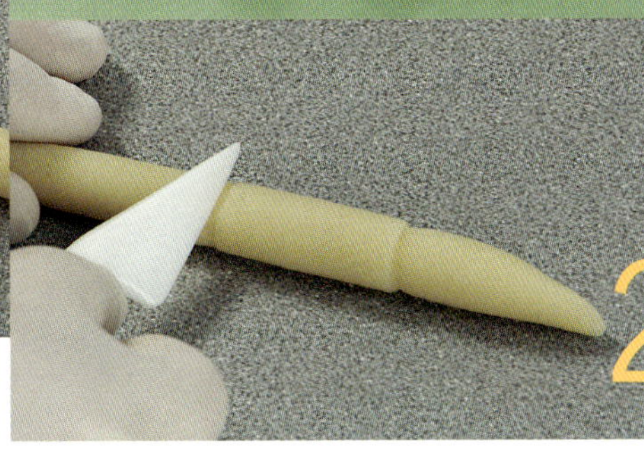
2

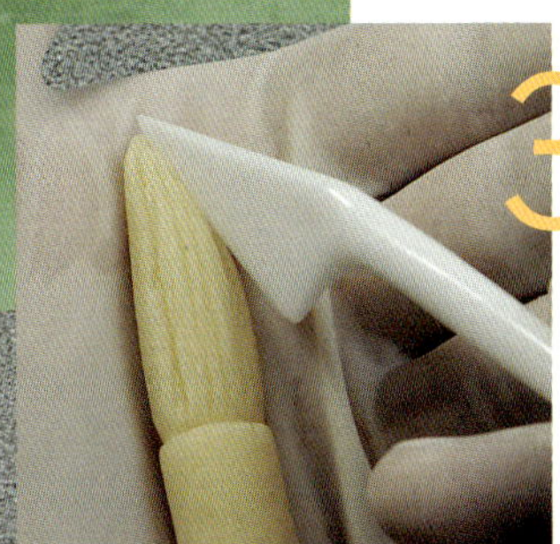
3

Rock around the clock

Rock around the clock

> Aus einer Marzipanplatte einen Halbkreis anfertigen, schminken und als Grundplatte verwenden.
Ein Rechteck für den Uhrenfuß vorbereiten. Mit M 7 und M 6 so einkerben, dass eine Tür mit Uhrenpendel zu erkennen ist. Für die Scharniere kleine Segmente in Form bringen und ankleben. Den oberen Uhrenkasten der Standuhr aus einem Quadrat herstellen und ein Ziffernblatt einkerben. Kleine Zeiger separat formen und mittig platzieren. Die Verzierung aus einer eingedrehten Marzipanstange aufsetzen. Die unterschiedlichen Marzipanblöcke zusammensetzen, gelb grundieren und mit Braun nachsprühen. Ziffernblatt und Pendeleinblick mit dem Pinsel nachschminken.
Für das Schaukelpferdchen zuerst die Kufen anfertigen. Dazu eine Platte ausrollen, ein Rechteck ausschneiden und zwei Quadrate heraustrennen, um die Kufen entstehen zu lassen. Das bearbeitete Unterteil über einer Rundung trocknen lassen. | 1 |
Den Grundkörper des Pferdchens aus einem grob dreieckigen Grundkörper beginnen. Für den Kopf eine Ecke etwas länger herausmodellieren. Die Ohren und die Schnauze mit den Fingern formen. Mit M 2 die Backen abgrenzen. | 2 |
Durch Einkerben mit M 1 die Ohren- und Augenpartie fertigen. Den Schweif ansetzen, die Beine durch Ausschneiden eines Keils herausholen. | 3 |
Die Kanten abrunden und auf dem Unterteil befestigen. Nach ausreichender Trocknung schminken und die Augen aufspritzen.
Ein Baby wie bei „Früh übt sich ..." (Seite 166) beschrieben herstellen und auf dem Schaukelpferdchen befestigen.
Die Standuhr, das Schaukelpferdchen sowie ein Schildchen auf der Grundplatte drapieren.

> Make a semi-circle from a marzipan slab, colour and use as a base slab.
Prepare a rectangular shape as a base for the clock. Use an M 7 and M 6 to outline the door and indicate the pendulum that one can see through the door. Attach small pieces to represent the hinges. Make the top box of the grandfather clock from a cube and mark the numbers for the clock face. Form small hands separately and attach in the middle. Make the embellishment from a rolled strip of marzipan and attach this to the top. Join the two separate marzipan blocks together, apply a yellow base coat and then follow on with a brown spray. Use the brush to add extra colour to the clock face and the pendulum.
To make the rocking horse, start with the runners. For this purpose roll out a marzipan slab, cut out a rectangular shape and remove two squares to make the runners. Place over a round shape and leave to dry. | 1 |
Start modelling the basic shape of the horse from a roughly triangular block. To make the head, model one corner into a longer shape. Form the ears and mouth with your fingers. Use an M 2 to delineate the cheeks. | 2 |
Use an M 1 to score the ears and the area of the eyes. Attach the tail and sculpt the legs by cutting out a wedge shape. | 3 |
Round off the edges and attach to the base. Once the figure has dried out sufficiently, paint and pipe on the eyes.
Make a baby as described in "Starting early" (page 166) and place onto the rocking horse. Arrange the grandfather clock, the rocking horse and a small sign on the base slab.

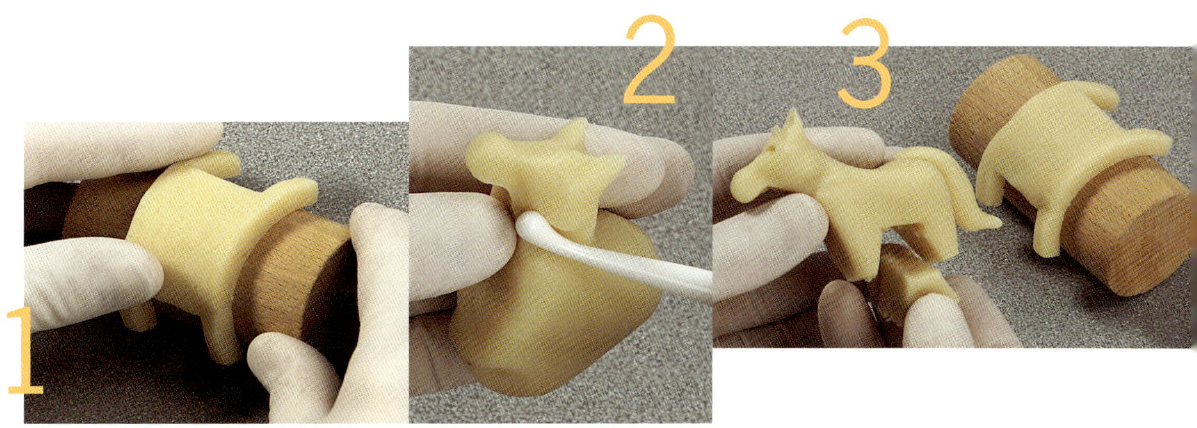

Zur Taufe

For the christening

> Für die Wiege ein Quadrat sowie zwei Rechtecke aus einer dünnen Platte schneiden und über einem Rundholz trocknen lassen. |1|
Aus den zwei Rechtecken die Grundform der Wiege schneiden. |2|
Mit M 3 die Schnittkanten abrunden. Die verschiedenen Zierkanten ebenfalls mit M 3 einarbeiten. |3|
Die gut getrockneten Teile mit Kuvertüre oder Eiweißspritzglasur zusammenfügen. |4|
Aus durchgefärbtem Marzipan oder weißer Dekormasse das Kissen und die Bettdecke herstellen. Kopf und Hände des Babys aus jeweils kleinen Kugeln modellieren und ein Haarbüschel gesondert ansetzen. Das Köpfchen auf dem Kissen ankleben, eine Decke leicht über den Kopf legen und die Hände anbringen.
Nach vollständiger Trocknung die Wiege mit dem Baby schminken und auf einer vorbereiteten Grundplatte mit einem kleinen Schildchen befestigen.
Verschieden große Herzen wie bei „Liebe auf den ersten Blick“ (Seite 44) beschrieben modellieren und um das Szenario herum verteilen.

> To make the cradle, cut a square and two rectangular shapes from a thin slab and leave to dry over a rolling pin. |1|
Cut the basic shape of the cradle from the two rectangles. |2|
Use an M 3 to round off the cut edges. Also use an M 3 to score the various decorative edges. |3|
Once the parts have dried sufficiently, join them together with couverture or royal icing. |4|
Make the pillow and the bedcover from tinted marzipan or white icing. Model the head and hands of the baby from small balls; attach the curl of hair separately. Attach the little head to the pillow, place the blanket slightly over the head and attach the hands.
After everything has dried completely, colour the cradle with the baby and fix to a prepared base slab, together with a small sign.
Make hearts of different sizes as under “Love at first sight” (page 44) and distribute all over the scenario.

PROFI **TIPP** *Kleine Details, in verstreuter Art und Weise auf Arrangements angebracht, sorgen für eine lockere unbeschwerte Gesamtwirkung. Ein Probelegen verhindert, dass allzu störende Größenunterschiede zu benachbarten Teilen oder eine völlige Isoliertheit entsteht.*

Small details that are scattered about the ensemble, ensure a relaxed and pleasing overall effect. In order to prevent a clash between different-sized items, or empty areas, it is worth laying out the pieces on a trial basis first.

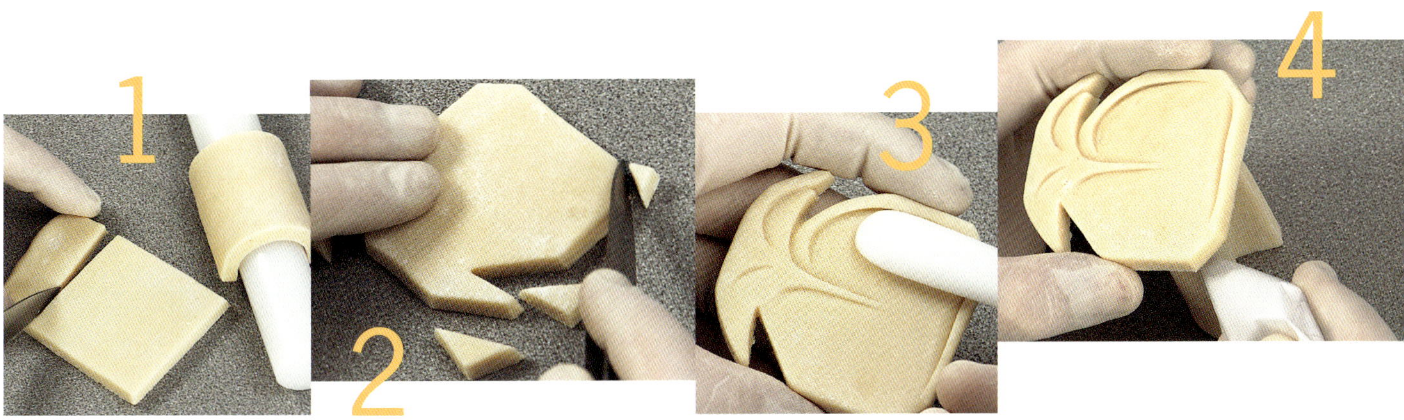

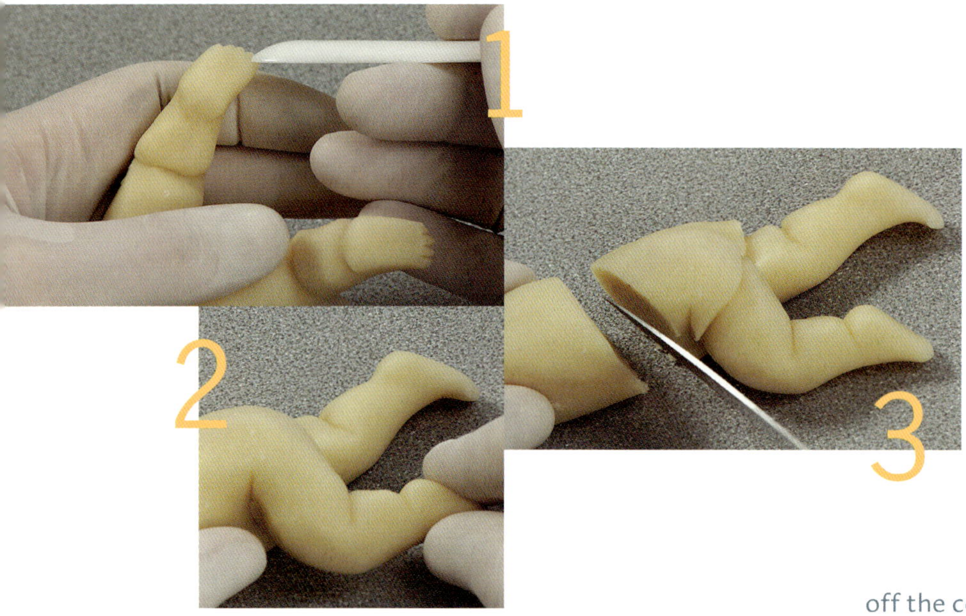

› Aus einem Quader mit abgerundeten Ecken das Fernsehgerät herstellen. Mit M 11 die Struktur der Lautsprechergitter und der Bildröhre einritzen. Die Gehäusekanten ebenfalls mit M 11 kennzeichnen. Die Rückwand aus einer Marzipanplatte zusammensetzen und mit „Kühlöffnungen“ versehen. Das Gehäuse und die Rückwand einfärben. Feine Konturen mit Schwarz nachziehen. Die Bildröhre weiß grundieren und kreisförmig mit Blau nachsprühen, um einen heller werdenden Farbverlauf zu erzielen. Ein Schildchen mit Aufschrift anfertigen und oben auf der Rückwand des Fernsehgeräts ankleben.
Für die Babyfüße einen kurzen Marzipanzylinder mit M 2 tief einkerben. Beide Beine mit den Fingern lang modellieren und mit Daumen sowie Zeigefinger die Füße abgrenzen. Mit M 1 die Kniebeuge einarbeiten. Die Fersen weiter ausformen und die Zehen mit M 1 andeuten. | 1 |
Am linken Beinansatz eine weitere Kerbe eindrücken, um das Bein sanft nach vorne schieben zu können. | 2 |
Um die Windel hervorzuheben, mit M 1 den Umriss kennzeichnen. Körper am oberen Ende der Windel abschneiden. | 3 |
Auf einer vorbereiteten Grundplatte die Babyfüßchen mit dem abgeschnittenen Ansatz zwischen Fernseher und Rückwand platzieren. Mit kleinen Details, wie einem Schraubenzieher und Schrauben, das Arrangement vervollständigen.

› Take a cube of marzipan and round off the corners to make the television set. Use an M 11 to score the texture of the loudspeaker grills and the screen. Also mark the edges of the box with an M 11. Cut out a marzipan slab as the back panel and cut out “ventilation openings”. Colour the box and the back panel. Accentuate delicate features in black. Apply a white base coat to the glass screen and then spray in a circular fashion with blue in order to achieve a slight gradation in colour intensity. Make a sign with the caption and attach to the top of the back panel of the television set.
To make the feet of the baby, use an M 2 to make a deep cut in a short marzipan roll. Model both legs with your fingers and use your thumb and forefinger to shape the feet. Use an M 1 to mark the back of the knee. Continue to shape the heels of the feet and use an M 1 to indicate the toes. | 1 |
Press in another groove at the top of the left leg so that it is possible to move the leg slightly forward. | 2 |
To accentuate the nappy use an M 1 to delineate its contours and remove the excess marzipan from the body. | 3 |
Place the feet of the baby on a prepared base slab, between the television set and the back panel. Complete the arrangement with small details such as a screwdriver and screws.

Jugend forscht

Young researcher

Zur Geburt, zur Taufe, zum Kindergeburtstag …

For birthdays, christenings and a new baby …

Message to you

Was ich dir sagen wollte ...

Trust me!

Trust me!

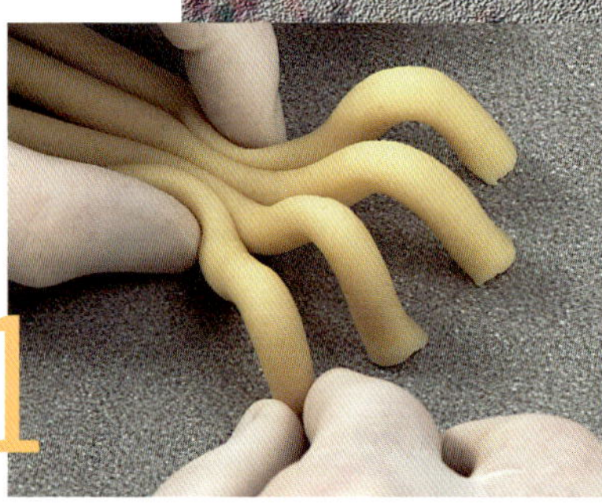

1

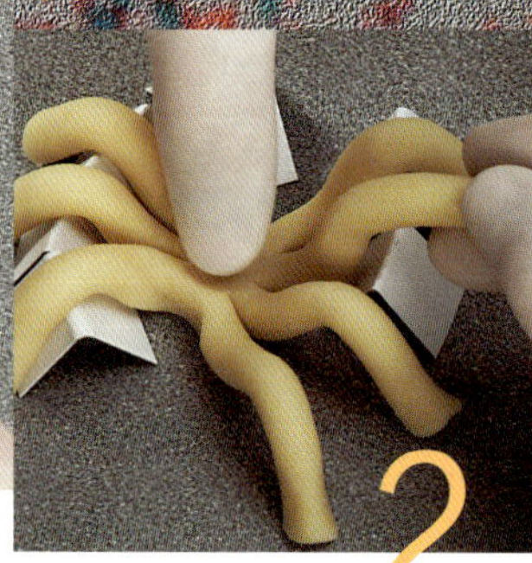

2

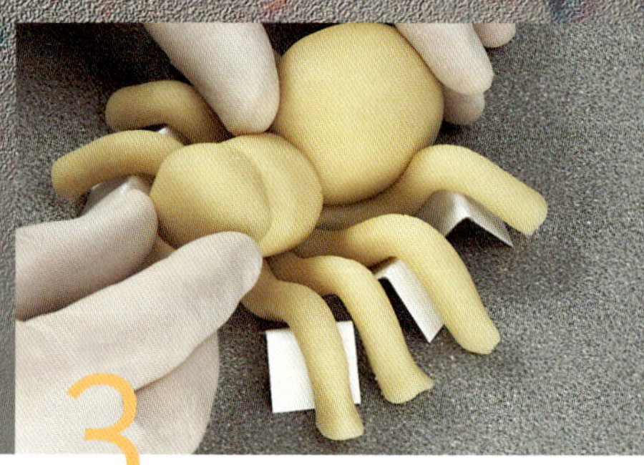

3

> Eine Marzipanplatte auswellen und mit M 1 erst die Spann- und dann die Fangfäden des Spinnennetzes einkerben. Nach Festlegen der Größe am äußersten Faden entlang die Grundplatte ausschneiden. Mit einem dünnen Pinsel die Vertiefungen schwarz nachziehen. Das gesamte Spinnennetz mit Blau schattieren und kräftig mit Wasser nachsprühen. Nach Belieben ein kleines Schild hinzufügen.
Für die Spinnenbeine vier Marzipanstränge parallel nebeneinander legen, mittig zusammendrücken und in Form bringen. | 1 |
Unter die abgewinkelten Beine als kleine Stütze geknickte Pappkartonblättchen stellen. | 2 |
Den Körper aus drei verschieden großen Kugeln zusammenfügen. | 3 |
Ein beidseitig angespitztes Röllchen für den Mund mit M 3 ausgestalten und die Augenhöhlen vertiefen. Aus einer kleineren Kugel die Nase sowie einen Zahn modellieren und ankleben. Ein Kreuz aus dünnen Marzipansträngen herstellen und befestigen. Die Figur gelb grundieren, mit Braun nachsprühen und vereinzelt schwarze Schattierungen auftragen. Die Augen aufspritzen. Den Kopf hautfarben besprühen. Feinheiten mit einem Pinsel nachschminken. Nach guter Trocknung kann die Figur problemlos – auch ohne Stützplättchen – bewegt und auf dem Spinnennetz positioniert werden.

> Roll out a marzipan slab and use an M 1 to mark first the radial lines and then the concentric lines of the spider's web. Once you have decided on a size, cut out the base slab along the outer line of the web. Use a fine brush to accentuate the pattern in black. Apply a blue colour coat to the entire web and then spray vigorously with water. Add a small sign if required. To make the spider's legs, place four rolled marzipan strips next to each other, with equal distance between them, press them together in the middle and then bend to the required shape. | 1 |
Make some miniature trestles from folded cardboard to support the bent legs. | 2 |
Join the body together from three balls of different sizes. | 3 |
Use a thin marzipan roll tapering at both ends and attach as a mouth. Use an M 3 to sculpt the rest of the mouth as well as the eye sockets. Model the nose and one tooth from a small ball and attach to the body. Make a cross from a thin rolled marzipan strip and attach to the body. Apply a yellow base coat to the figure, follow on with brown and add some black shading here and there. Pipe on the eyes. Spray the head with skin-coloured paint. Use a brush to accentuate the detail.
Once the figure has dried it can be moved – without the help of the trestles – and positioned on the web.

PROFI **TIPP** *Mit der richtigen Stütze lassen sich viele kompliziert wirkende Formen umsetzen. Ein Bogen lebensmittelechter Karton, der oft schon bei Lieferungen enthalten ist, sowie Schere und Tesafilm bieten schon die notwendigen Hilfsmittel, um solche Stützen zu realisieren.*

With the right support it is possible to realise many shapes, even if they appear difficult. Supports can be made from a sheet of food packaging card using some scissors and sticky tape. You may already have some card from earlier deliveries.

Don't
worry
be
happy

Don't worry, be happy

Don't worry, be happy

› Mit M 1 die kreisförmigen Wellen auf einer etwas dickeren Grundplatte eindrücken. Blaue Farbe als Grundierung auftragen. Um naturgetreue Lichtreflexionen hervorzurufen, kräftig mit Wasser nachsprühen.
Messer und Gabel modellieren. Gut trocknen lassen und mit silberner Lebensmittelfarbe glänzende Reflexe setzen. Die jeweiligen Griffflächen mit Braun schminken und schwarze Konturen nachziehen.
Den Hai aus einer vorn abgerundeten Stange formen. Das Maul einschneiden und im 90°-Winkel biegen. Das Grinsen sowie die Kiemen beidseitig mit M 11 einarbeiten. Beide Flossen separat in Form bringen, ansetzen und mit dem Besteck bestücken. Die Zähne wie bei „Dem süßen Heimwerker" (Seite 104) beschrieben vorbereiten und in das bereits geschminkte Maul kleben. Erst nach kurzer Trocknung eine kleine Zunge ankleben. Die Augenpartie gestalten. Den Hai mit grauer Farbe schminken. Zähne und Zunge mit dem Pinsel nachfärben.
Das Entchen in einfachster Ausführung mit zwei Tropfen für Körper und Schnabel sowie einer Kugel für den Kopf zusammensetzen und schminken.
Den Hai in die „Wellen tauchen" und das Entchen beifügen. An Stelle eines aufgelegten Schildchens den Schriftzug direkt aufschreiben.

› Use an M 1 to sculpt the circular waves on a somewhat thicker base slab. Apply blue paint as base coat. Spray vigorously with water in order to generate natural light reflections.
Model knife and fork. Leave to dry well and use silver food colouring to apply shiny surfaces on the metal parts. Colour the handles with brown and accentuate contours with black. Shape the shark from a roll that has been rounded at the front. Cut in the mouth and bend the head downwards. Work in the grin as well as the gills on both sides with an M 11. Form both fins separately, attach to the fish and then arrange the cutlery to suit. Prepare the teeth as described under "For the sweet DIYer" (page 104) and insert into the mouth after it has already been coloured. Leave to dry for a short while and then attach a small tongue. Sculpt the area of the eyes. Spray the shark in grey colour. Use a brush to add extra colour to the teeth and tongue.
Make the little duck in the simplest form with two drops, for the body and the beak, and a ball for the head, join together and apply the colour.
Place the shark on the base so that it appears to be in the waves and then add the duck. Instead of a sign one can write the caption directly onto the slab.

Auf zu neuen Gipfeln

Quest for new heights

1

2

3

> Die Grundform für den Rucksack aus einem Stangenabschnitt grob vormodellieren, dabei die Unterseite standfest glätten und die Kanten abrunden. Mit M 1 die Umrisse der Außentaschen und anschließend der Laschen einkerben. Verschlussriemen ebenfalls einarbeiten oder aus dünnen Bändern herstellen. Aus einer dünnen Marzipanplatte ein Stück herausschneiden, zur Decke einrollen und befestigen. Ein kleines Rechteck für den Rucksackdeckel über die Decke stülpen und auf der Rückseite anmodellieren. Beide Trägerriemen zurechtschneiden und gleich anbringen. Nach ausreichender Trocknung der Riemen mit dem Schminken beginnen und die Verschlussschnallen aufspritzen.
Marzipan auswellen und eine Grundplatte anfertigen. Für die Herstellung der Graselemente Marzipankugeln durch ein Sieb drücken. Die einzelnen Büschel zusammen mit dem Rucksack auf der Platte fixieren und gelb-grün schminken.
Aus zwei Marzipanstangen und einem dünnen Röllchen für den Henkel den Eispickel zusammensetzen und gut trocknen lassen. Beim Formen des Seils eine lange Schnur aus Modelliermarzipan zügig vorbereiten, da das verwendete Material schnell trocknet und zum Brechen neigt. | 1 |
Auf einer glatten Arbeitsunterlage die Schnur in Schlangenlinien auflegen. | 2 |
Das Seil vorsichtig von der Fläche nehmen und mit dem offenen Ende umschlingen. | 3 |
In die endgültige Form bringen, ausreichend trocknen lassen und schminken.
Zur Vervollständigung des Arrangements den Eispickel und ein Schildchen auf der Grundplatte befestigen.

> Roughly model the basic shape of the rucksack from a short roll, ensuring that the edges are rounded off and the underside is flat so that it stands firm. Use an M 1 to mark the contours of the outside pockets and their flaps. Also work in the straps; alternatively you can make these from thin ribbons. Cut out a piece from a thin marzipan slab, roll it into a blanket and attach to the rucksack. Cut a small rectangular piece as cover flap and attach it over the blanket. Cut the two carrier straps and attach straight away. Once the straps have dried sufficiently, start applying the colour and pipe on the buckles.
Roll out some marzipan and prepare a base slab. To make the grass elements, press some marzipan balls through a strainer. Fix the grass tussocks together with the rucksack on the slab and spray in yellow-green colour.
Make up the ice pick from two rolled strips of marzipan and an even thinner rolled strip for the strap and leave to dry well. For the rope, prepare a long string from modelling marzipan, working swiftly, since the material dries out quite fast and will soon become brittle. | 1 |
Arrange the rope on a smooth working surface in curvy lines. | 2 |
Carefully lift the rope from the surface and tie a loop through the open end. | 3 |
Form it to the final shape, leave to dry sufficiently and apply colour. To finish off the ensemble, attach the ice pick and a small sign on the base slab.

PROFI **TIPP** *Für fragile Details, wie hier das Bergsteigerseil, bietet es sich an, fertiges Modelliermarzipan zu verwenden, da dieses länger weich und flexibel bleibt.*

For fragile details such as the mountaineering rope in the above example, it is best to use ready-made modelling marzipan since this stays soft and flexible for longer.

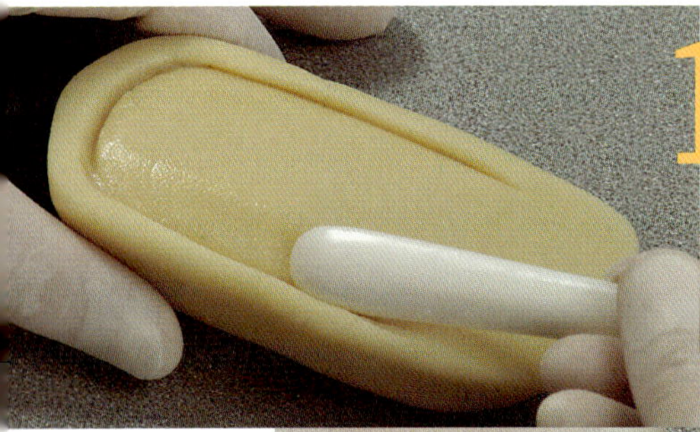
1

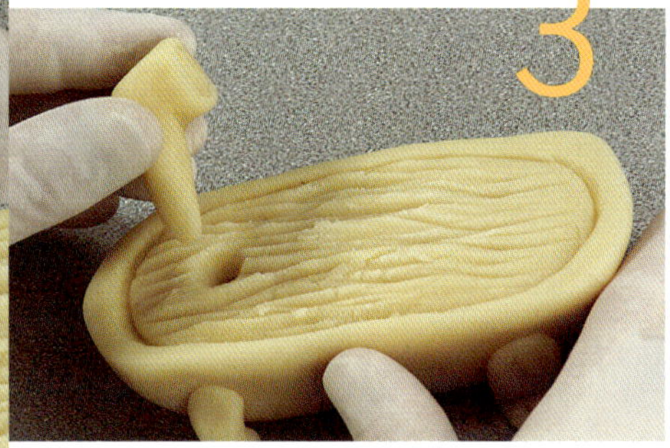
3

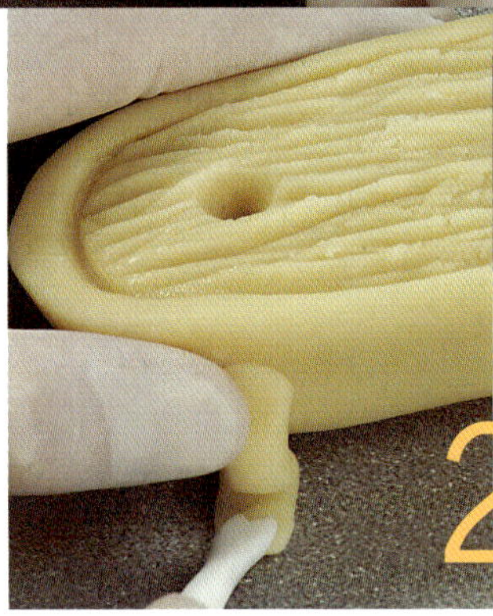
2

› Einen dicken Marzipanzylinder längs in der Mitte durchtrennen. Eine Hälfte an die Arbeitsfläche anmodellieren und die Oberseite abrunden. Die Wannenform drehen und mit M 3 die Wasserkante markieren. | 1 |
Durch Vor- und Zurückdrehen des M 1 die Wellen einarbeiten und für das Sehrohr eine kleine runde Vertiefung einstechen. Vier kurze Stangenabschnitte S-förmig biegen, die entstandenen Füße mit M 1 einkerben und ankleben. | 2 |
Das Sehrohr in der dafür vorgesehenen Stelle einfügen. | 2 |
Eine Vertiefung für den Oberkörper der Figur modellieren. Die obere Hälfte des Körpers wie im Grundlagenkapitel „Modelliertechniken“ (ab Seite 232) beschrieben herstellen. Die Figur mit dem Messer abschneiden und mit M 3 sowie ein wenig Wasser den Ansatz „unsichtbar“ machen. Die Armaturen an einer schräg abgeschnittenen Stange anbringen. Beim Schminken die Einzelteile – um Farbfehler zu vermeiden – getrennt behandeln. Die Wanne mit Weiß grundieren und am Rand ein Schildchen befestigen. Die Wannenränder mit Papier abdecken und das Wasser mit Blau besprühen. Für die Konturen und Feinheiten des Arrangements den Pinsel verwenden.

› Cut a thick marzipan cylinder from top to bottom into two halves. Place one half on the work surface and round off the top. Turn the bathtub form and use an M 3 to mark the waterline. | 1 |
Turn the M 1 backwards and forwards to create the impression of the waves and push in a small round indentation for the periscope. Cut four short sections of a marzipan roll and bend in an S-shape to make the feet; score the feet with an M 1 and attach. | 2 |
Attach the periscope in the hole prepared for this purpose. | 3 |
Carve out an indentation for the top half of the figure. Make the top half of the body as described in the chapter “Modelling Techniques” (from page 232). Cut the figure off with a knife and use an M 3 as well as a little water to smooth out the join.
Attach the tap to a roll that has been cut at an angle at the top. When applying the colour, work on the different parts separately in order to avoid any mixing of colours. Apply a white base coat to the tub and attach a small sign on the edge. Cover the edges of the tub with paper and spray the water in blue. Use a brush to accentuate the contours and finer detail of the ensemble.

See you

See you

Eine lustige Aufforderung für ein Wiedersehen

A humorous invitation to renew a contact

> Als Grundplatte eine Schriftrolle gestalten, die in der Herstellung mit den beiden kleinen Rollen identisch ist. Aus einer dünnen Platte einen Streifen in passender Größe schneiden. Eine Marzipanstange mit dem Streifen einrollen. Den Ansatz dabei sauber glätten, um eine Unwucht zu vermeiden. | 1 |
Das Siegelband aus einem schmalen Reststück ausschneiden und anbringen. | 2 |
Zwei aufgeklebte Kügelchen an der Rollenstange befestigen und ein weiteres zu einem Siegel formen. | 3 |
Die Schriftrollen in Form bringen und trocknen lassen. Bei der Grundplatte zusätzlich die Kanten des Schriftstücks abflachen und mit einem Schneiderad geschwungen abschneiden. Mit brauner und schwarzer Farbgebung werden Brandstellen vorgetäuscht.
Den Elefanten wie bei "No way out!" (Seite 148) beschrieben modellieren, mit einem Doktorhut ausstatten und auf der Grundplatte platzieren. Hierfür einen kurzen Stangenabschnitt sowie ein quadratisches Plattenstück aufeinander kleben und mit einer Quaste vervollständigen.

> Design the base slab in the form of a scroll, which is prepared quite similarly to the other two small scrolls. Cut a wide strip of appropriate length from a thin slab. Roll the strip around a stick of marzipan. Smooth the point of attachment carefully in order to avoid any unevenness. | 1 |
Cut out the ribbon for the seal from a small off-cut and attach. | 2 |
Attach two little balls at the ends of the stick and use another one to shape a seal. | 3 |
Arrange the scrolls to the desired shape and leave to dry. For the base plate, the edges of the scroll are flattened down and cut off in wavy shapes with the cutting wheel. Use brown and black colour shades to imitate scorch marks from fire.
Model the elephant as described under "No way out!" (page 148). Put a graduate's hat on it and place it on the base slab. To make the hat, stick a short section of roll together with a square piece of slab and complete with a tassel.

PROFI **TIPP** *Schriften mit dem Lebensmittelfarbdrucker auf essbare Trägerfolie drucken. Wenn auf normales Papier gedruckt wird, den Käufer unbedingt informieren.*

Print the text onto edible carrier foil using a food colour printer. If you use normal paper for the printout, you must inform the customer.

Keep me in mind

Keep me in mind

Heute geschlossen
Closed today

> Für die Rasenfläche eine Grundplatte anfertigen und die Strafraummarkierung mit M 6 einritzen. Mit M 10 die Grasstruktur einarbeiten. Vor dem Tor eine kleine halbrunde Fläche freilassen. Die Platte schminken und trocknen lassen. Auf einem grob vorgeformten Rechteck mit M 7 die Bretter des Fußballtors einritzen. Mit einer scharfen Messerspitze die Durchbrüche herausschneiden. | 1 |
Um den Bretterverschlag vom Torpfosten abzugrenzen, die Pfosten seitlich tiefer eindrücken. | 2 |
Nach dem Gestalten von Brettern und Durchbrüchen das Tor in die endgültige Form bringen. Für die Nägel mit M 2 einzelne Löcher einstechen. | 3 |
Mit M 8 die Holzmaserung einritzen. Das Tor am besten liegend schminken. Die Bretter gelb-braun färben und mit Wasser nachsprühen.
Die Torpfosten mit dem Pinsel weiß einfärben. Nach vollständiger Trocknung das Fußballtor sowie ein vorbereitetes Schildchen auf die Rasenfläche stellen. Zwei vorgefertigte Bügel ankleben.
Den Fußballspieler wie im Grundlagenkapitel „Modelliertechniken" (ab Seite 232) beschrieben modellieren und schminken.
Für den Fußball eine Kugel weiß grundieren, trocknen lassen und mit schwarzen Konturen versehen. Die Figur und den Ball vor dem Tor positionieren. Die Szenerie mit einem kleinen Hämmerchen und aufgemalten oder modellierten Nägeln fertig stellen.

> To simulate the grass area, prepare a base slab and mark the penalty area with an M 6. Use an M 10 to work in the grass texture. Leave out a small semi-circular area in front of the goal. Colour the slab and leave to dry.
Cut out a rectangular shape and use an M 7 to score the boards of the goal. Use a sharp knife point to cut out the gaps. | 1 |
In order to distinguish the boards from the goalposts, set the posts back on the sides. | 2 |
Once you have made the boards and the gaps, shape the goal to its final desired form.
To simulate the nails, use an M 2 to punch individual holes. | 3 |
Use an M 8 to score the grain of the wood. The colour is easiest applied with the goal lying flat. Colour the boards in yellowish-brown paint and follow on with a spray of water. Use a brush to paint the goalposts white. Once it is completely dry, place the goal as well as the small sign onto the lawn. Make two hoops and attach them at the back.
Model the football player as described in the chapter "Modelling Techniques" (from page 232) and colour to suit.
For the football, apply white base coat to a ball, leave to dry and mark with black contours.
Place the figure and the ball in front of the goal. Complete the scenario with a small hammer and nails painted on or modelled separately and attached.

PROFI **TIPP** *Torpfosten und Bretterverschlag lassen sich auch gut separat herstellen und zusammenfügen.*

It is also easy to make the goalposts and the boards separately and join them together.

1
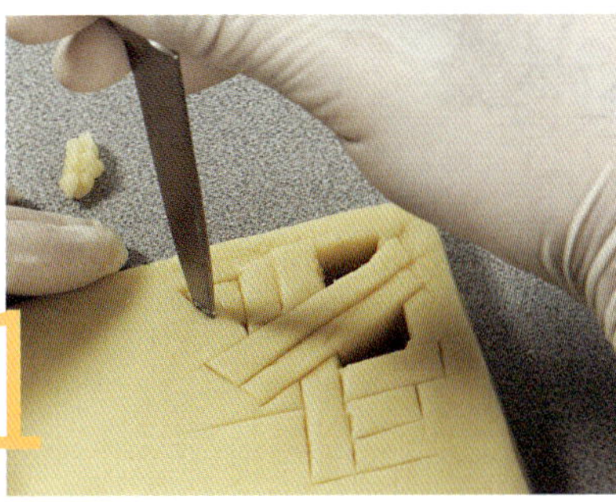

2
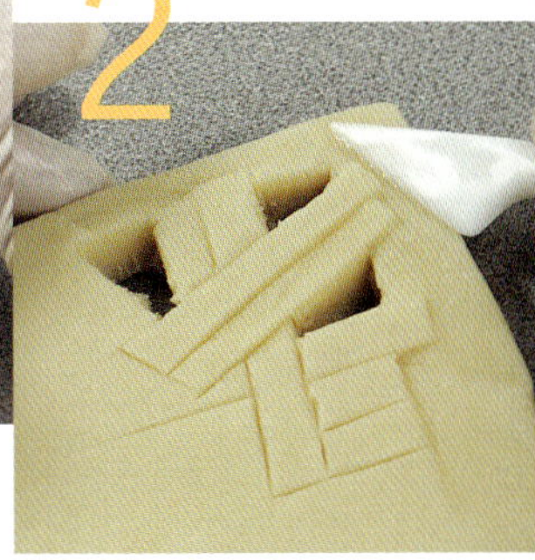

3

Mensch ärgere dich nicht

Ludo

Ein ideales Versöhnungsgeschenk

An ideal present for making peace

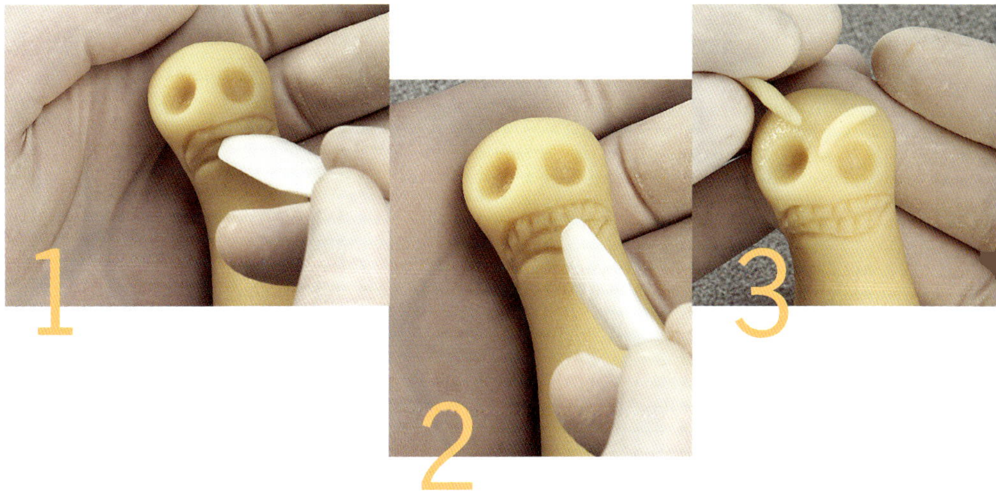

> Die Grundplatte aus einem Rechteck schneiden. Mit einer Lochtülle die einzelnen Spielpunkte eindrücken. Alles weiß grundieren. Mit dem Pinsel die Punkte in unterschiedlichen Farben anlegen und schwarz umranden.
Den Würfel mit einem Backhörnchen aus einer Kugel zurechtdrücken. Die Punkte mit M 2 einbringen. Die beiden streitenden Kegel entstehen aus je einer länglichen Birnenform. Die Arme aus dünnen, vorn abgeflachten, zu Händen geformten Stangen herstellen und charakteristisch in Pose bringen. Sehr wichtig sind hier die Gesichter: Die Augen als Ausgangspunkt festlegen. Mit M 11 zuerst die äußere Form des Munds anzeichnen, dann eine mittige Kerbe einbringen. | 1 |
Die einzelnen Zähne einkerben. | 2 |
Den verkniffenen Ausdruck erhalten die Figuren durch die angesetzten Augenbrauen in V-Form. | 3 |
Beide Figuren mit unterschiedlichen Farben schminken. Die Zähne strahlend weiß aufzeichnen und trocknen lassen. Abschließend mit dem Pinsel Mund und Brauen schwarz nachziehen.
Arrangement zusammensetzen, das mit dem Lebensmittelfarbdrucker erstellte Schildchen anbringen.

> Cut a square base slab. Use a round piping nozzle to mark all the various dots on the playing board. Cover everything with white base coat. Use the brush to paint the dots in their different colours and paint a black surround.
Make the dice from a ball squashed into shape. Push in the number points with an M 2. Make the two "players" from a longish bulb shape each. Form the arms from thin rolled strips that have been flattened at the front to make the hands and attach them in the characteristic expression. Very important here are the faces: first mark the eyes as a starting point. Use an M 11 to draw on the outside shape of the mouth and then enter the groove in the middle. | 1 |
Score the individual teeth. | 2 |
The figures are given their intense expression through the V-shaped eyebrows. | 3 |
Colour the two figures with different colours. Paint the teeth in brilliant white and leave to dry. Then use the brush to accentuate the mouth and the eyebrows in black.
Put it all together and apply the little sign you have produced with the food colour printer.

> Für den Schneckenkörper Marzipan ausrollen, mit den Fingern an die Unterlage modellieren, so dass beidseitig unten scharfe Kanten entstehen. Mit der gezackten Seite des M 8 wird der Körper längs gekerbt. M 1 grenzt eine Linie nach unten ab. | 1 |
Die Fläche unterhalb der abgrenzenden Linie schräg einkerben. Den Schneckenkörper vorn geschwungen anheben und mit M 5 die Stecklöcher für die „Fühler" einbringen. Über ein Rundholz gestützt werden die Fühler angebracht und mit M 2 die Augenhöhlen eingedrückt. | 2 |
Mit M 3 den Mund modellieren. | 3 |
Die Schnecke hautfarben grundieren und leicht mit Braun nachsprühen. Augen einsetzen, Gesicht schminken.
Eine lange, sich verjüngende Stange herstellen und zu einem Schneckenhaus einrollen. Mit M 11 Rillen eindrücken. Alles gelb grundieren und spiralförmig mit Braun nachsprühen. So entstehen die ersten Streifenmuster. Mit weißer Farbe in die noch feuchte Grundierung den Mittelstreifen schminken.
Die Tasche aus einem Stück modellieren, Lasche und Riemen mit M 1 abgrenzen.
Getrennt von der Schnecke schminken und schließlich ansetzen.
Das Schildchen "No stress!" vervollständigt die Express-Schnecke.

> To make the body of the snail, roll out some marzipan, use your fingers to model it to the work surface so that sharp edges are created on both sides. Use the jagged edge of the M 8 to insert the grooves along the body. Use M 1 to mark a line towards the ground. | 1 |
Make a slanted groove in the surface underneath the demarcation line. Lift the body of the snail at the front in a curve and use an M 5 to push in holes for the horns. Attach the horns, with support from a round block of wood, and use an M 2 to sculpt the eye sockets. | 2 |
Use an M 3 to model the mouth. | 3 |
Apply a skin-coloured base coat to the snail and follow on with a light touch of brown. Insert the eyes and colour the face.
Roll a long tapered marzipan strip and roll up to form a snail's shell. Use an M 11 to score the grooves. Apply a yellow base coat to everything and then spray with brown in a spiral motion. This makes the first stripe patterns. Use white paint to mark the centre stripe into the base coat while it is still wet.
Model the briefcase from one piece, using an M 1 to score the flap and straps.
Colour separately from the snail and then attach when ready. Make a little sign with the inscription "No stress!" to complete the ensemble.

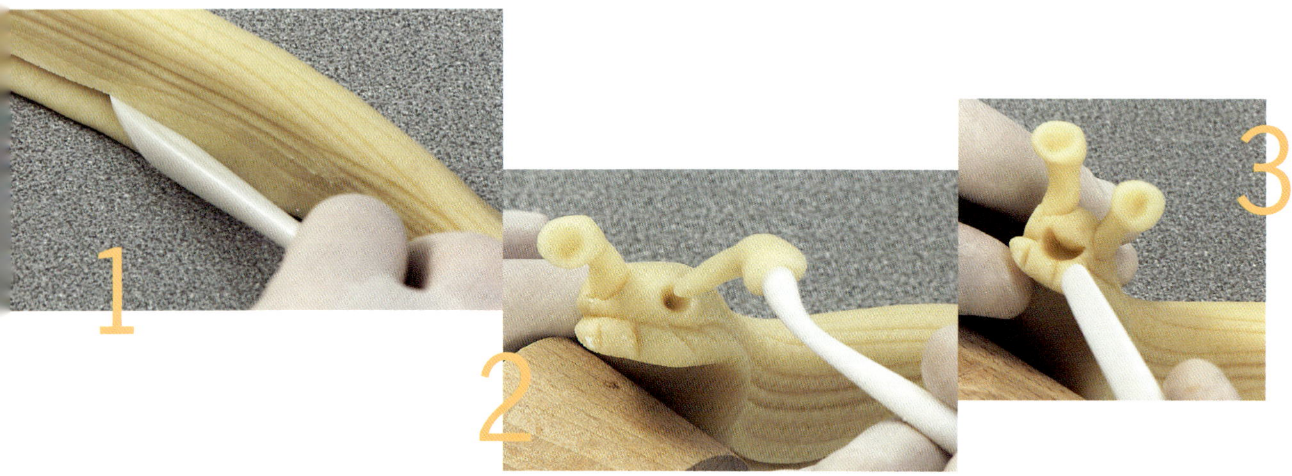

No stress!

No stress!

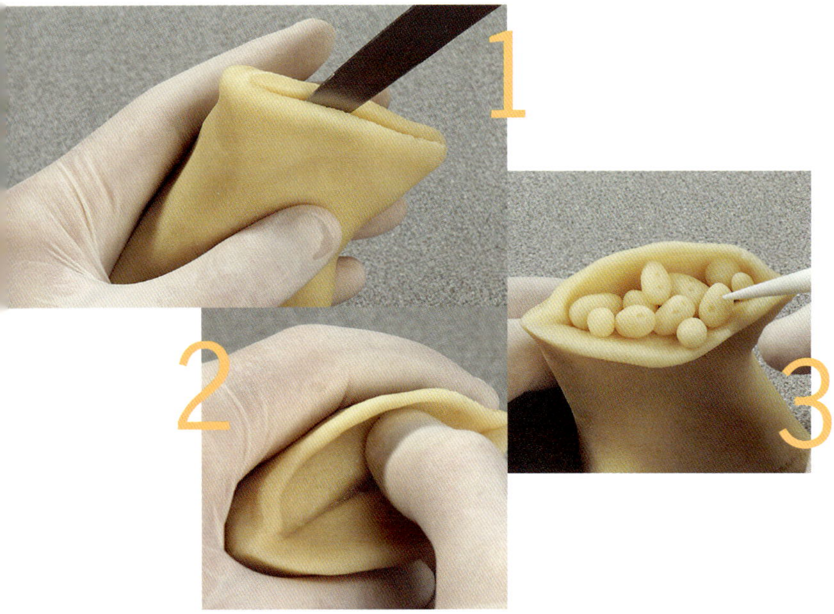

> Runde Grundplatte ausstechen und mit M 10 Fugen einbringen. Weiß grundieren und mit Braun schattieren. Fugen nachziehen.
Für den Sack ein kurzes Stück einer Marzipanrolle abschneiden, beide Enden flach drücken und Spitzen ausformen. Mit dem Messer die obere Öffnung einschneiden. | 1 |
Mit Daumen und Zeigefinger die Öffnung etwas erweitern. | 2 |
Viele unregelmäßig geformte Minikartoffeln rollen, in den Sack legen und dann mit M 4 „Augen" eindrücken. | 3 |
Die Figur des Kochs modellieren. Den Mund vorsichtig rund formen und mit M 4 eindrücken.
Die Kochmütze aus einer Marzipanstange fertigen. Für den Überhang die Stange über eine scharfe Tischkante rollen. Alle Falten mit M 1 einkerben. Den Koch gut abstützen und trocknen lassen. Beim Schminken der Figur die Augenbrauen nicht vergessen. Hoch angesetzte Brauen machen einen verwunderten bzw. erwartungsvollen Ausdruck.
Hühnchen modellieren und schminken.
Szene zusammensetzen und mit einem Schildchen versehen.

> Cut out a round base slab and use an M 10 to score the joints of the tiles.
Apply white base coat and spray with brown in different shades. Accentuate the joints.
To make the sack, cut off a short piece from a marzipan roll, press both ends flat and model into points. Cut the opening at the top end with a knife. | 1 |
Use thumb and forefinger to increase the opening a little. | 2 |
Roll a lot of irregularly shaped mini-potatoes, put them into the sack and use an M 4 to push in the characteristic eyes. | 3 |
Model the figure of the chef. Form the mouth carefully into a round shape and use an M 4 to make the hole in the middle. Make the chef's hat from a short roll of marzipan. To create the overhanging top end, roll the hat along a sharp edge of a table, then use an M 1 to score the folds. Support the chef well and leave to dry. Do not forget the eyebrows when you apply the colouring. If you set the eyebrows high, it will achieve a somewhat expectant or bemused expression.
Model the chicken and colour to suit.
Assemble the scene and finish off with a little sign.

A good chick ...

A good chick ...

Für die Jäger des erlesenen Geschmacks

For the punters chasing a select taste

> Für den Wäschekorb eine Styroporunterlage bereitlegen. Aus einer ungeraden Zahl von Schaschlikstäben ein Oval stecken. Eine Marzipanplatte als Boden einlegen. | 1 |
Dünne Marzipanstränge wellenlinienförmig um die Schaschlikstäbchen legen. | 2 |
Ist die gewünschte Höhe des Korbgeflechts erreicht, Körbchen beiseite stellen. Marzipanstäbe fertigen und mit dem Körbchen gut trocknen lassen. Die Hölzer entfernen und durch Marzipanstäbe ersetzen. Eine gedrillte, mit Spritzglasur angeklebte Marzipankordel bildet den oberen Abschluss des Körbchens. Zwei Griffe komplettieren den Korb. | 3 |
Alles gelb grundieren und nur ganz leicht mit Braun nachsprühen.
Wäschestücke aus einer Platte schneiden, mit M 11 Arm-, Bein- und Rumpföffnungen leicht einkerben.
Den Hund modellieren, die Schnauzenhaare mit der Schere einschneiden und nach der Grundierung etwas dunkler absetzen. Ein Marzipan-Shirt auf seine Pfoten legen, in Form bringen, ein paar Löcher einmodellieren und abgestützt gut trocknen lassen.
Die Grundplatte in Form eines Kleidungsstücks schneiden. Alles farbig schminken und zu einem Arrangement zusammensetzen. Ein frecher Spruch vervollständigt das Ganze.

> To make the laundry basket it is best to work with a polystyrene base. Spike an uneven number of wooden skewers into the base, making an oval shape. Place the marzipan slab between them as base for the basket. | 1 |
Prepare thin strands of marzipan which you weave around the wooden skewers. | 2 |
Once you have reached the required height of the woven sides for the basket, put it aside and leave to dry. Make some marzipan sticks and also leave to dry. Remove the wooden skewers and replace them with the marzipan sticks. The top edge of the basket is formed from a twisted marzipan string which is attached with icing. Finally add two handles to complete the basket. | 3 |
Apply a yellow base coat to everything and only a very light touch of brown spray.
Cut the pieces of laundry from a slab, then use an M 11 to lightly score the openings for arms, legs and the body.
Model the dog, using scissors to separate the whiskers; apply the base coat colour and then go over the whiskers in a darker shade. Place a marzipan shirt onto its paws, drape into the required shape, make a few holes so that it looks torn and then leave to dry on an appropriate support.
Cut the base slab in the shape of a piece of clothing. Apply colour to suit and then assemble the miniature. You can use the suggested caption or any other message that suits the occasion.

1

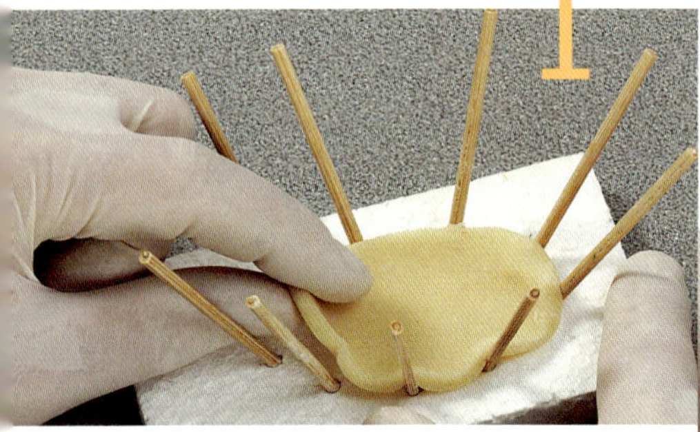

2

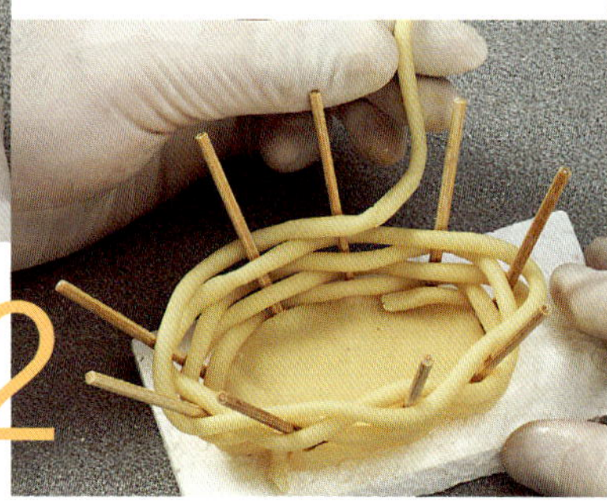

3

Time to say good-bye

Time to say good-bye

1

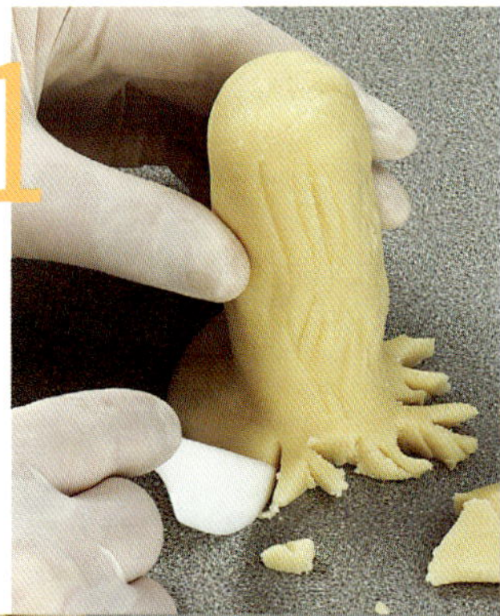

3

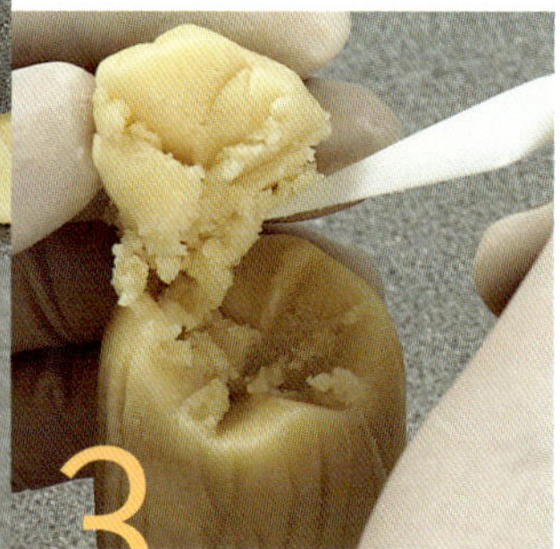

2

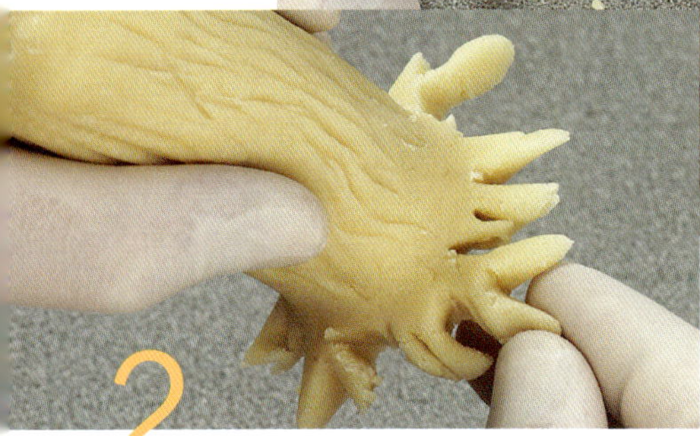

› Für den Baumstamm eine dicke Marzipanrolle fertigen, mit Daumen und Zeigefinger den Wurzelstock vorbereiten. Die Rinde entsteht mit M 1, das hin- und hergekippt durch das Marzipan gezogen wird. Auf den Sockel gestellt, werden die Wurzeln grob ausgeschnitten. | 1 |
Mit den Fingern abrunden. | 2 |
Für die Bruchstelle oben am Baumstamm Marzipan mit M 7 grob herausschneiden. | 3 |
Den Baum gelb grundieren und bis auf die Bruchstelle gut mit Braun nachsprühen. Ein vorsichtiges Übersprühen mit Wasser verstärkt die optische Struktur der Rinde. Den Besenstiel aus ummanteltem Holzstäbchen herstellen. Durch den Baum treiben und „Strohteil" anstecken.
Die Beine der Hexe vormodellieren, aber erst in getrocknetem Zustand anbringen. Körper mit Armen aus einem Stück formen und befestigen. Den Kopf aus einer einfachen Kugel andrücken. Die Haare durch ein Sieb drücken und üppig verteilen. Den Hut aus einer runden Scheibe herstellen, die partiell mit M 4 aus der Mitte heraus dünner gerollt wird. Daraus ergibt sich das Wellenmuster der Krempe. Den restlichen Teil des Huts aus einem Kegel formen. Mit M 1 das Band abgrenzen und den Knick einbringen. Die Figur gut trocknen lassen und mit dem Pinsel schminken, denn durch die vielen, dicht beieinander liegenden Farben eignet sich der Airbrush nicht besonders.

› To make the tree trunk, prepare a thick marzipan roll and shape the spread-out roots with thumb and forefinger. Use an M 1 to create the bark pattern, applying a rocking action while drawing it along the marzipan. Place the trunk on its base and cut out the root shapes. | 1 |
Use your fingers to round them off. | 2 |
Where the trunk has broken off, use an M 7 to model the wooden splinters. | 3 |
Apply a yellow base coat to the tree and then follow on with brown spray except where the tree is broken. Carefully spray with water to enhance the visual appearance of the bark. Make the broomstick from a skewer encased in marzipan. Drive it through the tree and push on the straw broom at the other end. Model the legs of the witch as a first step, but do not attach them until they are dry. Form the body and arms from one piece and attach them to the trunk. Shape the head from a single ball and push it onto the body. Make the hair by pressing marzipan through a strainer and spread it generously over the head. Make the hat from a round disc, which is rolled from the centre outwards using an M 4. This results in the wavy shape of the rim. Make the top part of the hat from a cone, using an M 1 to delineate the ribbon and to press in the kink. Allow the figure to dry well and then use a brush to decorate, since an airbrush is not particularly suitable here due to the many different colours in close proximity.

Don't drink and fly

Don't drink and fly

Alkohol am Steuer – nein danke!

Drinking and driving? No thanks!

Schreib' mal

Drop me a line

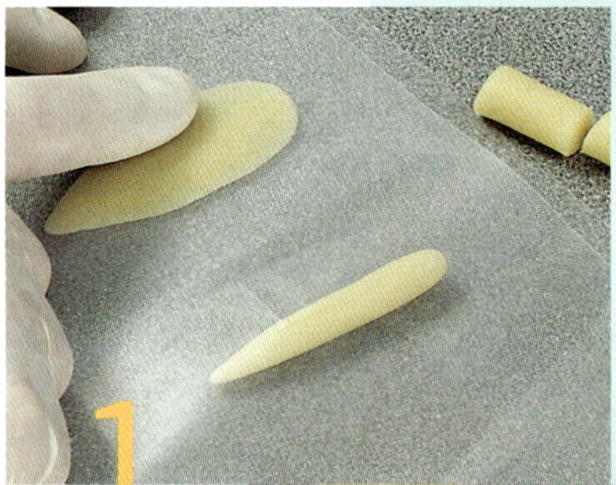

1

2

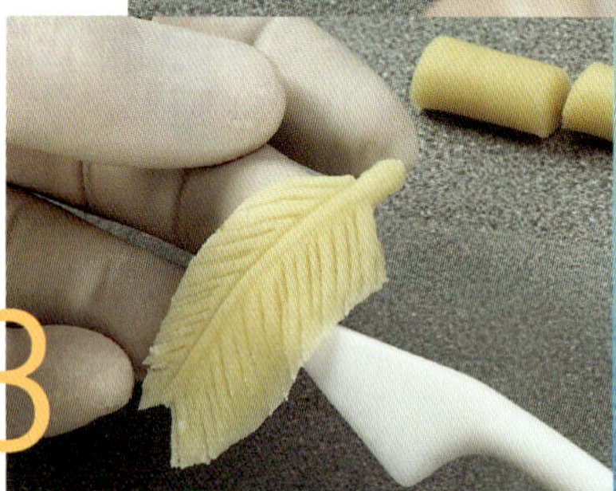

3

4

> Auf die ausgestochene „Wasserplatte“ kommt eine glatte Insel. Das Wasser flach und nur von einer Seite mit Blau besprühen. So ergeben sich sofort erste Lichtreflexionen. Eine kleine Aussparung für die Flasche ausstechen.
Für die Palme einen Ring aus einer Marzipanrolle formen. Aus gleich großen Marzipanstücken spitze Stangen rollen und zwischen zwei Folien platt drücken. Die Mitte etwas dicker lassen und nur die Ränder dünn machen. | 1 |
Mit der Doppelkante des M 10 den Mittelast des Blattes einkerben, mit M 7 die Rippen eindrücken. Die Spitze dreieckig kappen. | 2 |
Den Strunk des Blattes zuschneiden und alles von der Folie lösen. | 3 |
Die Blätter reihum über den Ring legen, dann noch einmal mittig. | 4 |
Ist das Blätterdach geschlossen, so muss es mehrere Tage trocknen, damit es freitragend stabilisiert ist. Mit Gelb sowie Grün färben und leichte braune Schattierungen anbringen. Der Stamm entsteht aus einer Marzipanstange, in welche ein Holzstab eingearbeitet ist. Mit M 1 Rillen eindrücken. Gut trocknen lassen, dann Kokosnüsse anbringen. Baumkrone mit Kuvertüre oder Spritzglasur gut ankleben. Zwei einzelne Palmblätter kaschieren den Ansatz des Stamms auf der Insel.
Die Flasche wird modelliert und in eine ausgestochene Aussparung in der Grundplatte eingefügt. Der einsame Insulaner kann aus einem Stück gefertigt werden.
Das Schild wird auch hier mit dem Lebensmittelfarbdrucker hergestellt.

> Cut out a round base plate, the surface of which you shape with wavy lines to represent the water. Spray blue on one side of the waves only to create the appearance of light reflections on water. Press on another smaller round disc for the island and cut out a hole for the bottom.
To make the palm, form a ring from a marzipan roll. Use marzipan pieces of equal size, roll them with a point and press them flat between two pieces of foil, making them thinner at the edges and thicker in the middle. | 1 |
Use the double edge of the M 10 to score the central rib of the leaf, and an M 7 to press in the ribs. Cut a triangular shape out of the tip. | 2 |
Trim the stalk of the leaf and lift everything from the foil. | 3 |
Place the leaves in a circular fashion around the previously prepared ring and then go round once again joining them at the centre. | 4 |
Once the canopy of leaves has been prepared it needs to dry out for several days so that it can support itself. Colour with yellow and green and also apply light brown shadings. The trunk is made from a marzipan roll which is reinforced with a wooden skewer. Use an M 1 to score the circular grooves. Leave to dry well, then apply the coconuts. Attach the head of the tree with couverture or with icing. Two individual palm leaves hide the join of the trunk with the island.
Model the bottle and stick into the previously cut hole. The lonely island inhabitant can be made from one piece.
Make the sign using your food colour printer.

PROFI **TIPP** *Als Inselbewohner bietet sich jede Figur an, die leicht von der Hand geht. Das kann vom Hasen bis zum Kamel reichen.*

The creature on the island can be any figure you find easy to make – it could be a rabbit or camel or anything else.

Motivation ist alles!

Motivation is everything!

› In eine lang gezogene Grundplatte mit der Doppelseite des M 1 Wellen einkerben. Den Schwimmer partiell modellieren und mit einem scharfen Messer an der Wasserkante abschneiden. Den Arm des Schwimmers zum Trocknen gut stützen. Schwimmer auf der Grundplatte anbringen, die Übergänge von der Figur zum Wasser mit etwas Flüssigkeit und M 3 kaschieren. Dazu mit dem Modellierholz einfach die Körperkontur nachfahren und leicht an die Grundplatte drücken. Das vermittelt den Eindruck, der Schwimmer würde im Wasser einsinken. Die kleinen Schaumkronen entstehen aus ungleichmäßig abgerissenen Marzipanteilchen, die mit M 12 leicht gepunktet werden.
Die Tauchermaske des „Begleiters" entsteht aus einem dünnen Marzipanband. Zwischen zwei Folien eine Platte ausrollen. Obere Folie ablösen, zwei unterschiedlich breite Streifen schneiden. Den breiteren direkt am Gesicht zu einer Taucherbrille formen und festkleben. | 1 |
Mit einer kleinen Schere die Länge anpassen. | 2 |
Der zweite dünnere Strang ergibt den Kopfriemen. Einfach anlegen und abschneiden. | 3 |
Die Hautfarbe mit dem Airbrush auftragen. Die kleinen Teile mit dem Pinsel schminken. Das Wasser blau besprühen. Da sich die Hautfarbe und das Blau des Wassers an den Übergängen vermischen, verstärkt sich der Eindruck von Transparenz des Wassers. Die Schaumkronen werden mit Weiß bepinselt und gesprüht.

› Score a long drawn-out base slab with the double side of the M 1 to represent the waves. Model the top part of the swimmer and then cut off with a sharp knife to leave just the part above the water. Support the arm of the swimmer whilst it is drying. Place the swimmer onto the base slab, making sure to smooth out the join between the figure and the water with a little liquid and an M 3. To do this simply use the modelling tool to follow the contours of the body and press slightly downwards towards the slab. This creates the impression that the swimmer is about to sink into the water. The small tufts of froth are made from unevenly torn-off pieces of marzipan which are then spiked a little with an M 12.
The diving mask of the "pursuer" is made from a thin marzipan ribbon. Roll out a slab between two foils, detach the upper foil and cut out two ribbons of different widths. Use the wider one to shape into goggles directly on the face of the swimmer and attach. | 1 |
Use small scissors to adjust the length. | 2 |
The second, narrower ribbon is used for the head strap. Simply place on the head and cut off. | 3 |
Apply the skin colour by airbrush but use a brush for the small parts. Spray the water in blue. This will lead to the colours of the skin and the blue of the water merging, which will increase the appearance of transparency of the water. Brush the tufts of froth with white and then spray.

1
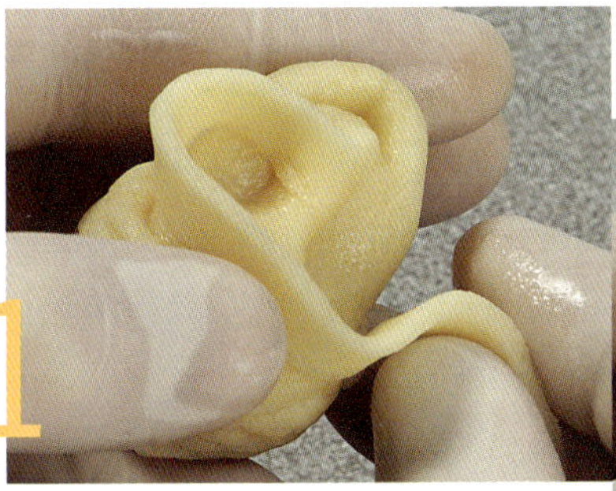
2
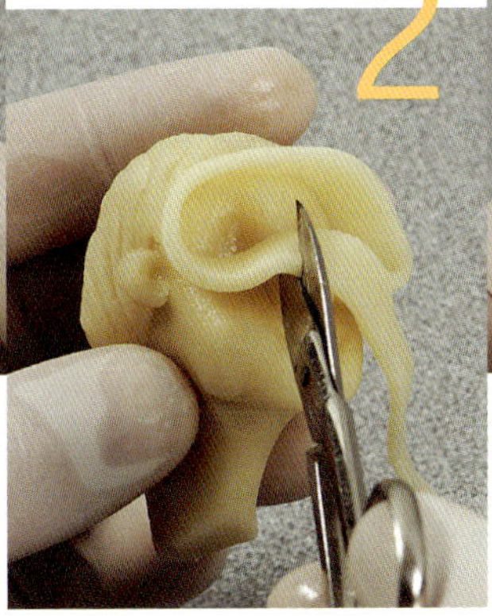
3
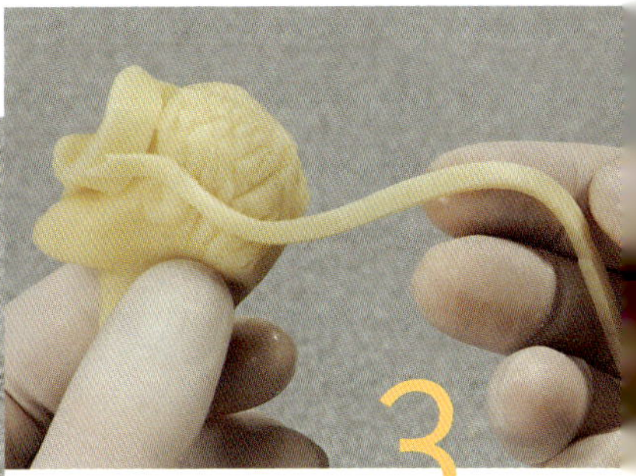

Keep cool!

Keep cool!

> Eine unregelmäßig geformte Grundplatte glatt ausrollen. Mit M 1 eine Eisscholle durch beherztes Eindrücken abgrenzen. Mit den Fingerkuppen das Wasser so gestalten, dass die Scholle erhaben hervortritt. Grundplatte weiß grundieren, Scholle vorsichtig mit Blau nachsprühen.
Den Körper des Eisbären aus einer platt gedrückten Kugel formen. Dafür zwei Seiten mit M 2 einkerben. Mit Daumen, Zeige- und Mittelfinger die Gliedmaßen länger modellieren. Ständiges schnelles Tippen verhindert das Reißen des Marzipans und ergibt eine runde Form ohne Druckstellen. | 1 |
Die Enden von Beinen und Armen platt drücken. Arme und Beine am Rumpf mit M 1 tief einkerben und einklappen. | 2 |
Mit M 2 den Bauch hervorheben. | 3 |
Den fertigen Körper nur noch in die richtige Form drücken und fixieren.
Den Bärenkopf aus einer ganz kurzen Birne modellieren. Die Schnauze einschneiden und eine Zunge anbringen. Für die Ohren zwei kleine Kügelchen mit M 2 eindrücken und am Kopf befestigen. Den Eisbären weiß grundieren. Leichte schwarze Schattierungen lassen das Eisbärenfell lebendiger wirken.

> Roll out an irregularly shaped base slab. Use an M 1 to mark out an ice-floe. Use your fingertips to shape the water surface so that the floe stands proud of the water. Apply white base coat to the base slab and lightly spray the floe in blue.
Shape the body of the polar bear from a flattened ball. Use an M 2 to indent the two sides. Model the limbs of the bear by elongating parts of the ball between your thumb, forefinger and middle finger. While doing this, constant rapid tapping with the fingertips prevents the marzipan from tearing and also results in a round form without flat areas. | 1 |
Press the ends of the arms and legs flat. Work a deep score where the arms and legs join the trunk, using an M 1, and fold into the desired position. | 2 |
Use an M 2 to accentuate the belly. | 3 |
Bend the completed body into the desired shape and fix into place.
Make the head of the bear from a very short bulb shape. Cut the snout and attach a tongue. To make the ears, sculpt two small balls with an M 2 and attach to the head. Apply a white base coat to the bear. Very light black shadings give more life to the fur of the polar bear.

PROFI **TIPP** *Farbige Vorlagen sind sehr hilfreich beim Schminken. Es empfiehlt sich, eine Sammlung von Abbildungen anzulegen – einfach aus Zeitschriften ausschneiden und nach Gruppen, z. B. Tiere, Technik, ablegen.*

When colouring a model it is very useful to have an image to copy from. We therefore recommend keeping a collection of pictures; they can be simply cut out from magazines, and filed under their respective headings, such as animals, technology etc.

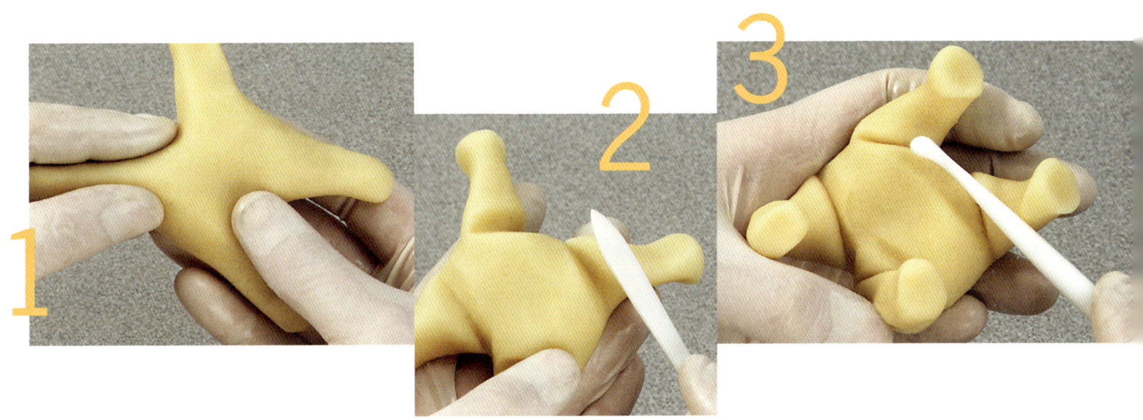

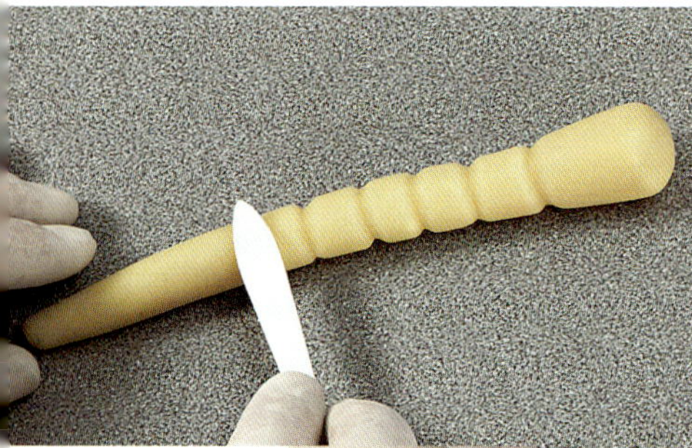

1

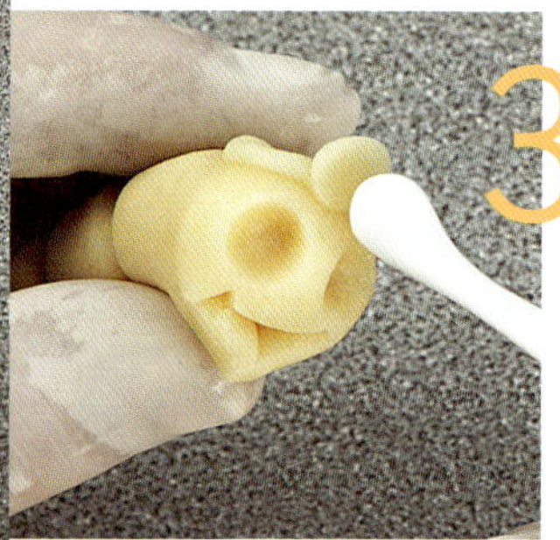

3

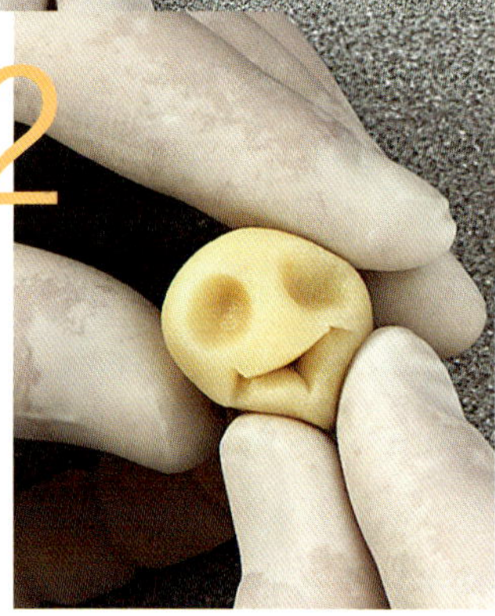

2

› Aus einer Kugel einen Apfel formen. Mit M 2 die Augen eindrücken. M 3 zum Einkerben des Munds und der Augenbrauen verwenden. Mit M 5 seitlich Vertiefungen zum Ansatz des Wurms eindrücken. Blatt und Stiel vorfertigen und trocknen lassen, dann mit Kuvertüre befestigen. Apfel gelb grundieren und mit „gerupftem" Borstenpinsel streifig röten. Die Farben Weiß und Schwarz mit feinem Pinsel auftragen.
Den Wurm aus einer Stange formen. Mit M 1 die Glieder einkerben. | 1 |
Kopf dicker lassen und nach den Augen ebenfalls mit M 1 den Mund eindrücken. Daumen und Zeigefinger formen das Kinn. | 2 |
Kleines Band als Spiegelhalterung anbringen. Aus kleiner Kugel mit M 2 den Spiegel an das Band drücken. | 3 |
Wurm teilen, die Schnittstellen zur Passung spitz modellieren, mit dem Airbrush flächig färben. Beide Teile am Apfel befestigen und mit Hölzchen bis zur Trocknung abstützen. Nach der Stabilisierung fertig schminken und Augen einspritzen.

› Form an apple from a ball. Use an M 2 to push in the eye sockets and an M 3 to score the mouth and the eyebrows. Use an M 5 to make impressions on the side to attach the worm. Make the leaf and stalk separately and leave to dry, then attach with couverture. Apply a yellow base coat to the apple and then use a bristle brush with uneven length bristles to paint on the red stripes. Use a fine brush to apply the white and black colours.
Shape the worm from a rolled strip and use an M 1 to score the segments. | 1 |
Leave the head a little thicker and then use an M 1 to push in the eye sockets and the opening for the mouth. Shape the chin with your thumb and forefinger. | 2 |
Attach a small ring on the head to hold the mirror. Make the mirror using an M 2 and push onto the ring. | 3 |
Separate the worm, narrowing the cuts to a point so that they fit into the holes and then colour the parts of the worm evenly with the airbrush. Attach both parts to the apple and support with sticks until dry. Once the exhibit is stable, complete the colouring and pipe on the eyes.

An apple a day keeps the doctor away

An apple a day...

Gutes Holz wärmt zweimal

Good wood warms twice

1

2

3

› Grundplatte unregelmäßig aus einer Marzipanplatte brechen. Mit M 12 wahllos riffeln. Aus verschieden dicken Marzipanstangen Stücke schneiden. Mit M 1 die Rinde imitieren. M 3 grenzt an der Schnittstelle die Rinde vom Holz ab. Alles mit Gelb grundieren und die Rinde mit Braun nachschminken.
Den Hackklotz auf der Oberseite mit M 7 wild einkerben, um ihm ein benutzes Aussehen zu verleihen. Eine tiefere Kerbe muss gesetzt werden, um später die Axt einzuklemmen.
Den Holzstapel schafft man rationell, indem man eine dickere Platte ausrollt. Mit M 8 die Rindenstruktur eindrücken. Die Breite der Holzscheite mit einem scharfen Messer vorgeben. | 1 |
Mit entgegengesetzten, schrägen Schnitten die Scheite schneiden. | 2 |
Die frischen Teile lassen sich einfach stapeln. | 3 |
Das Ganze gelb grundieren und mit dem Pinsel die Rinde braun nachschminken.
Die Axt entsteht aus einem Stück. Gut trocknen lassen und schminken. Wenn sie ausreichend stabil ist, in die Kerbe des Hackklotzes eindrücken.
Die Figur wie im Grundlagenkapitel „Modelliertechniken“ (ab Seite 232) beschrieben herstellen und in die entsprechende Haltung bringen. Gut gestützt härten lassen, dann schminken.

› Make an irregular shape from a slab of marzipan for the base slab. Use an M 12 to apply the irregular pattern.
Cut pieces from marzipan rolls of different thickness. Use an M 1 to create the bark pattern and an M 3 to score the demarcation between the bark and the wood. Apply a yellow base coat to everything and then colour the bark in brown.
Use an M 7 to apply a rough texture to the chopping block in order to give it a well-used appearance. One score needs to be quite deep in order to allow for the axe to be wedged into it later.
An efficient way of making the pile of wood is to roll out a thicker slab and using an M 8 to create the bark texture. Use a sharp knife to insert cuts for the width of the logs. | 1 |
Again using the knife, cut the individual logs inserting the cuts at different angles. | 2 |
The cut logs can be piled up into a stack while still fresh. | 3 |
Apply a yellow base coat to the whole pile and use the brush to colour the bark brown.
The axe is made from one piece. Leave to dry well and colour. When it is sufficiently firm, press the axe into the groove in the chopping block.
Make the figure as described in the basics chapter “Modelling Techniques” (from page 232) and shape into the desired position. Support well, leave to harden and then apply the colour.

PROFI **TIPP** *Kunden schätzen es sehr, wenn ein Exponat speziell auf den Beschenkten abgestimmt ist. Daher sollte immer nach der charakteristischen Kleidung, nach Haarlänge und -farbe sowie nach Bart, Zopf oder Ähnlichem gefragt werden, wenn die Bestellung aufgenommen wird.*

Customers place a particular value on an exhibit that has been specially designed with a particular person in mind. Therefore one should always ask about their favourite clothing, the length and colour of hair and beard and other characteristics when accepting the order.

› Die Grundplatte mit einem runden Ausstecher in Blumenform ausstechen. Gelb grundieren und die Ränder mit Rot nachsprühen. Weiße Striche ergeben eine hübsche Abgrenzung.
Die Blumentöpfe aus Stangenteilen schneiden. Durch ein Sieb gedrücktes Marzipan, gelb-grün besprüht, ergibt die Grundlage der weißen Blümchen. Diese entstehen einfach aus kleinen Kügelchen, die mit M 2 gedrückt werden. Die große Blume wird separat modelliert und getrocknet. Um genügend Halt zu garantieren, kann ein Holzstäbchen mit eingearbeitet werden. Nach guter Trocknung kann die Blume „gepflanzt“ werden.
Die Gießkanne entsteht aus einer platt gedrückten Rolle. Mit M 6 wird diese ein wenig ausgehöhlt. | 1 |
Eine dünn ausgerollte Platte mit einer Lochtülle ausstechen. Den Gießkannenkörper leicht anfeuchten und auf das Loch in der Platte stürzen. Mit M 7 den Rand abschneiden. | 2 |
Fein geglättet, ist der Ansatz nicht mehr zu sehen. Eine sich verjüngende Stange bildet den Gießrüssel. Aus einer längeren Marzipanrolle den Griff formen und an die Kanne ankleben. Mit entsprechender Unterbauung behält der Griff seine Form, bis er getrocknet ist. | 3 |
Die stabile Gießkanne gelb grundieren und grün nachsprühen. Auf die trockene Farbe können noch weiße Zierstreifen aufgemalt werden.

› To make the base slab cut out round shapes with a cutting tool and arrange into a flower. Apply a yellow base coat and then spray the edges in red. The white lines add extra attractive detail.
Cut the flowerpots from round sections. Some marzipan pressed through a strainer and sprayed in yellow-green colour makes the basis for the white flowers. These are simply made from small balls that are pressed with an M 2. The big flower is modelled separately and then dried. In order to guarantee enough structural strength you may want to incorporate a wooden stick. Once it has dried out well, the flower can be planted.
The body of the watering can is made from a flattened roll. Use an M 6 to hollow it out a little. | 1 |
To make the top, roll out a slab thinly and punch out a hole with a round piping nozzle. Slightly moisten the body of the watering can and then turn it onto the rolled-out slab, over the hole.
Use an M 7 to cut off any overhang. | 2 |
Smooth the join until it is no longer visible. The watering spout is made from a tapered roll, while the handle is made from a longish marzipan roll which is then attached to the can. Support the handle sufficiently until it is dry. | 3 |
Once the watering can has dried sufficiently, apply a yellow base coat and then spray in green.

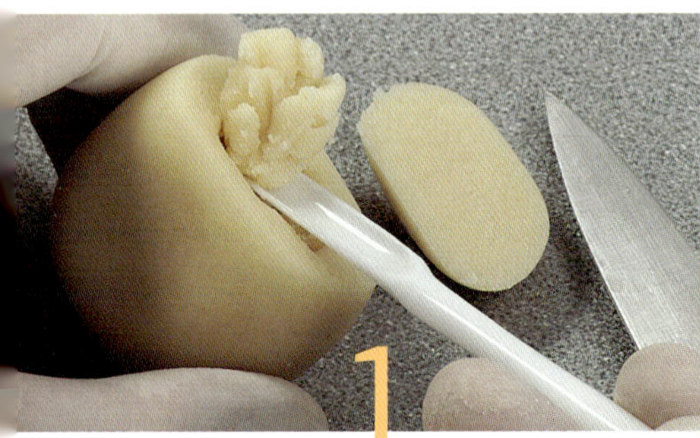
1

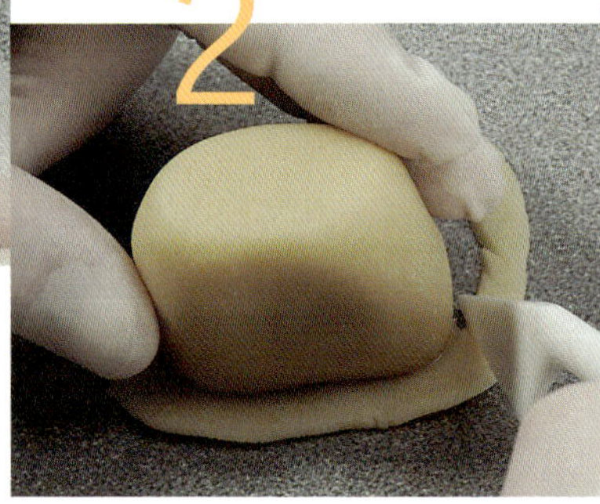
2

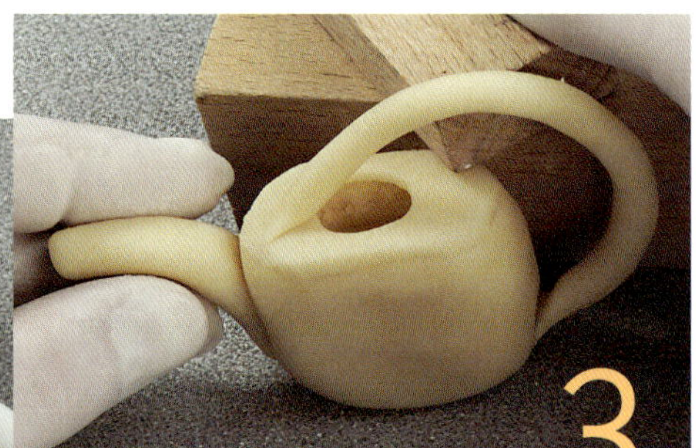
3

Danke fürs Urlaubs-Gießen

Thank you ...

Danke für die Hilfe

Thanks for your help

› Die Grundplatte aus drei Schichten herstellen und die jeweiligen Schichten aufeinander legen. In die unterste Platte mit M 11 den Gullydeckel einmodellieren. Die nächste Schicht gerade abschneiden und mit M 7 die Bordsteinkante herstellen. Die dritte und oberste Schicht ist unregelmäßig und bildet den Schnee. Eine Kerbe für die Schaufel einbringen. Alles weiß grundieren und die Straße leicht mit Schwarz schattieren. Den Gullydeckel mit dem Pinsel schminken.
Für den Baum einen Marzipankegel herstellen und mit der Schere die Äste einschneiden. Den Baum nur in die Schnittstellen hinein mit Grün schminken. Dann von oben mit viel Weiß nachsprühen. Die Schneeschaufel aus einer rechteckigen, über runder Unterlage getrockneter Platte herstellen. Die Schleifkante mit M 7 abgrenzen, mit Nagellöchern versehen und grau schminken. Den Rest gelb-braun besprühen.
Für den Stiel der Schneeschaufel eine lange Marzipanstange mit M 4 einkerben. Einen Schaschlikstab einlegen. | 1 |
Mit den Fingern das Marzipan um den Stab drücken und gleichmäßig über dem Holz verteilen. | 2 |
Wichtig ist, dass keine Lufteinschlüsse entstehen. Zum Schluss den Stab auf einer Unterlage rollen, bis er ebenmäßig ist. | 3 |
Mit der Schaufel verklebt ergibt sich die Schneeschippe.

› Make the base slab from three layers and place on top of each other. Use an M 11 to model the drain into the bottom layer. Cut off the next layer in a straight line and use an M 7 to model the edge of the pavement. The third and topmost layer is irregular and is textured to represent the snow. Insert a groove for the shovel. Apply a white coat to everything and a light shading of black to the road. Paint the colour for the drain with a brush.
To make the tree, use a cone-shaped piece of marzipan and cut the branches with scissors. Apply the green colour to the tree only in the area of the cuts, and then spray from the top with a lot of white. Make the snow shovel from a thin rectangular slab which is left to dry over a round support. Use an M 7 to mark out the front lip of the shovel, push in some nail holes and colour grey. Spray the rest in yellow-brown.
To make the handle of the snow shovel, cut a groove into a long marzipan roll with an M 4. Insert a wooden skewer. | 1 |
Dress the marzipan around the skewer with your fingers and spread evenly over the wood. | 2 |
It is important that no air bubbles remain inside. Finally roll the handle on a worktop until it is completely smooth and even. | 3 |
Attach the handle to the blade to complete the snow shovel.

PROFI **TIPP** *Wen es stört, dass der Stiel nicht essbar ist, der findet im Süßwarenangebot gebackene Sticks, die sich auch eignen. Vorsicht ist nur beim Verpacken geboten, da die Stabilität sehr begrenzt ist.*

If you don't like the fact that the handle cannot be eaten, you will find baked sticks that can be used and are available in the trade. However great care needs to be taken as these items are quite fragile.

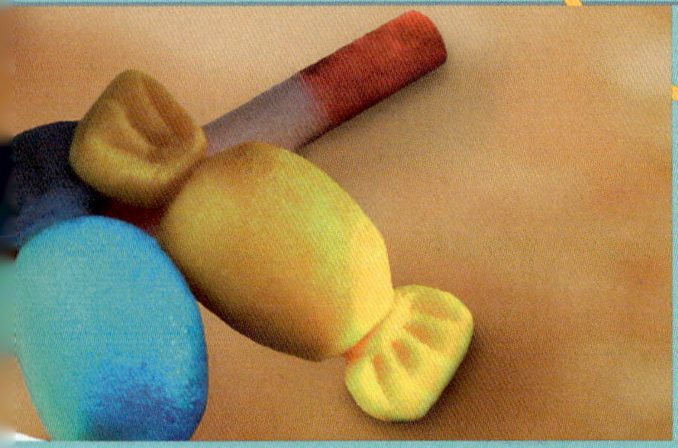

Best wishes

Das wünsch ich dir

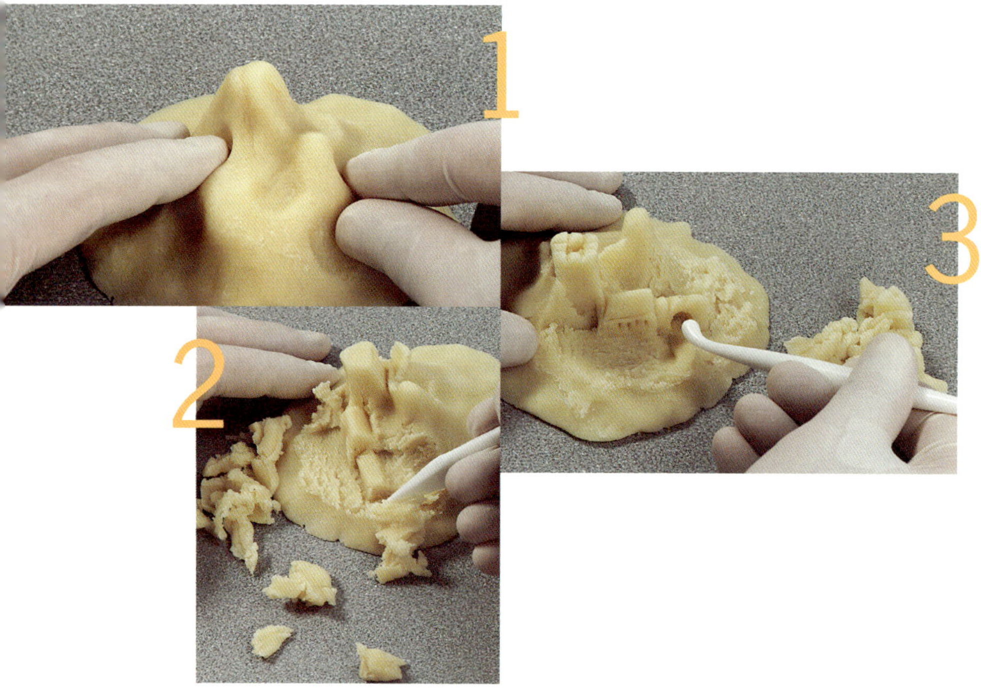

› Aus einer Kugel grob die Form einer Insel mit Erhöhung drücken. | 1 |
Mit verschiedenen Modellierhölzern, vornehmlich mit M 7, die Umrisse einer Burg ausschneiden. | 2 |
Fenster und Torbögen eindrücken. | 3 |
Sandburg mit Gelb grundieren, zart mit Braun nachsprühen und dann kräftig mit Wasser einschwemmen. Dadurch kommen die Vertiefungen gut zur Geltung.
Den Seestern ausstechen und alle Kanten abrunden.
Eimer und Tragebügel getrennt herstellen und trocknen lassen. Mit etwas Spritzglasur zusammenkleben.
Schaufel und Rechen modellieren.
Alle Einzelteile trocknen lassen, schminken und dann arrangieren.

› Use a ball to roughly shape an island with a mound. | 1 |
Cut out the contours of a castle using several different modelling tools, primarily with an M 7. | 2 |
Shape the windows and arches for the doors. | 3 |
Apply a yellow base coat to the sandcastle, followed by a slight brown spray and then quite a vigorous spray of water. This highlights the indentations.
Cut out the starfish and smooth off all edges.
Make the bucket and handle separately and leave to dry; then join together with icing. Model the spade and rake.
Leave all parts to dry, apply the colour and arrange to suit.

Nice days at the beach

Nice days at the beach

Die besten Wünsche für einen entspannenden Urlaub
Best wishes for a relaxing holiday

PARIS
BERLIN
Gute Reise
MILANO
Roma

Gute Reise
Have a nice trip

> Aus ausgerolltem Marzipan die Grundplatte in Form eines Pfeils schneiden. Mit Gelb und Rot schminken, trocknen lassen und dann mit konzentrierter weißer Farbe die Schrift und die Zierlinie aufbringen. Das geschieht am besten mit zwei verschieden dicken Pinseln. Mit Schwarz die Buchstaben abgrenzen.
Den Wanderstock aus einer Stange biegen und trocknen lassen.
Aus einem dicken Marzipanrechteck entsteht der Koffer. Alle Kanten abrunden und mit M 7 den Öffnungsspalt und die Beschläge einritzen. Ein kleiner Marzipanstrang bildet den Griff. Koffer und Stock erst gelb, dann braun besprühen. Mit silberner Lebensmittelfarbe die Spitze des Stocks schminken. Für die Beschläge bietet sich hier goldene Farbe an. Städteschilder mit dem Lebensmittelfarbdrucker erstellen.
Die Hutschachtel von einer dicken Marzipanrolle abschneiden und mit einer Deckelkante versehen. Den Tragebügel aus einer dünnen Platte schneiden, zurechtbiegen und trocknen lassen. Erst nach guter Trocknung senkrecht stellen und anbringen.

> Roll out some marzipan and cut out the base slab in the shape of an arrow. Apply yellow and red colour, leave to dry and then put on the writing and the decorative line in concentrated white paint. This is best carried out with two brushes of different thickness. Accentuate the letters in black.
Bend the walking stick from a rolled strip of marzipan and leave to dry.
The suitcase is made from a thick marzipan rectangle. Smooth off all edges and use an M 7 to score the line where the two halves meet as well as the buckles. A small marzipan strand is used to make the handle. Apply a yellow spray coat to the suitcase and walking stick, followed by brown. Paint the tip of the walking stick with silver food colouring. The buckles are best coloured in gold. Make the names of the cities with the help of your food colour printer.
Cut the hatbox from a thick marzipan roll and sculpt an edge on it to represent the lid. Cut the carrying handle from a thin slab, bend to shape and leave to dry. Once dry, place vertically and attach.

PROFI **TIPP** *Um die weiße Lebensmittelfarbe zu höherer Konzentration zu bringen, sollte frühzeitig ein großer Schuss Farbe in ein kleines Behältnis geschüttet werden. Nach einigen Stunden ist ein Teil der Flüssigkeit verdampft, und die weißen Pigmente sind konzentrierter. Mit solcher Farbe lassen sich feine Linien aufmalen, die an den Konturen nicht ausfließen.*

To make white food colouring in a stronger concentration, pour some of the colouring into a small container in good time. After some hours, part of the moisture will have evaporated and there will be a greater concentration of white pigment. This can then be used to paint on fine lines that will not run.

> Grundplatte in Form einer Zahnbürste mit scharfem Schneiderad aus einem Stück schneiden. Die Borsten mit M 7 eindrücken.
Instrumente aus einer Stange formen. Das Spiegelglas mit M 3 eindrücken. Die Griffe mit M 9 längs kerben. Auf einer schrägen Unterlage gestützt, trocknen die Spitze und der Spiegel abgewinkelt. Weiß grundieren und mit Schwarz leicht nachsprühen.
Der Zahn entsteht aus einer Marzipanstange. Diese unten spitz modellieren. Mit einem scharfen Messer drei Stücke teilen. | 1 |
Die drei Zacken mehr oder weniger rund modellieren. Oberhalb der Wurzeln den Zahn leicht taillieren und mit M 2 die Oberfläche „zahntypisch“ formen. | 2 |
Mund mit M 3 einritzen. Die Augenbrauen aus kleinen Segmenten anbringen. | 3 |
Den Zahn einfach weiß schminken und abgestützt trocknen lassen.
Sind alle Einzelteile stabil, werden sie erst probeweise gelegt und dann geklebt.

> Use a sharp cutting wheel to cut the base slab from one piece in the shape of a toothbrush. Use an M 7 to sculpt the bristles.
Form the instruments from a rolled piece. Indent the mirror glass with an M 3 and use an M 9 to score the handles lengthwise. Support the point of the instrument and the mirror at an angle on a sloping support. Apply a white base coat and then spray lightly with black.
The tooth is made from a marzipan roll. Model this to a point at the bottom and use a sharp knife to separate the end into three parts. | 1 |
Model the three jagged points more or less round. Above the roots, give the tooth a slight indentation, then use the M 2 to shape the tooth in the typical fashion. | 2 |
Use an M 3 to score the mouth. Attach the eyebrows from small segments. | 3 |
Simply apply white colour to the tooth and leave to dry while supported.
Once all parts have dried sufficiently, put them into place on a trial basis and then attach together.

PROFI ***TIPP*** *Besteht ein Exponat aus mehreren Einzelteilen ist es meist sinnvoll, diese getrennt voneinander zu schminken und zu trocknen. Ehe das Arrangement zusammengeklebt wird, sollten die Einzelteile zur Probe gelegt werden.*

If an exhibit consists of several individual parts it usually makes sense to colour and dry these separately. Before putting the scene together permanently, it is advisable to place them together on a trial basis.

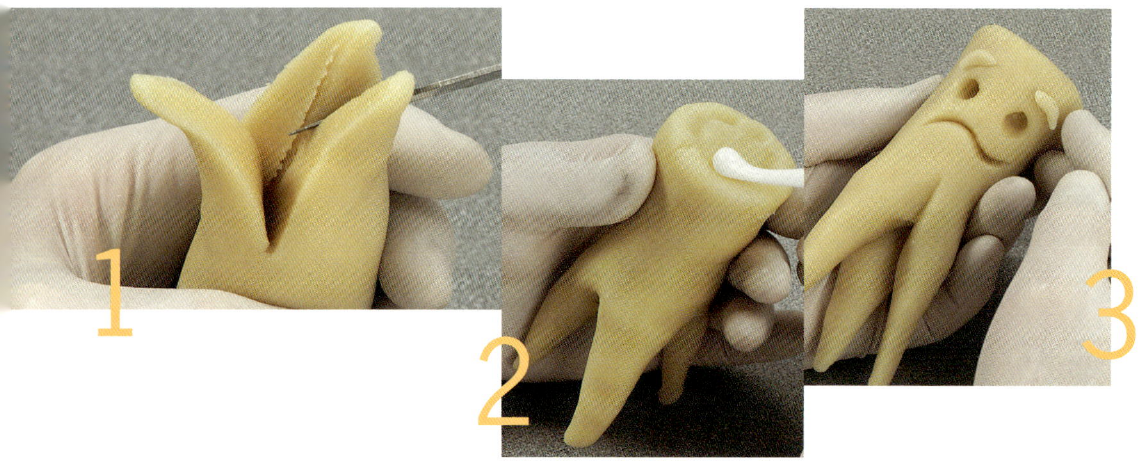
1 2 3

No panic

No panic

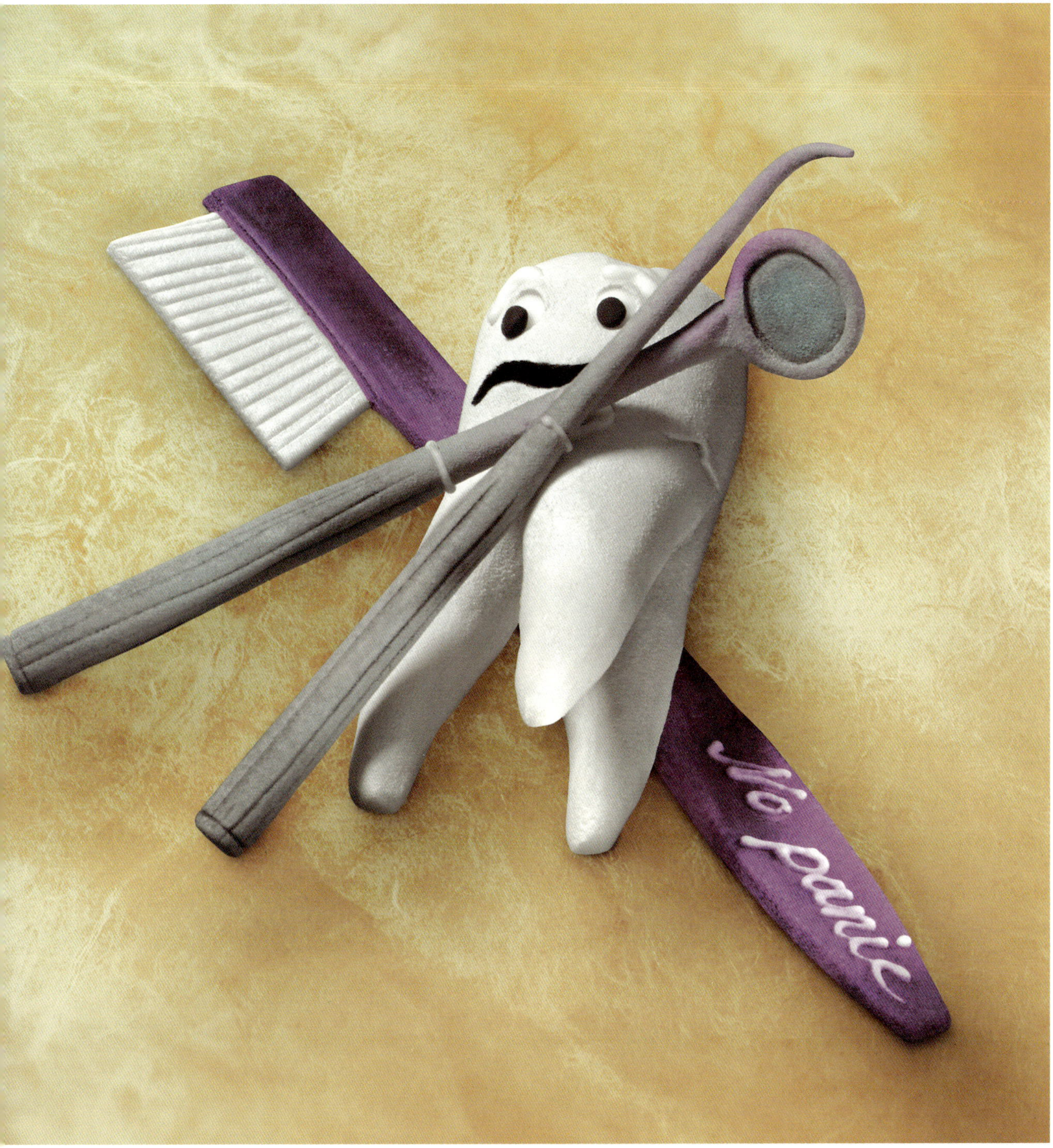

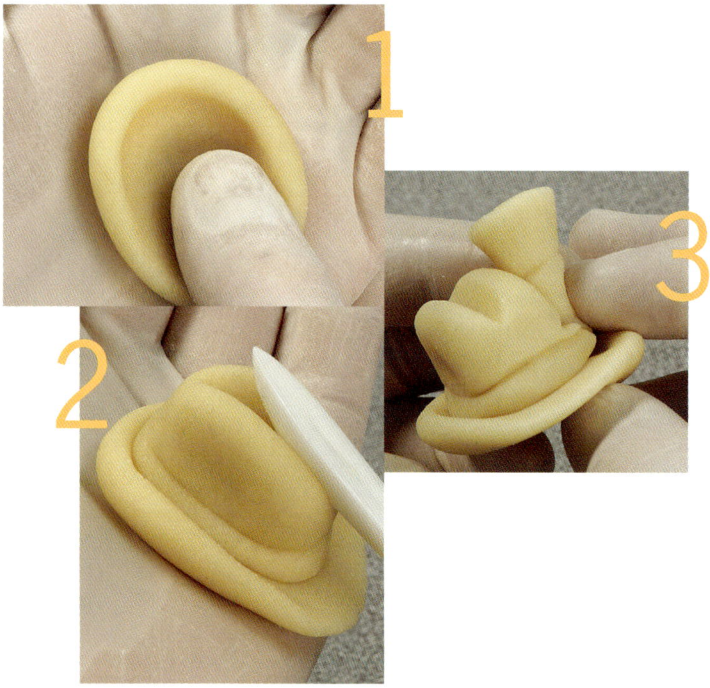

› Grundplatte frei ausschneiden, umdrehen, Kanten abrunden und zurückdrehen.
Mit M 10 kleine Grasflächen einrollen. Gelb grundieren, Grasflächen grün, den Rest braun nachsprühen.
Wie in "Don't drink and fly" (Seite 196) beschrieben den Baumstumpf modellieren.
Das Gewehr aus einer spitz zulaufenden Stange modellieren. Mit M 1 Lauf und Holzteil gegeneinander abgrenzen. Gut trocknen lassen, damit das Gewehr gleich an den Hasen anmodelliert werden kann.
Den Hasen wie gewohnt herstellen, nur die Arme etwas länger halten, damit sie um die Flinte herumreichen. Beim Modellieren das Gewehr gleich integrieren und abgestützt trocknen lassen.
Den Förster modellieren und stützen. Den Kopf flach abschneiden. Aus einer Kugel die Hutkrempe drücken. Dazu reicht der Daumen, denn nach vorn ist die Krempe offen bzw. flach. | 1 |
Eine zweite Kugel an die Unterlage modellieren. Mit M 1 das Hutband andeuten. Zusammengefügt braucht es nur noch eine Mittelkerbe. | 2 |
Aus einem Kegel entsteht der „Gamsbart". | 3 |
An den Hut kleben und alles grün grundieren.
Den Gamsbart mit dem Pinsel schwärzen und die Halterung grau schminken.

› Cut out the base slab in a free shape, turn over to smooth the edges and then turn back.
Use an M 10 to roll the small patches of grass.
Apply a yellow base coat, then spray green on the grass areas and brown on the other surfaces.
Model the tree trunk as described in "Don't drink and fly" (page 196).
Model the rifle from a strip that has been rolled to a point, using an M 1 to score the demarcation between the wood and the barrel. Leave to dry well so that the rifle can be used to drape the hare around.
Make the hare in the usual fashion, except that the arms should be a little longer so that they reach around the rifle. When modelling the figure it is best to integrate the prepared rifle; provide adequate support for drying.
Model the forester and support for drying. Cut off the head flat. Use a ball to make the rim of the hat. To do that you only need your thumb because towards the front the rim remains open, i.e. flat. | 1 |
Model a second ball onto the rim and use an M 1 to mark the ribbon for the hat. Once joined together, it only needs a groove in the middle. | 2 |
Make the tufted hat decoration from a cone. | 3 |
Attach this to the hat and then apply a green base coat to everything. Use the brush to paint the hat decoration black and the holder grey.

Weidmannsheil!

Happy hunting!

Damit der Schuss nicht nach hinten losgeht!
So that the shot does not backfire!

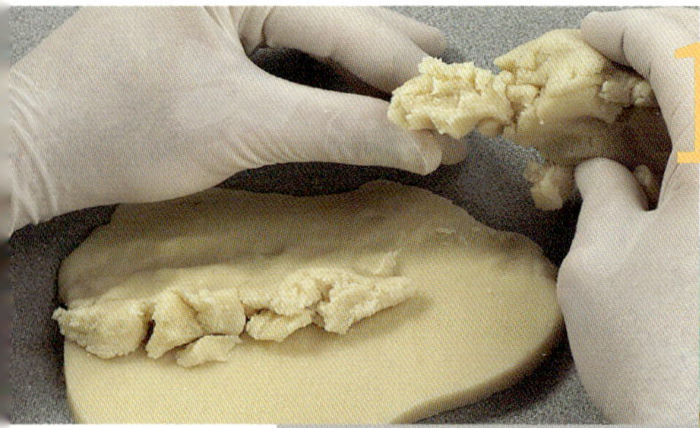

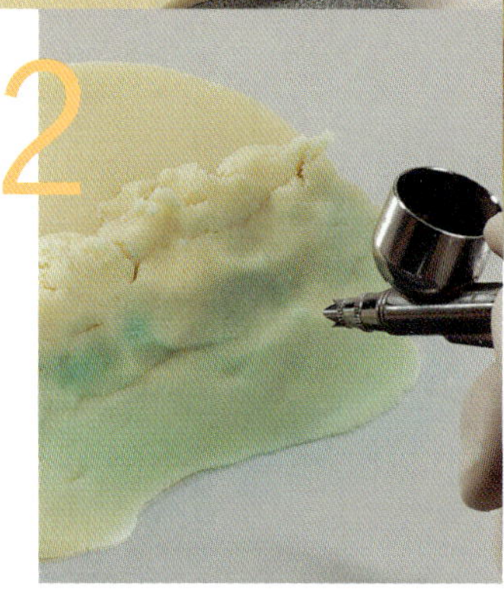

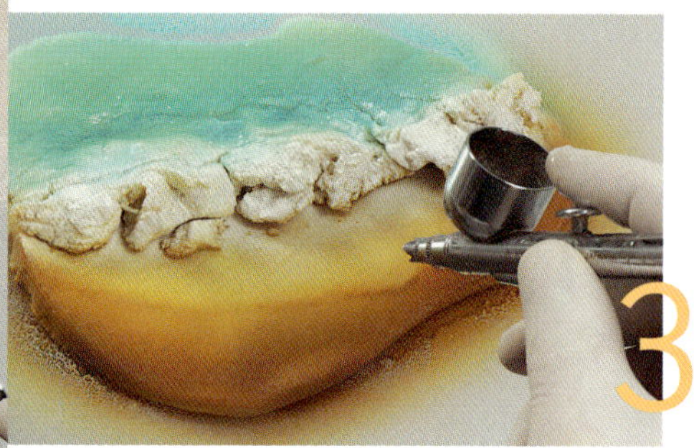

> Die Grundplatte frei ausschneiden, Kanten abrunden. Aus einem angetrockneten Marzipanstück Teile abbrechen. Die krümelige Struktur nach vorn ausrichten, um den Wellenschaum zu imitieren. |1|
Nach hinten die Teile flach modellieren. Die entstehenden Dellen sind durchaus erwünscht, da sie der Wellenform entsprechen. Das Wasser von hinten her blau schminken. Zur Gischt hin soll die Farbe auslaufen. |2|
Den Strand mit Gelb grundieren, die Wellenkrone weiß besprühen. Vom Rand her mit Braun färben, aber zur Welle hin verblassen lassen. Ganz zum Schluss ein Band im Übergangsbereich von der Welle zum Land mit Wasser nachsprühen. Das ergibt eine sehr natürliche Farbmischung. |3|
Die beiden Holzpfähle entstehen aus Marzipanstangen, in deren Innerem je ein Holzstab steckt. Die oberen Enden mit dem Finger flach tippen und entsprechend schminken. Zwei dünne Marzipanbänder verbinden beide Pfähle.
Einfache Accessoires, wie Ball, Schwimmring und Seestern, beleben die Szenerie.

> Cut out the base slab and round off the edges. Break bits out of a dried piece of marzipan, arranging the jagged edges forward in order to imitate the froth on the waves. |1|
Model the parts flat towards the back. The indentations are a welcome side effect as they simulate the waves. Apply blue paint to the waves from behind. Towards the froth the colour should run out. |2|
Apply a yellow base coat to the beach, and white to the peaks of the waves. Start on the edge with brown colouring but let this fade away towards the wave. At the very end, spray some water in the transition zone from the wave to the land. This will result in a very natural mixture of colours. |3|
Make the two wooden posts from marzipan sticks, reinforced with a wooden skewer. Slightly tap the top ends with your fingers until flat and colour to suit. Two thin marzipan ribbons are used to connect the posts.
Simple accessories, such as the ball, the rubber ring and the starfish add extra interest to the scene.

Viel Spaß am Meer

Have fun by the sea

Sonne, Strand und Erholung pur!

Pure bliss with sun, sea and sand!

Take it easy

Take it easy

> Die Grundplatte besteht aus drei Hantelscheiben mit verschiedenen Gewichten. Dafür aus einer etwas dickeren Platte drei im Durchmesser abgestufte Scheiben ausstechen. Das Mittelloch ist bei allen gleich. Mit M 3 die äußere und innere Abgrenzung einarbeiten. Die Gewichtsangaben mit M 7 einritzen. Ganz leichte weiße Grundierung, gefolgt von starkem, schwarzem Auftrag, ergibt nach dem Übersprühen mit Wasser die gewünschte Optik.
Die Hantel des Gewichthebers aus zwei dicken Stangenteilen herstellen. Diese mit M 7 so einkerben, dass jeweils der Eindruck von drei aneinander gereihten Scheiben entsteht. Zwei kleine Scheiben bilden mit einem kleinen Stangenteil den Abschluss. Die Hantelstange ist ein Holzstab. Diesen grau schminken, während die Scheiben schwarz gehalten werden.
Der Körper des Affen zeichnet sich durch eher kurze Hinterbeine und durch besonders lange und kräftige Arme aus. Dies beim Modellieren berücksichtigen. Den Kopf extra herstellen. Aus einer Birnenform die Schnauze herausmodellieren. Mit M 3 den Mund einkerben. | 1 |
Die Zähne mit M 7 andeuten und mit M 1 die Stirnfalten eindrücken. | 2 |
Zwei kleine Kugeln ergeben die Ohren. | 3 |
Die Nasenlöcher mit M 1 einbringen. Am Hals abschneiden und mit etwas Feuchtigkeit am Rumpf befestigen. Beim Schminken Hände und Gesicht mit Hautfarbe besprühen. Die Zähne mit konzentrierter weißer Farbe nachschminken.

> The base slab consists of three dumb-bell discs of different weights. To make these, cut three discs from a somewhat thicker slab, which are different in diameter. The central hole for all discs is of the same size. Use an M 3 to sculpt the demarcations inside and outside. Use an M 7 to indicate the weight. Apply a very slight white base coat, follow up with a heavy application of black and then with a spray of water in order to achieve the desired visual effect.
Make the dumb-bells from two thick roll sections, which are scored with an M 7 so that the impression of three discs in a row is created. Two small discs and a piece of bar form the ends. The bar itself is a wooden skewer. Paint this grey whereas the discs are kept in black.
The body of the monkey has rather short hind legs and particularly long and strong forearms, which is particularly important here. Make the head separately. Form the snout from a bulb shape and use an M 3 to score the shape of the mouth. | 1 |
Indicate the teeth with an M 7 and use an M 1 to mark the wrinkles on the forehead. | 2 |
The ears are made from two small balls. | 3 |
Push in the nostrils with an M 1. Cut off at the neck and attach to the body using a little liquid. Spray hands and face with skin colour and paint the teeth with concentrated white.

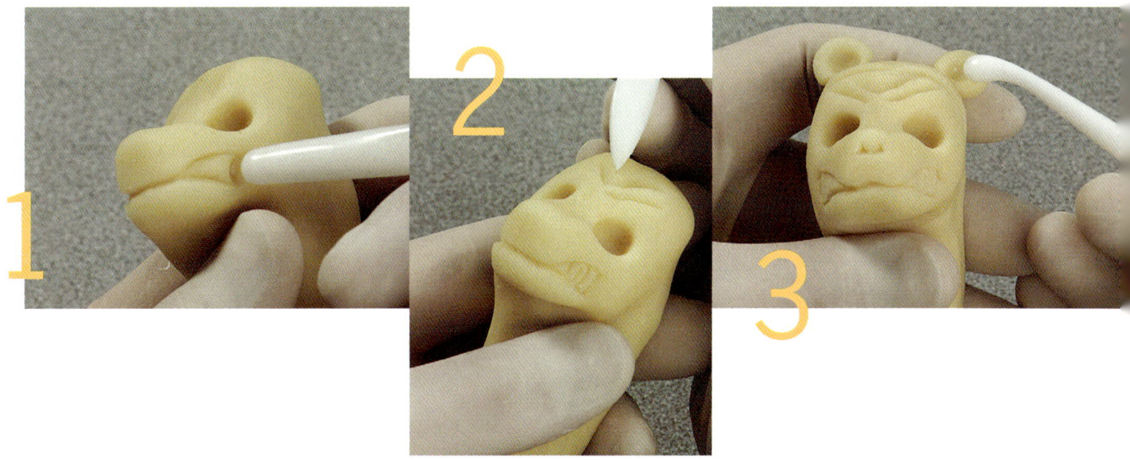

Happy diet!

Happy dieting!

› Den Körper des Nilpferds aus einer dicken Stange beginnen. Mit M 2 Arme und Beine an beiden Enden vorkerben. Mit den Fingern die Gliedmaßen rund modellieren. Die Fußsohlen glatt machen und mit M 1 Zehen eindrücken. Mit dem gleichen Modellierholz die Beinfalten einkerben. Einen Arm als Kopfstütze nach hinten legen, den anderen rechtwinklig aufstellen. Den Kopf aus einer Kugel beginnen. Diese mittig dünner modellieren. Mit scharfem Messer den Mund einschneiden. M 3 hilft beim Glätten der Schnittkante und beim Abgrenzen der Lippe. Ein platt gedrücktes Kügelchen ergibt eingekerbt die Zunge. Zwei kleine Tropfen bilden mit der Spitze nach oben und mit M 1 eingedrückt die Ohren. Zwei Nasenlöcher mit M 5 geformt vervollständigen den Kopf. Das Nilpferd mit Weiß grundieren, zart mit Schwarz nachsprühen. Maul, Nase, Ohren und Fußsohlen mit Rosa absetzen. Die Zähne rein weiß mit dem Pinsel schminken. Die Bartstoppeln entstehen ebenfalls mit feinem Pinsel.
Zuckerstangen und Bonbons modellieren und gut trocknen lassen.
Arrangement zusammenfügen und mit Schildchen vervollständigen.

› Start the body of the hippopotamus from a thick marzipan roll, using an M 2 to do the initial scoring of arms and legs on both sides. Then use the fingers to model the limbs into a round shape. Make the soles of the feet flat and use an M 1 to indicate the toes. Again use an M 1 to score the folds on the legs. Use one arm as a support for the head, place backwards and arrange the other one at right angles. Start modelling the head from a ball which you shape thinner in the middle. Cut in the mouth with a sharp knife. An M 3 is useful for smoothing the cut edge and marking the lip. Use a little ball with a groove in it to model the tongue. Two small drops with the pointed end upwards and sculpted with an M 1 represent the ears. Use an M 5 to push in the nostrils – the head is now complete.
Apply a white base coat to the hippopotamus, followed by a light spray of black. Use pink for the mouth, nose, ears and the soles for the feet. Use a brush to paint on the stubble and also to colour the teeth in pure white.
Model sugar candy and sweets and dry well.
Put the scenario together and complete with a sign.

Happy Diet !!

Have fun at the concert

Have fun at the concert

> Seerosenblatt aus einer Marzipanplatte schneiden. Mit M 3 die Ränder glätten und die Abgrenzung des Blattes eindrücken. M 1 zum Einkerben der Blattadern verwenden.
Für den Froschkörper eine große Birne formen. Aus der kleineren Rundung ein Froschmaul herausmodellieren. Mit einem scharfen Messer einschneiden und öffnen. Die Grübchen mit M 1 eindrücken. Aus zwei Kugeln entstehen mit M 2 die Augen. Den hinteren Teil des Körpers leicht spitz machen und dann abgestützt stellen. Aus vier Stangen entstehen die Gliedmaßen. Die längeren ergeben die Sprungbeine. Mit beiden Händen zwei Verjüngungen einrollen. | 1 |
Das untere Ende platt drücken und mit M 1 die Schwimmhäute andeuten. | 2 |
Die Beine in der Mitte knicken und am Körper befestigen. In gleicher Manier entstehen die anderen Teile. Die Arme sind kürzer und werden in dafür angebrachte Löcher eingeführt. | 3 |
Das erleichtert das Anbringen und stabilisiert den Arm. Mit Gelb grundieren und kräftig mit Grün nachsprühen. Maul und Augenbrauen mit dem Pinsel nachschminken.

> Cut the leaf of the water lily from a marzipan slab and use an M 3 to smooth the edges and mark the contours of the leaf. Use an M 1 to score the veins of the leaf.
To make the body of the frog, use a large bulb. Model the mouth of the frog from the narrower end, insert a cut with a sharp knife and open it up. Press in the dimples with an M 1. Make the eyes with an M 2 from two balls. Model the end of the body with a slight point and then place on an appropriate support. The four limbs are made from four rolled pieces, the longer ones being used for the hind legs. Roll between your hands to make a tapered shape. | 1 |
Press the lower end flat and use an M 1 to indicate the webbing. | 2 |
Bend the legs in the middle and then attach to the body. The other parts are made in the same manner. The arms are shorter and are inserted in the holes made for this purpose. | 3 |
This makes it easier to attach the arms and gives them some stability. Apply a yellow base coat and then spray liberally with green. Use the brush to paint the mouth and the eyebrows.

PROFI **TIPP** *Kleinere Figuren, wie hier die Biene, sind zwar sehr filigran in der Herstellung, beleben aber einfache Exponate. In Serie gefertigt wird der Aufwand geringer.*

Small figures such as the bee in this exhibit require quite a lot of detail when being produced but add extra interest to otherwise simple exhibits. When produced in series there is less effort involved.

1
2
3

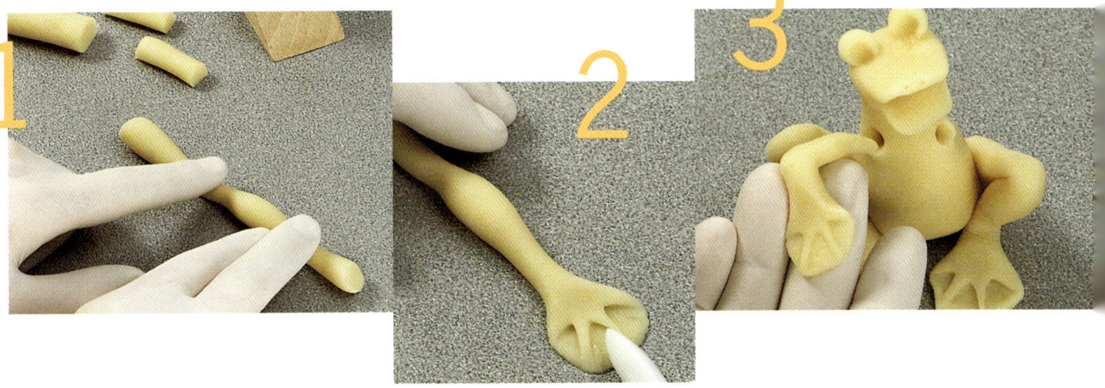

Basic Techniques

Grundtechniken

Modellieren

Modelling

› Für die Erstellung der Szenen in diesem Buch bedarf es meist der Verwendung von selbst angewirktem Marzipan ohne Frischhaltemittel. Handelsübliches Modelliermarzipan eignet sich nur für nicht tragende, flache oder statisch einfache Gebilde.
Es ist empfehlenswert, ausschließlich Marzipan von guter Qualität zu verwenden, das nicht zum Ölen neigt. Im Verhältnis zwei Teile Marzipan und ein Teil Puderzucker ergibt sich eine Rohmasse, die flexibel genug ist, um sich sauber formen zu lassen; dabei aber auch schnell genug trocknet, um gewagtere Figuren zu erstellen.
Das wichtigste Werkzeug sind unsere Hände. Wie wir die natürlichen Wölbungen der Handflächen verwenden, um Grundformen herzustellen, ist sicher jedem Leser geläufig. Kugel, Tropfen und Birne sind die Basis für die meisten Körper. Auch das Formen gleichmäßiger Stangen sollte keine Probleme bereiten. Mit diesem Können ist man bereits gut gerüstet, um sich in die Welt der kleinen Szenen zu wagen.
Eine Steigerung ihrer Brauchbarkeit erfährt die Hand durch den Einsatz von Modellierhölzern.

› To make the miniatures shown in this book you will in most cases need marzipan without preservative that you have prepared yourself. Modelling marzipan available in the trade is only suitable for structurally not supporting, flat and uncomplicated parts. In our experience consumers do not eat these exhibits but want to keep them as mementoes. For this reason, keeping the marzipan soft and fresh is not too important. This opens up some options and possibilities, which you will discover when reading these notes.
We would recommend only using good-quality marzipan, with no tendency to oiliness. When mixing two parts of marzipan and one part of icing sugar you obtain a basic mixture that is pliable enough to be moulded into the required shapes; at the same time it also dries quickly enough so that it is possible to make more daring constructions.
By far the most important tools are our hands which we always have with us. Each of us will know from experience how to use the natural shapes and curves of our hands, which are useful for many basic shapes. Most bodies are made of basic components such as balls, drops and bulbs. Another basic shape is the rolled bar or strip which we can produce without any problem. If you can master these simple things you are already well equipped to have a go in the world of miniatures. But to enhance the usefulness of your hands there are a number of modelling tools that make certain jobs easier.

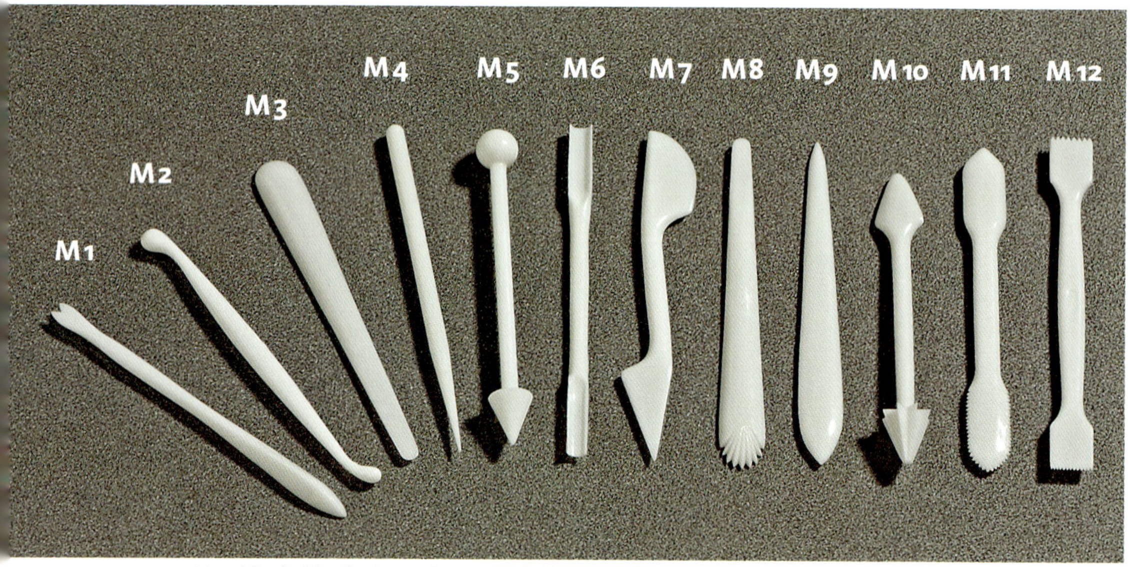

Die Modellierhölzer
Modelling tools

M = Modellierholz *M = Modelling tool*

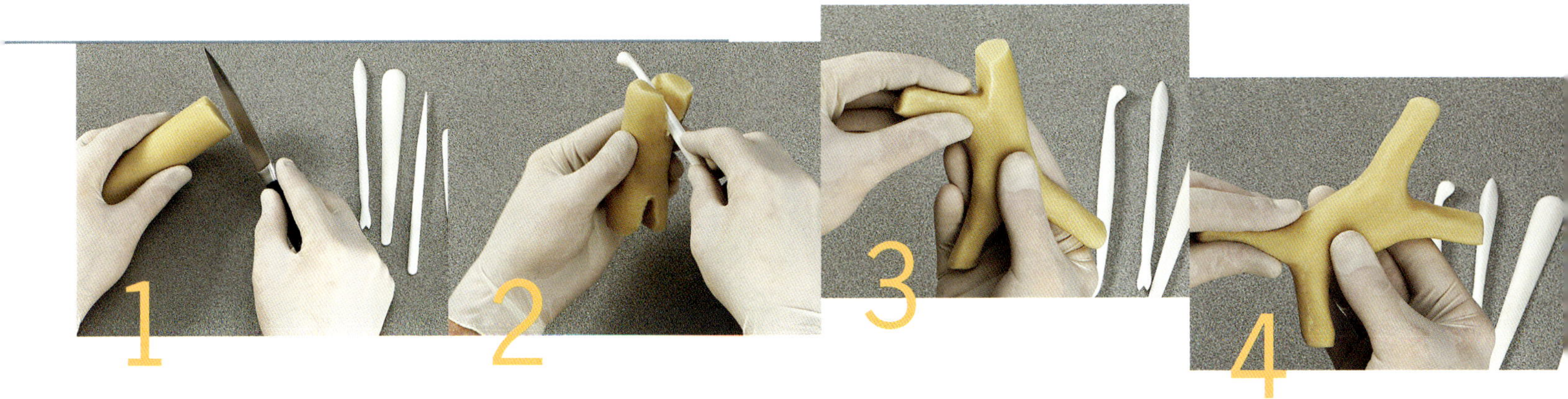

› Die zweifellos schwierigste Figur ist der Mensch. Gut vertraut mit seinen Formen fallen uns Fehler in einer Marzipanfigur schnell auf. Hände mit vier Fingern oder falsch ausgerichtete Daumen stechen sofort unangenehm ins Auge. Desgleichen verhält es sich mit den Füßen. Besonders die Proportionen stehen im Vordergrund. Ein zu großer oder zu kleiner Kopf „verdirbt" den Gesamteindruck. Proportionsgefühl kann man jedoch nicht einfach vermitteln, es muss mit jeder neuen Figur erarbeitet werden. Fangen Sie daher immer mit dem Körper eines Exponats an. Ist dieser gelungen, lässt sich die Kopfgröße durch das Anlegen einer entsprechenden Marzipankugel grob bestimmen. Scheint der „Kugelkopf" zum Rumpf zu passen, wird er ausgeformt. Mit diesen Grundsätzen gewappnet, wollen wir uns an die Erschaffung einer männlichen Figur heranwagen. Es entsteht ein Bräutigam. Die nun folgende Vorgehensweise steht stellvertretend für alle menschlichen Figuren, egal ob männlich, weiblich, alt oder jung.

Wir beginnen mit dem Körper. Eine Marzipanstange bildet die Ausgangsform. |1|

Schon hier legen wir die ungefähre Größe unseres Bräutigams fest. Mit M 2 oder M 4 arbeiten wir an beiden Enden der Stange eine tiefe Kerbe ein. |2|

Die entstehenden Teilstücke bilden fortan Arme und Beine. Proportional gehen wir bei jeder Kerbe um ein Drittel der Gesamtlänge in die Stange hinein. So bleibt ein Drittel der Form unversehrt. Dieses bildet fortan den Rumpf. Alle vier Gliedmaßen werden nun durch Tippen mit dem Daumen und Zeigefinger rund modelliert. |3| |4|

› No doubt, the most difficult figures to model are people. We are, as onlookers, quite familiar with people's shapes and appearance and any mistake in a marzipan figure will soon be noticed. Luckily, the human body also features a great variety of proportions so there is no disadvantage witha certain freedom of improvisation. Whether large or small, fat or thin, stocky or lanky, these are all things we accept without hesitation as they reflect the variations that occur naturally. However, the limbs are a little more tricky. You will immediately notice a hand with only four fingers or a thumb on the wrong side of the hand. And the same applies to the feet. Proportions are an important issue you should focus on. If a head is too large or too small, the overall impression is spoiled. A feeling for proportions cannot simply be taught. It has to be worked out with every new figure we try to model. For this reason I recommend that you always start with the body. Once you have successfully modelled the body, the size of the head can be roughly determined by making a marzipan ball of the right size. If it seems to be in the right proportion to the body, you can proceed with working on the details.

Having established these principles we will now try to create the figure of a man, in this case a bridegroom.

The procedure described below can be followed for all human figures, whether male or female, old or young.

We start with the body, beginning with a rolled piece of marzipan as the basic shape. |1|

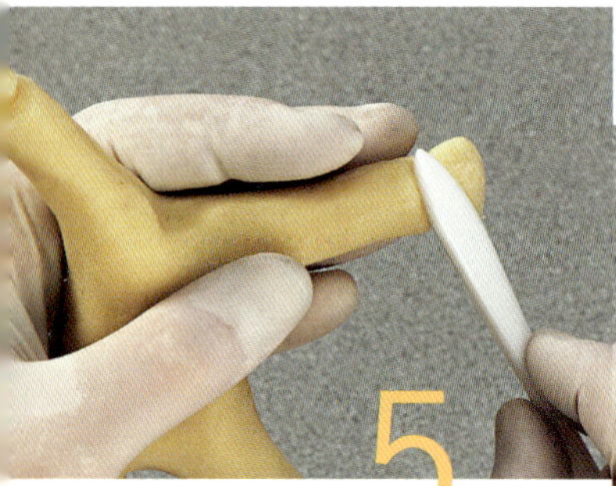
5

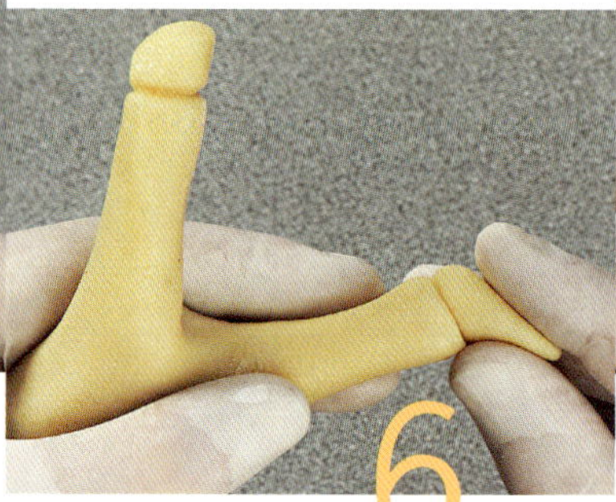
6

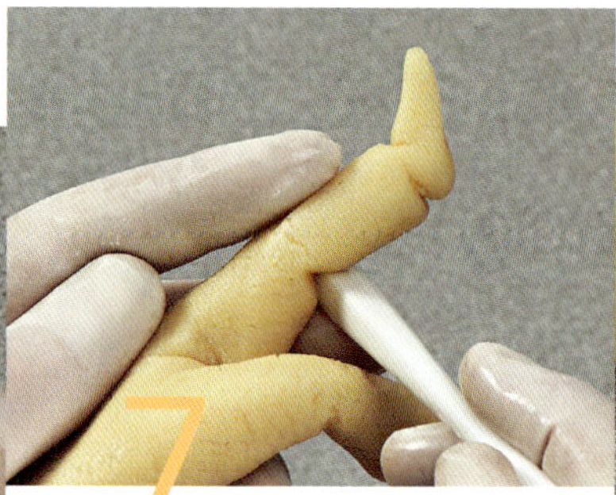
7

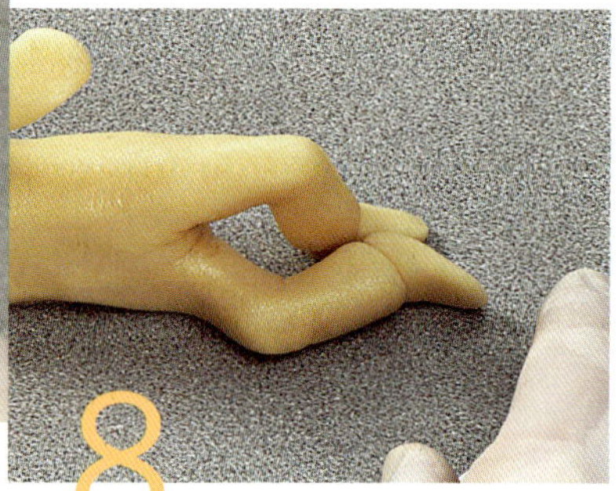
8

Die Enden abstumpfen. Mit der schärferen Kante des M 1 kerben wir die Hosenkante am Ende des Beins. | 5 |
Es entstehen die Füße. Diese beugen wir im 90°-Winkel und drücken sie an der Sohle platt. | 6 |
Die somit neu definierte Beinlänge wird von der Fersenseite her mit stumpfer Seite des M 1 mittig eingekerbt. So entsteht die Kniebeuge, und das Bein kann in anatomisch korrekte Formen gebogen werden. | 7 |
Das entstehende Knie muss jedoch mit Daumen, Zeige- und/oder Mittelfinger ausmodelliert werden, da durch den Beugevorgang Risse entstehen können. | 8 |
Sind die Beine so weit gerichtet, wird der Arm zum Körper gebeugt. | 9 |
Auch hier darauf achten dass sich im Schulterbereich keine Risse bilden. Mit M 1 wird die Hand abgegrenzt. | 10 |
Eine scharfe Schere hilft beim Ausschneiden eines Dreiecks zur Trennung des Daumens von den restlichen Fingern. | 11 |

Right at the beginning we determine the size of our bridegroom. Using an M 2 or an M 4 we insert a deep groove at both ends of the roll. | 2 |
The separated pieces will now make arms and legs. To get the proportions right, we cut the groove at each end about one-third of the way along the overall length of the roll. This means that one-third of the roll remains intact, which will form the trunk of the body. Proceed by tapping all four limbs with your thumb and forefinger to model them into a round shape. | 3 | | 4 |
Flatten the ends and then use the sharper edge of the M 1 to mark the line for the end of the trousers at the bottom of the leg. | 5 |
Now for the feet. Bend these at an angle of 90 degrees and press them flat at the soles. | 6 |
We now have the correct length of the leg and use the blunt side of an M 1 to score an indentation at the back of the leg. This makes the back of the knee and we can now bend the leg into the anatomically correct shape. | 7 |
However, the knee requires further modelling with our thumb, forefinger and/or middle finger since the bending process can lead to cracks. | 8 |

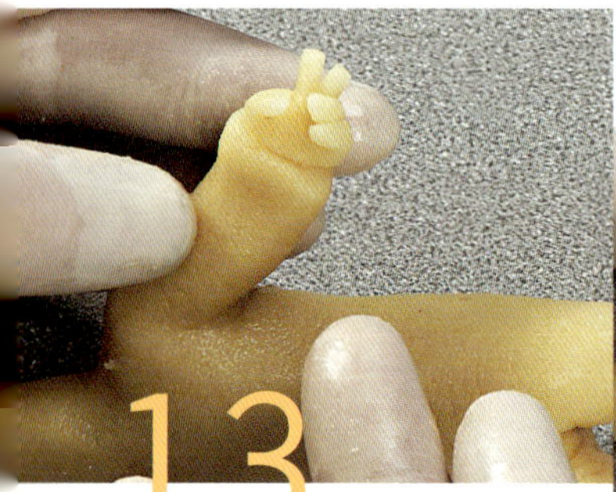
13

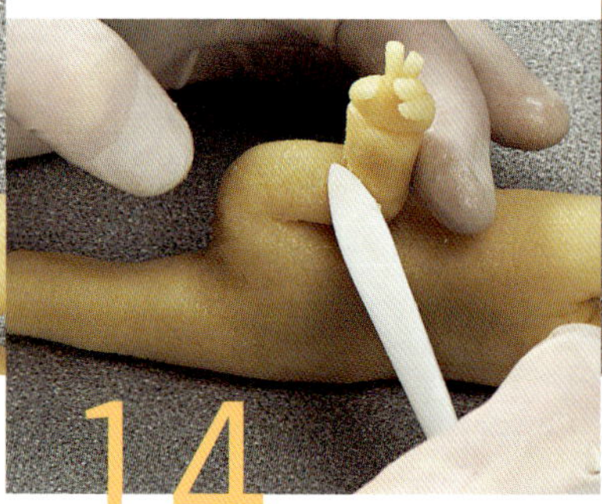
14

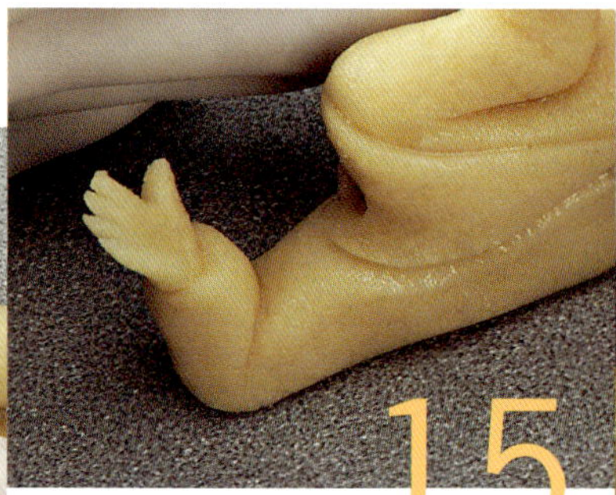
15

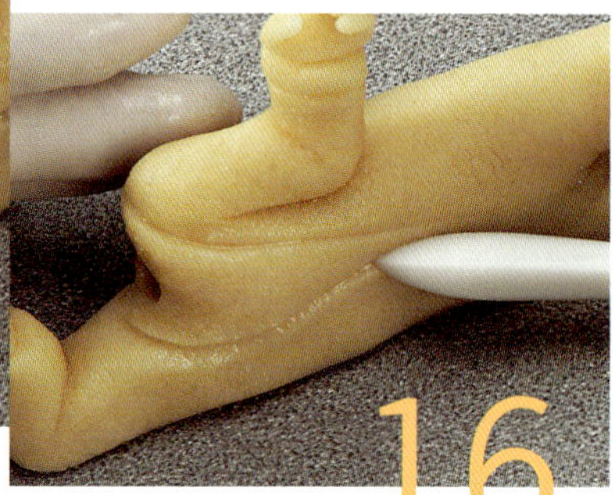
16

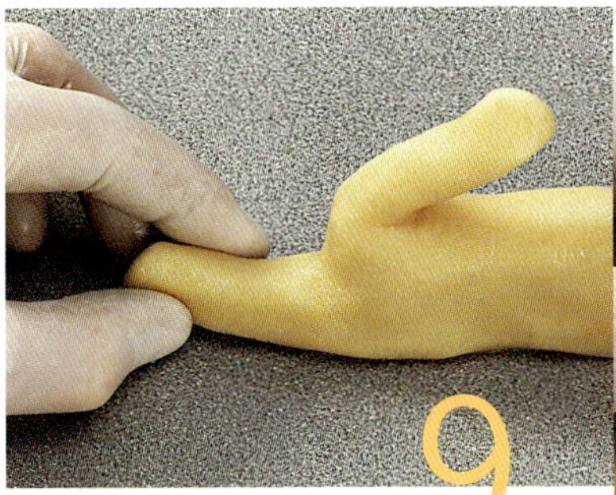

9

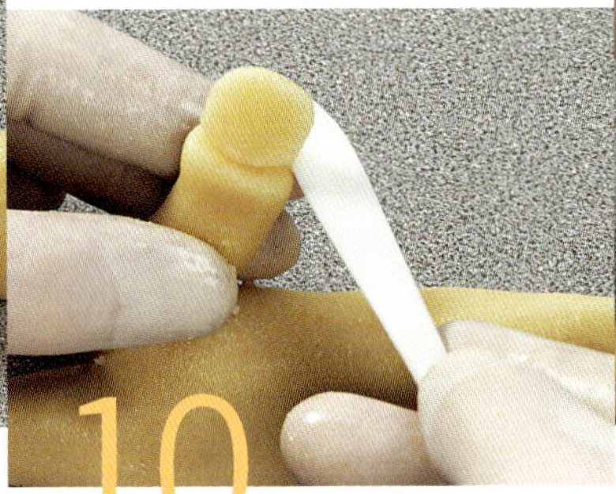

10

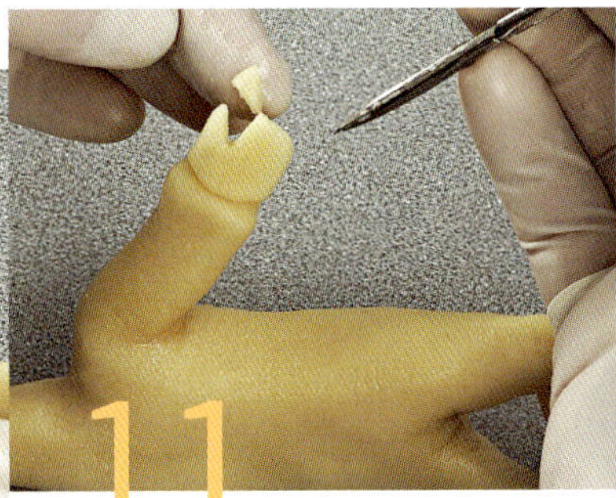

11

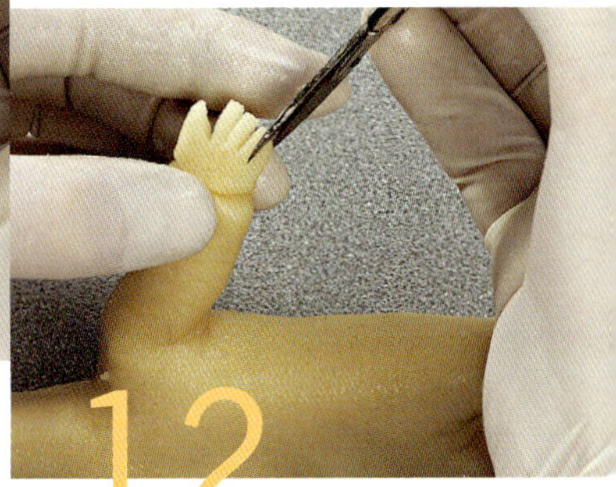

12

Diese werden gleichmäßig mit feuchter Schere eingeschnitten. | 12 |
Die einzelnen Finger lassen sich in die gewünschte Haltung biegen. | 13 |
Mit M 1 die Armbeuge einkerben und den Arm anlegen. | 14 |
Den zweiten Arm und die zweite Hand modellieren und in Form bringen. | 15 |
Das gleiche Modellierholz kerbt die Außenkante des Revers ein. | 16 |
Ebenso geschieht es mit den anderen Kleidungsübergängen. | 17 |
Die Aussparung im Kragen entsteht durch flaches Eindrücken mit der Unterseite des M 1. | 18 |
Hemdkragen und Krawatte entstehen entsprechend. | 19 |
Auch die Brusttasche durch Kerben anzeichnen.
Als letzte Aktion die ersten Linien noch einmal nachziehen. | 20 |

Once the legs are complete we bend the arms towards the body. | 9 |
Here again we need to take care that no cracks appear in the shoulder area. Use an M 1 to delineate the hand. | 10 |
You can use some sharp scissors to cut out the triangle which separates the thumb from the other fingers. | 11 |
Insert even cuts with some dampened scissors to separate the fingers. | 12 |
You can now bend the fingers into the required position. | 13 |
Use an M 1 to score a groove at the front of the elbow and place the arm in the required position. | 14 | | 15 |
The same modelling tool is used for scoring the edge of the lapel. | 16 |
Proceed in a similar fashion with the other contours of the items of clothing. | 17 |
The indentation in the collar is made by using the underside of the M 1, simply pressing into it. | 18 |
Proceed in the same way with the short collar and the necktie. | 19 |
Finally go over the first lines again. | 20 |

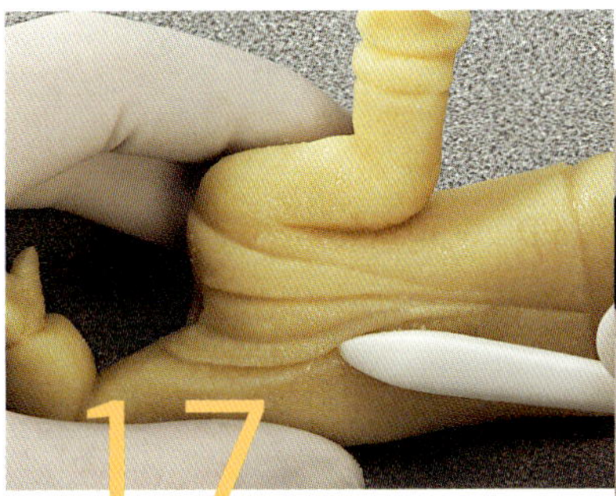

17

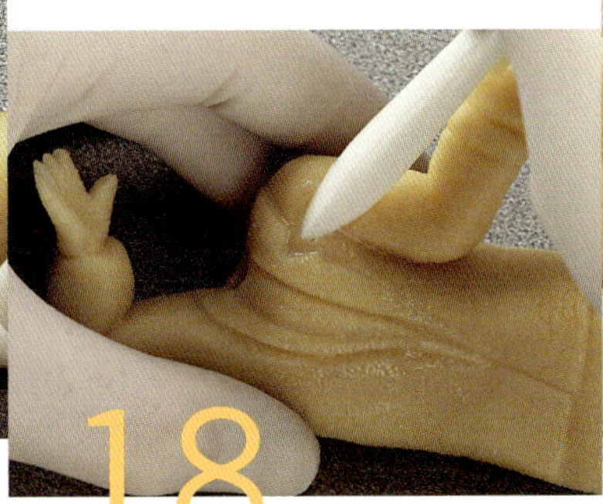

18

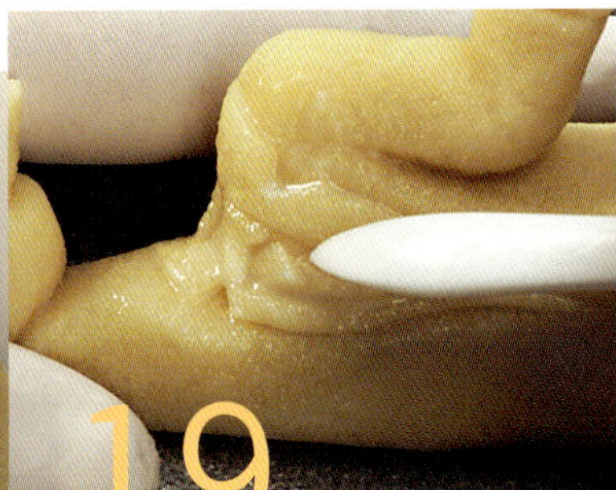

19

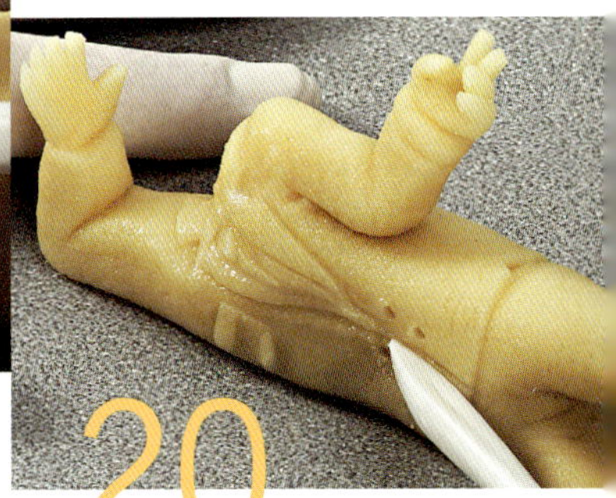

20

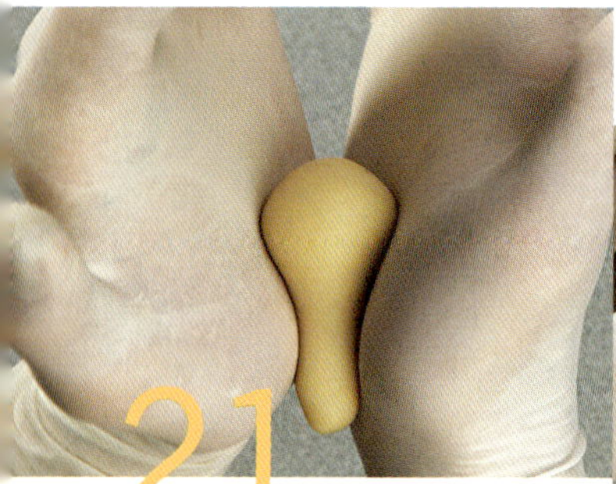
21

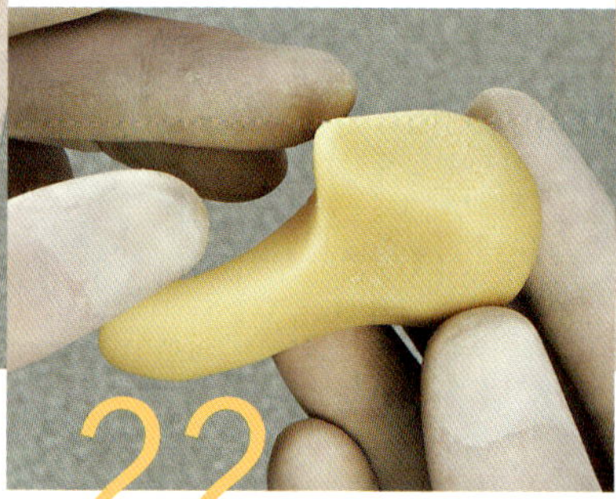
22

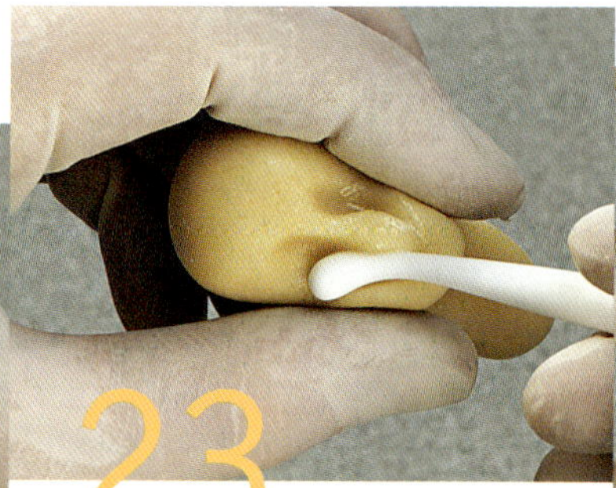
23

24

Den Kopf beginnen wir mit einer Birnenform. Der Hals wird verlängert. | 21 |
Über die Daumenkuppe wird das Kinn gedrückt. Das Gesicht wird abgeflacht und leicht kantig angelegt. | 22 |
Mit M 2 die Augen eindrücken. Die äußeren Ränder abflachen und von beiden Seiten her die Nase eindrücken. | 23 |
Den unteren Abschluss der Nase formen. Mit der gegebenen Fingerwölbung wird der Übergang von Stirn und Nase bestimmt. | 24 |
Die Kieferkonturen werden eingedrückt. | 25 |
M 1 ergibt den Mund. | 26 |
Mit M 4 entstehen die Nasenlöcher. Kleine Falten oder Grübchen ergeben Charakter und die Lachfalten. | 27 |
Den Hals auf passende Stärke modellieren und kürzen. Aus einem platt gedrückten und geriffelten Marzipanstrang entstehen die Haare. Diese an der einen Kopfseite ansetzen und herumführen. | 28 |
Die Stirnhaare gesondert anbringen. Mit einem scharfen Messer die Auflagefläche für den Zylinder schaffen. | 29 |

We start the head with a bulb shape. Elongate the neck. | 21 |
Form the chin by moulding it over the thumb. Flatten the face and make it slightly squarer in appearance. | 22 |
Use an M 2 to press in the sockets for the eyes. Flatten the outer edges and sculpt the nose by pressing from both sides. | 23 |
Shape the lower end of the nose. Use the natural curve of your finger to shape the natural dip between the nose and the forehead. | 24 |
Shape the contours of the jaw. | 25 |
Use an M 1 to shape the mouth. | 26 |
Use an M 4 to push in the nostrils. Small folds or dimples add character or create facial expressions such as laugh lines. | 27 |
Model the neck to an appropriate thickness and cut it to the length required. Make the hair from a roll of marzipan that has been pressed flat and textured. Attach the hair to one side of the head and drape it over the top to create the hairstyle. | 28 |
Apply the hair at the forehead separately. Use a sharp knife to cut the base surface for the top hat. | 29 |

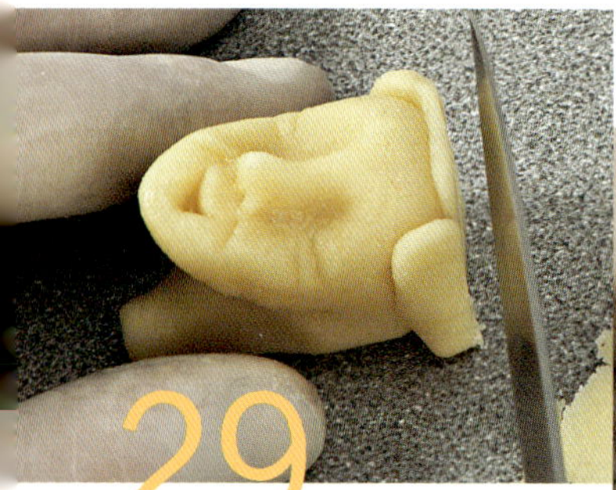
29

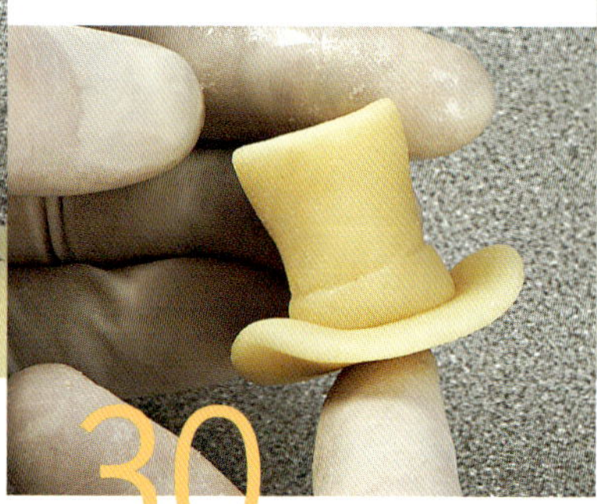
30

31

32

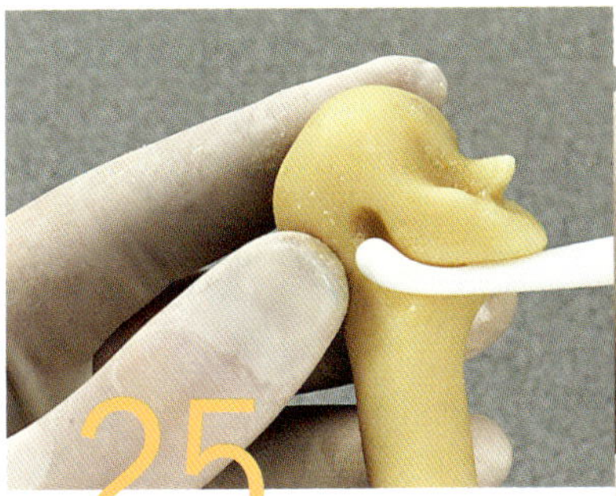
25

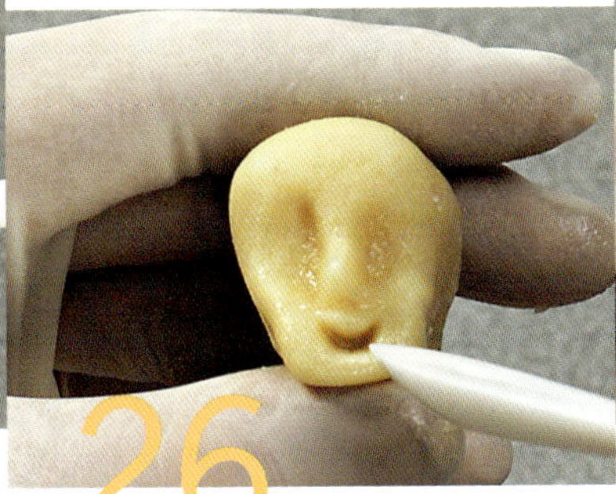
26

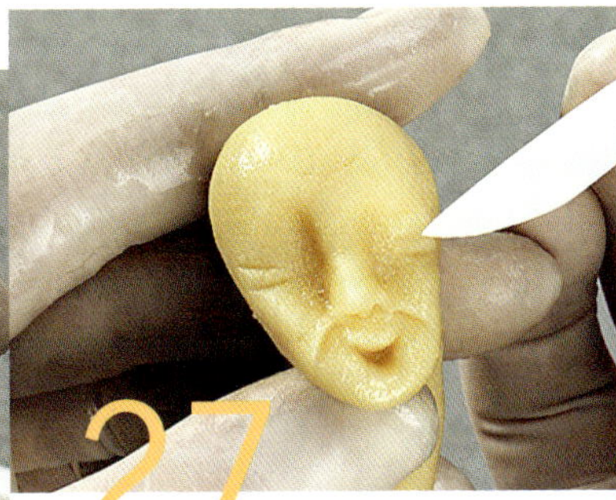
27

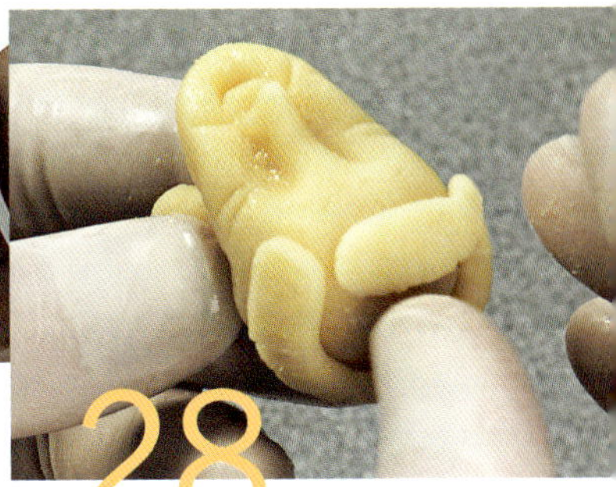
28

Zwei kleine Kugeln ergeben mit M 3 die Ohren. Den Zylinder unten glatt formen. | 30 |
Mit Eiweißspritzglasur oder Kuvertüre festkleben. Mit entsprechenden Stützen versehen, bis die Trocknung Stabilität bringt. | 31 |
Geschminkt wird zuerst die Hautfarbe. | 32 |
Mit einem Papier werden die Konturen abgedeckt. Den restlichen Teil der Figur, aber ohne den Hemdbereich, mit Schwarz besprühen. Beim Zylinder das Hutband aussparen. | 33 |
Mit dem Pinsel wird konzentrierte weiße Farbe für das Hemd benutzt. Die Krawatte mit Rot schminken. | 34 |
Die Krempe des Zylinders wird mit dem Pinsel fertig geschminkt, um eine Farbüberlagerung beim Sprühen zu verhindern. Haare, Mund, Hutband und Augenbrauen mit dem Pinsel färben. | 35 |
Die Augen einspritzen oder aus zwei gefärbten Kugeln eindrücken. Mit roter Farbe sehr gefühlvoll die Wangen röten. | 36 |

Use two small balls and an M 3 to make thc cars. Shape the top hat flat at the bottom. | 30 |
Attach with royal icing or couverture. Devise some suitable props as supports until the figure has dried out sufficiently to be stable. | 31 |
For the colouring process we start with the skin colour. | 32 |
Use a piece of paper to cover the contours. Spray the remaining part of the figure with black, except the shirt area. When colouring the top hat, make sure to leave out the ribbon. | 33 |
Use a brush to apply concentrated white paint for the shirt. Apply red paint for the necktie. | 34 |
Use a brush to complete the colouring of the rim of the top hat since any spraying would likely also go on the figure below. Use a brush to paint the hair, the mouth, the ribbon and the eyebrows. | 35 |
Pipe on the eyes or press in two coloured balls. Apply some red colour to the cheeks, being careful not to exaggerate this feature too much. | 36 |

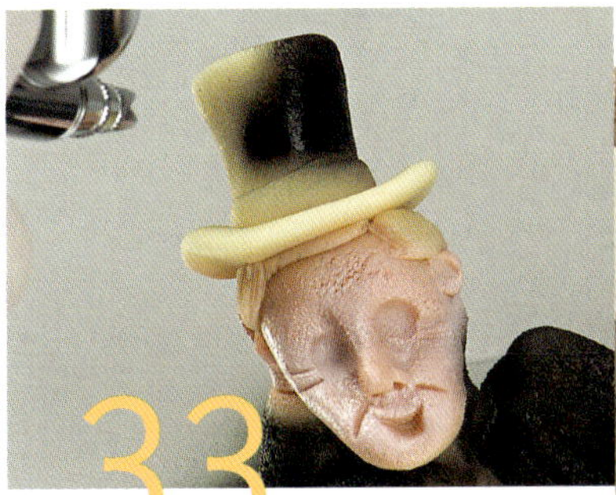
33

34

35

36

Schminken

Colouring

> Die verschiedenen Schminktechniken lassen sich an Hand des Exponats "Dangerous love" am leichtesten erklären.
Die getrockneten einzelnen Bestandteile werden bereitgestellt. | 1 |
Da gelb für leuchtende Effekte sorgt, wird es gern als Grundierung verwendet. Vor allem unter Grün und Braun ist die Farbe Gelb sehr effektiv. Es werden die entsprechenden Teile mit Gelb grundiert. | 2 |
Bevor die nächsten großflächigen Farben aufgetragen werden, entfernt man alle Exponatteile, die nicht angesprüht werden sollen, aus dem „Gefahrenbereich". Auf dieser Grundplatte befinden sich nun mehrere verschiedenfarbige Bereiche. Was als Gras angelegt ist, wird grün besprüht. | 3 |
Der Kaktus erhält ebenso eine großflächige grüne Einfärbung. Hier dürfen ruhig hellere und dunklere Stellen entstehen, denn die Natur lässt auch verschiedene Farbnuancen zu. | 4 |
Ein wenig Wasser nachgesprüht, lässt die Farbe in die Vertiefungen laufen und verstärkt so deren Wirkung. | 5 |
Die nächste Farbe, die verwendet wird, ist Schwarz. Felsen und Schlange werden sehr dünn damit grundiert. Das erreicht man durch zaghaftes Ziehen am Farbzufuhrhebel der Schminkpistole und durch eine gewisse Entfernung vom Objekt, die es dem Farbnebel ermöglicht, sich fein zu verteilen. | 6 |
Kleinere Exponatteile, die zusätzlich noch an einem größeren Teil befestigt sind, stellen eine neue

> The various colouring techniques can best be explained using the example of the exhibit "Dangerous love".
You start from the individual components once they have dried out sufficiently. | 1 |
Since yellow results in radiant effects, it is favoured as a base coat. The colour yellow is particularly effective under green and brown. Apply yellow base coat to the components. | 2 |
Before spraying any larger areas, remove all components that are not being sprayed out of harm's way. This particular base slab features several areas of different colours. The grass area is going to be sprayed in green. | 3 |
Likewise, the cactus is also being sprayed in green. It doesn't matter if the sprayed areas end up somewhat darker or lighter since in nature there are also often different intensities in colour. | 4 |
Follow on by spraying on a little water so that the paint runs into the grooves and thus accentuates the effect. | 5 |
The next colour is black. Apply a very thin base coat to the rocks and the snake. You can achieve that by pressing the trigger of the spray gun very gently and also by keeping a certain distance from the object so that the mist is distributed more finely. | 6 |
Small items which are still attached to a larger piece are specially challenging. In order to avoid adding unwanted colour to the main section we

5

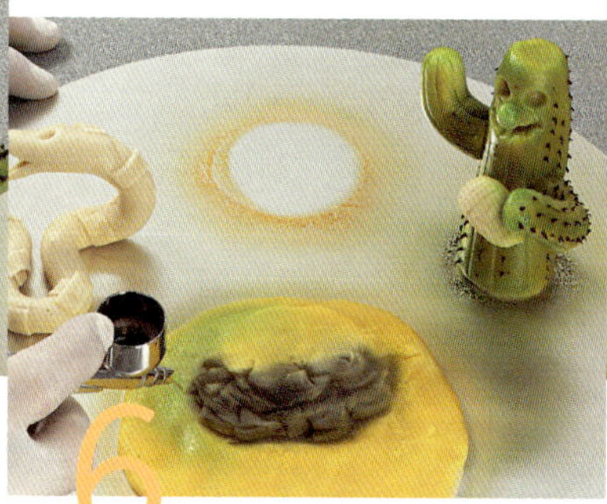
6

7

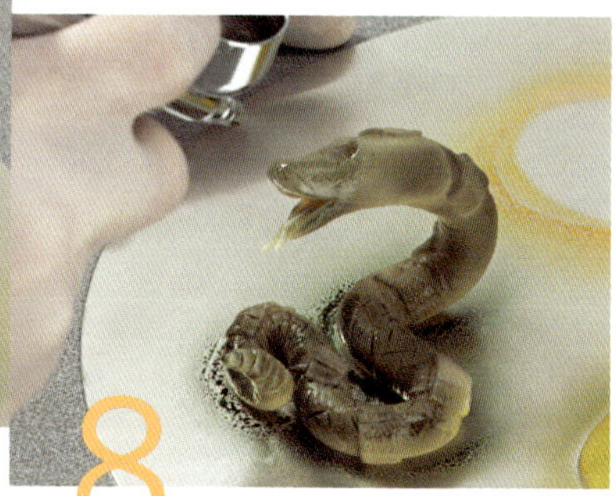
8

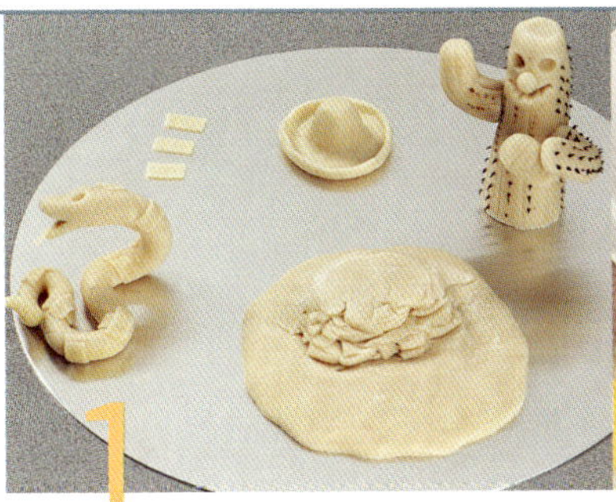

1

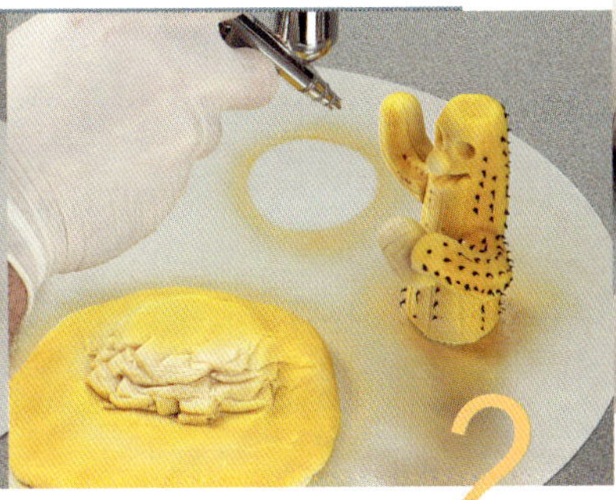

2

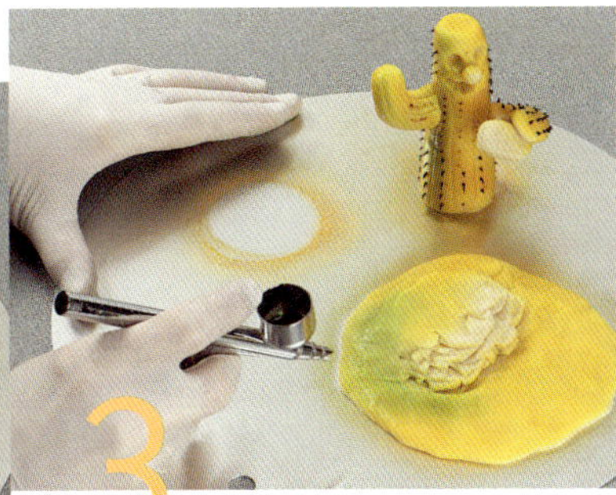

3

4

Herausforderung dar. Um das dahinter liegende Farbbild nicht zu beeinträchtigen, muss entweder mit dem Pinsel geschminkt werden oder es wird mit einem Papier abgedeckt. Hier wird schwarze Farbe aufgesprüht. Dies geschieht ebenfalls dünn, muss aber, um besser zielen zu können, aus nächster Nähe erfolgen. Das abdeckende Papier wird immer so platziert, dass der Hintergrund von Farbe verschont bleibt. | 7 |
Auch hier werden alle Konturen auf fast magische Art sichtbar, wenn man mit feinem Wassernebel nachsprüht. Bei der Schlange (und dem Rasierapparat) erfolgt das eher zaghaft, um zum einen das Exponat nicht zu sehr zu befeuchten, es könnte sonst wieder in sich zusammensinken, und zum anderen, um die anschließende Trocknungszeit kürzer zu halten. | 8 |
Für die Felsstrukturen muss man sich nicht so sehr zurückhalten. Durch Befeuchten mit kräftigem Wassernebel werden die vorderen Felsenteile fast farblos. Nur die Vertiefungen behalten ordentlich schwarze Farbe. | 9 |
Es folgt die Farbe Braun. Durch Umsprühen der Grundplatte ergibt sich ein einfacher Farbverlauf, der sich zur Mitte hin verliert.

need to use a brush or a piece of paper to protect the item. In this case we're spraying in black. This is done very thinly but has to be carried out from quite close up so as not to miss the target. Place the masking paper so that no colouring can get onto the background. | 7 |
Again, the contours become more accentuated, almost magically, if we follow on with a fine spray of water. In the case of the snake (and the razor) we should do this not too liberally in order to avoid too much moisture on the exhibit, which could make it collapse, and also to keep the required drying time as short as possible. | 8 |
For the texture in the rock we need to be less careful. By applying a fairly strong mist of water, the front parts of the rock almost lose their colour completely. Only the indentations retain their strong black colour. | 9 |
Now we follow on with brown. By spraying around the base slab we obtain a simple run of colour that thins out towards the middle. We can also add extra nuances at the top end of the rock. | 10 |
We colour the snake brown by spraying from a larger distance (about 30 cm). | 11 |

9

10

11

12

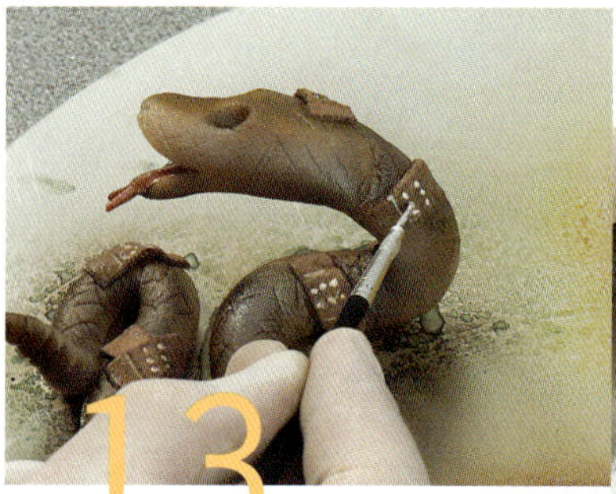

13

14

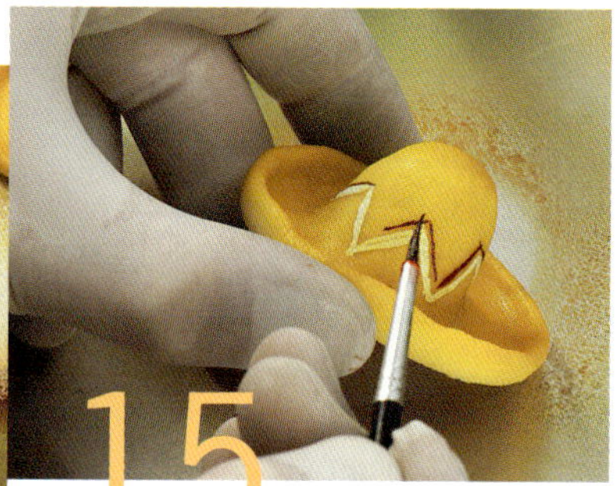

15

Auch oberhalb des Felsens lassen sich noch leichte Farbnuancen anbringen. | 10 |
Aus großer Distanz (etwa 30 cm) wird die Schlange leicht gebräunt. | 11 |
Die letzte Aktion mit der Schminkpistole ist der Auftrag von weißer Farbe auf die Felsen. Dieser Vorgang sollte aus fast senkrechter Position nass in nass ausgeführt werden. Das bedeutet, dass die weiße Farbe aufzutragen ist, wenn die Felsen vom Wasser noch feucht sind. Es entsteht ein zufälliges Farbspiel in vielen Grautönen, das sehr natürlich wirkt. | 12 |
Grundsätzlich gilt: Saubere Farbränder erhält man nur, wenn trockene Grundflächen bemalt werden. Ist das Exponat noch feucht, zerfließen alle aufgepinselten Farben. Die Pflaster der Schlange werden mit einer Farbmischung grundiert. Ist diese dann gut getrocknet, können die Punkte und Konturen mit konzentrierter weißer Farbe aufgetragen werden. | 13 |
Um die weiße Farbe in ihrer Konsistenz zu komprimieren, kann eine kleine Menge in einem Gefäß getrocknet werden. Die Pigmentkruste kann mit einem feuchtem Pinsel angelöst werden. Die Deckungskraft ist erstaunlich. Das geöffnete Maul und die Zunge der Schlange werden in unterschiedlichen Rosatönen geschminkt. | 14 |
Ebenso kann der Mund des Kaktus mit dunkler Farbe abgesetzt werden. Feine Linien entstehen aus konzentrierten Farben. Der Vorgang funktioniert auch mit allen anderen Flüssigfarben. Werden zwei verschiedenfarbige Linien dicht aneinander geschminkt, so sollte die erste gut getrocknet sein, bevor die zweite aufgetragen wird. | 15 |
Man verhindert damit ein „Auslaufen" der Linien. Nun müssen nur noch die Augen eingespritzt und die Einzelteile zusammengefügt werden. Das fertige Exponat kann unter "Dangerous love" begutachtet werden.

The last action to be carried out with the spray pistol is the application of white colour to the rocks. This process should be carried out from an almost vertical position, wet in wet. This means that the white is applied when the rocks are still damp from the water spray. It creates a random play of colours with many tones of grey which have a very natural effect. | 12 |
The principle here is that we can only obtain clear edges for our coloured area if we paint on dry surfaces. If the exhibit is still damp, all brushed-on colouring will run. Although this may be a desirable effect in some instances, it is not usually what we want. The plasters on the snake are given a base coat from a mixture of colours. Once this has dried well we can add the points and contours with concentrated white paint. | 13 |
In order to concentrate the consistency of the white paint, a small quantity is left to dry in a container. The "paint" will form a crust, which can be dissolved with a damp brush, as with watercolours. The covering capacity of this type of colouring is remarkable. Now paint the open mouth and the tongue of the snake in different shades of pink. | 14 |
The mouth of the cactus can be highlighted in a dark colour. For fine lines we need concentrated colouring, as already explained above. The same process applies to all other liquid colourings. If two lines of a different colour are painted very close to each other, the first one should have dried out before applying the second one. | 15 |
This prevents the lines from running. Now all that is left to do is to pipe on the eyes and put the individual components together. To see the finished exhibit look up the pictures under "Dangerous love".